After national service in the South African Air Force, Ian Pringle migrated to Rhodesia to work as an industrial chemist and flew aircraft as a hobby. He was drafted into the Police Reserve Air Wing as a pilot, and was involved in numerous enemy contacts.

Pringle read his MBA in the UK and worked for Castrol International and BP plc at a senior executive level, spending much of his career in Asia and Europe. He learnt to fly helicopters and ex-military jets in England. He retired to Cape Town in 2004, bringing two Cold War jets with him, and he teamed up with Thunder City, where he still flies the Hawker Hunter, Buccaneer and aerobatic aircraft.

On 23 November 1977, an armada of helicopters and aeroplanes took off from Rhodesian airbases and crossed the border into Mozambique. Their objective: to attack the headquarters of the Zimbabwe African National Liberation Army, where thousands of enemy forces were concentrated. Codenamed *Operation Dingo*, the raid was planned to coincide with a meeting of Robert Mugabe and his war council at the targeted HQ. It would be the biggest conflict of the Rhodesian Bush War.

In this fascinating account, Ian Pringle describes the political and military backdrop leading up to the operation, and he tells the story of the battle through the eyes of key personalities who planned, led and participated in it. Using his own experience as a jet and helicopter pilot and skydiver, he recreates the battle in detail, explaining the performance of men and machines in the unfolding drama of events. *Dingo Firestorm* is a fresh, gripping recreation of a major battle in southern African military history.

DINGO
FIRESTORM

Ian Pringle

DINGO FIRESTORM

THE GREATEST BATTLE OF THE RHODESIAN BUSH WAR

Helion & Company Limited
26 Willow Road
Solihull
West Midlands B91 1UEEngland
Tel. 0121 705 3393
Fax 0121 711 4075
Email: info@helion.co.uk
Website: www.helion.co.uk
Twitter: @helionbooks
Visit our blog http://blog.helion.co.uk

This edition published by Helion & Company 2013 under license from Zebra Press, an imprint of Random House Struik (Pty) Ltd, PO Box 1144, Cape Town, 8000, South Africa. This paperback reprint 2014.

Cover photographs: Nine Alouette G-cars leaving Grand Reef airbase for Lake Alexander © Mark Jackson; Burning huts at the ZANLA base at New Farm, Chimoio © Keith Samler.

Maps by MapStudio

Zebra Press credits:
Publisher: Marlene Fryer
Managing editor: Robert Plummer
Editor: Mark Ronan
Proofreader: Lisa Compton
Cover designer: Michiel Botha
Text designer: Jacques Kaiser
Typesetter: Monique van den Berg
Indexer: Sanet le Roux
Set in 10 pt on 13.65 pt Sabon

Printed by Lightning Source Ltd, Milton Keynes, Buckinghamshire.

ISBN 978-1-909384-93-4

British Library Cataloguing-in-Publication Data.
A catalogue record for this book is available from the British Library.

For details of other military history titles published by Helion & Company Limitedcontact the above address, or visit our website: http://www.helion.co.uk.

We always welcome receiving book proposals from prospective authors.

This book is dedicated to the memory of
Lieutenant General Peter Walls MBE and
Air Marshal Norman Walsh OLM, BCR, ESM.

Contents

Author's note

Deploying virtually an entire air force (61 aircraft) over hostile foreign territory and dropping 184 troops to face an enemy numbering in the thousands in two bold attacks are what in essence make Operation Dingo such a remarkable story. It needed sound intelligence, excellent planning and bold decision-making to pull this operation off. The story that follows is, to the best of my knowledge, a fair and accurate account of what happened. It is primarily a story about people. To tell their story, I have interviewed a selection of key people involved in Dingo. I have also used a variety of sources, both published and unpublished, to bring authenticity to the story. Most of the text within quotation marks is what I have been told; the rest I have drawn from the battle log, autobiographies and previous accounts of the operation. In some cases, such as aircraft radio patter, I have assumed that standard radio language took place. Underpinning the story are the standard operating procedures used by the Rhodesian forces, which were well tried and tested, albeit on a smaller scale before Dingo.

Memories fade over time and, in some cases, I encountered discrepancies between what I was told, often very lucidly, and what has been written before. Although I have tried to seek consensus, sometimes this proved futile and, in most cases, I have gone with the accounts of those I interviewed and who were there during this operation. No doubt there will still be controversial and disputed elements in this book, something that is inevitable when looking back at an event that took place over three decades ago.

The other issue is the operations orders (ops orders). Like all good plans, they were modified, tweaked and improved, so what actually happened differed in a number of cases from the written plan. An accurate written summary of the operation, however, is provided by the high quality of the air-strike log; this is supplemented by radio messages and telexes. Very helpful too was the Operation Dingo debriefing, which helped me clear up a few grey areas. And the invaluable Super 8 movie footage I was able to view – the only filmed account of parts of Operation Dingo – has given me a vivid, virtually first-hand insight into certain aspects of the operation.

I was able to pilot a Hawker Hunter (from Thunder City in Cape Town) and simulate the attack profile that Rich Brand used to commence the Dingo attack, to give me a better feel for recording that tense moment. Granted, the adrenalin factor, precision, ground fire and weapons were missing, but it served a story-telling purpose. I apologise to residents in the Kommetjie area for disturbing their peace as I repeatedly rolled off my perch and dived at an imaginary target on the beach.

Being a helicopter pilot has also helped me describe parts of the story about those amazing Alouette pilots of the Rhodesian Air Force (RhAF). The parachuting details of the operation have been reinforced by my own skydiving experience.

There is an aerial bias to the book for which I do not apologise – every combatant in Operation Dingo got there and back by air.

Nomenclature

Place names, rivers, towns, and the like are presented in this book as they were at the time of the operation.

The Zimbabwe African National Liberation Army (ZANLA) headquarters complex in the Chimoio district of Mozambique was known as New Farm, but it was often simply called Chimoio, and these terms are used interchangeably. The town of Chimoio, formerly Vila Pery, is 17 kilometres south of New Farm; I refer to this as Chimoio Town to differentiate it.

The terms 'ZANU' (Zimbabwe African National Union), the political party, and its military wing, 'ZANLA', are used interchangeably according to the context: once the war started, the organisation's political and military identities very much merged.

Acknowledgements

Writing *Dingo Firestorm* has been possible only because of many people's generous support. When the idea came into my head to write this story, my first port of call was Peter Petter-Bowyer (PB), who agreed to help me without hesitation. PB, a former pilot, innovator and senior officer in the RhAF, and author of *Winds of Destruction*, has proved to be the key that opened many doors for me. His direct involvement in Operation Dingo, his book and our interviews have formed an invaluable foundation on which my story has been built. PB has corrected my interpretation of events a few times. I am deeply grateful to him for his enormous contribution and for repeating, without a word of complaint, our first interview, which I accidentally erased.

To make the story more interesting, I needed to speak to the man who opened the battle, the person who fired the first shots of Dingo. The chances of this happening were slim, as I was told repeatedly that former squadron leader Rich Brand, a highly successful businessman and aircraft builder, was unlikely to agree to be interviewed. PB gave me Rich's email address, and advised me to introduce myself first through my flying credentials. I am sure PB put in a good word for me because Rich readily agreed to chat to me from his home in Las Vegas. (His wife, Susan, even commented that he had never spoken on the phone to anyone for more than a minute.) For this reason, I am all the more grateful to Rich for generously interrupting his busy schedule to spend many hours telling me his story and explaining the finer details about how to really fly a Hawker Hunter.

Getting in contact with people has its challenges, yet one connection often spawns many more. I am most grateful to Dennis Croukamp for putting me in touch with Peter Walls. I spent five riveting hours interviewing General Walls at his home in Plettenberg Bay and a wonderful day in Knysna with him and his wife, Eunice. Over lunch on Thesen Islands, I mentioned to Peter that, try as I may, I had been unable to get in touch with one of the key Dingo personalities, Norman Walsh. Peter opened the door and thus began an invaluable dialogue with this remarkable man and the air force brains behind Operation Dingo.

I must also pay a huge tribute to Norman's wife, Merilyn, for facilitating my dialogue with Norman under very difficult times.

Sadly, both Peter Walls and Norman Walsh passed away shortly after I interviewed them; my great regret is that they never got to read *Dingo Firestorm*. For this reason and out of sheer respect, I have dedicated this book to the memory of these two great men.

I must also thank SAS Commander Brian Robinson, the army brains behind Operation Dingo, for the brief insights he shared with me. Brief, because Brian has no desire to be involved in writing about himself or the SAS, which I understand and respect. I hope I have done justice to his pivotal role in this story.

I started writing this book after interviewing Kevin Milligan, who helped me understand the intricacies of the mass parachute drop. Kevin also shared with me his vivid memories of Operation Dingo, for which I am very thankful. Then I tracked down Vic Wightman, Rich Brand's deputy at the time of Dingo, who helped me better understand the attack profiles and sight settings for various types of air-to-ground weapons delivery in the Hunter, especially flechette canisters. Thanks also to Vic for sharing his experience of ejecting from an English Electric Lightning supersonic interceptor.

Writing a story some 30 years after the event is always fraught with the ravages that time exerts on people's memories. In this respect, I have been incredibly fortunate to have documentary evidence of Operation Dingo in the form of the ops orders. I am most thankful to Chris Cocks for allowing me to use the ops orders for the first phase of Operation Dingo, as published in his book *Fireforce*. Chris then put me in touch with Professor Richard Wood, who had spent many hours meticulously copying parts of the original ops orders, air-strike logs, messages, telexes and the debrief summary for the Dingo section of his book *Counter-Strike from the Sky* and for *Operation Dingo*. These invaluable records were held at the British Commonwealth and Empire Museum in Bristol. Richard unselfishly sent me copies of these, for which I am most grateful. These documents underpin the architecture of the story I tell.

Then I had more luck. I remembered that my old skydiving buddy, Keith Samler, formerly a senior Police Special Branch (SB) officer attached to the Selous Scouts, had been a participant in Operation Dingo and had recorded it with a Super 8 camera. I was delighted to learn Keith still had the film, which he generously lent me and then talked me through it. The camera doesn't lie, and this footage enabled me to see parts of the operation first-hand. Keith also allowed me see ZANLA photographs he and his colleague recovered from the Chimoio base, some of which are reproduced in this book. I cannot adequately describe how valuable this material has been to my account of the story. I am grateful to Keith for the film and photographs and for sharing with me his own (considerable) experiences of Operation Dingo.

When Keith told Ron Reid-Daly, the former commanding officer of the Selous Scouts, that I was writing a story about Dingo, Ron asked to see me. Although he was not directly involved in the operation, Ron was keen to give me his perspective, which has certainly enhanced my understanding of the military landscape leading up to Dingo. I thoroughly enjoyed chatting to 'Uncle Ron', sipping red wine on his balcony overlooking False Bay. Sadly, Ron too passed away not long after our meeting.

SAS Captain Robert 'Bob' MacKenzie wrote a great account of his experiences of Operation Dingo in the magazine *Soldier of Fortune*. I am most grateful to Colonel Robert Brown, the editor of *Soldier of Fortune*, for granting me permission to use the article, which has effectively allowed me to bring the late Bob MacKenzie back to life.

My thanks also go to Jean Tholet, Ian Smith's daughter, for giving me permission to quote from his memoirs and to the Flower family for allowing me to use extracts from Ken Flower's memoirs.

As the project progressed, I found more leads. I was particularly looking for someone who knew Norman Walsh well, because Norman did not enjoy talking about himself. Merilyn Walsh obliged by asking Hugh Slatter, a close friend of Norman's and pilot of one of the attack aircraft used in Dingo, to contact me. Hugh's contribution filled a hole in my book. So did the valuable input from Dave Jenkins, who flew as technician/gunner with Norman Walsh and Brian Robinson in the command helicopter. Dave's perspectives of the battle from the command ship were most helpful.

Another 'door opener' was Eddy Norris, the moderator of one of the world's best websites dedicated to ex-servicemen, Old Rhodesian Air Force Sods (ORAFs). Eddy has always been quick and keen to help, pointing me in the right direction and connecting me with many people. One of the first was Rex Taylor, who set up a major helicopter refuelling and transit base during the second phase of Dingo on a mountain in Mozambique known as the Train. Rex made life easy for me by jotting down his experiences, which have certainly added colour to the story.

Peter Stanton, an SB officer who worked closely with Brian Robinson and Scotty McCormack to identify and select the Dingo targets, is gifted with an excellent memory. I am grateful to Peter for shedding light on the mysteries of intelligence gathering, particularly as it related to this story. Another man with an incredible memory is Neill Jackson, a Rhodesian Light Infantry (RLI) officer during Dingo, who remembers the operation as if it were yesterday. I am grateful to Neill for selflessly sharing his experiences.

I needed to speak to a K-car (helicopter gunship) pilot. PB and Dennis Croukamp immediately pointed me to Mark McLean, a passionate helicopter (and fixed wing) pilot, who took a bullet through his helmet over Chimoio during Dingo. Mark recalled his experiences, particularly as a K-car pilot, with infectious passion and vivid clarity. It was a fascinating interview, enhanced by the wonderful view from the veranda of Mark's home in Barrydale in the Western Cape.

Steve Kesby, one of the last pilots in the world to fly the de Havilland Vampire in action, vividly depicted the important contribution these super little jets made to Dingo. Derek de Kock, the officer in command of the Parachute Training School, helped me understand the finer details of how paratroopers envelop their target. Darrell Watt, a tough-as-nails SAS officer who was shot at Chimoio, shared that awful moment with me. John Norman of the RLI was also shot at Chimoio, and I am grateful to him for eventually agreeing to talk about it. Through John I got talking to Mark Adams, a fellow troop commander on Dingo, who gave me some great insights. Mark, in turn, connected me, through a book he and Chris Cocks are writing called *Africa's Commandos: The Rhodesian Light Infantry*, to Simon Haarhoff and Graeme Murdoch, who gave good accounts of their Dingo experiences.

Thanks to Mark Jackson for allowing me to use his photo collection and to Bob Manser for unselfishly trekking around New Farm to take pictures for me of the shrine and some of the gravesites there. Bob Manser also helped me pinpoint exactly where some of the major battles took place.

I am grateful to David Linsell for editing my original script, and for giving me honest and open critique. I would also like to thank Mark

Ronan, who edited the final script and whipped the book into shape, as well as correcting some of the Shona words I used.

The final hurdle, especially for a first-time author, is to find a publisher. I was fortunate: the first publisher I sent my manuscript to, Zebra Press at Random House Struik, accepted it. I am grateful to them, and in particular to Robert Plummer, the managing editor, and his team for managing the process of turning *Dingo Firestorm* into a book so professionally and seamlessly.

There are others, too many to mention, who have helped in some way. To you all, my sincere thanks.

And finally, my biggest thanks goes to my wife, Nina, and my family for their love, patience and unwavering support during the research and writing phases, which have taken up a huge chunk of my time over the last few years.

IAN PRINGLE
CAPE TOWN, JANUARY 2012

South-east Africa, 1977

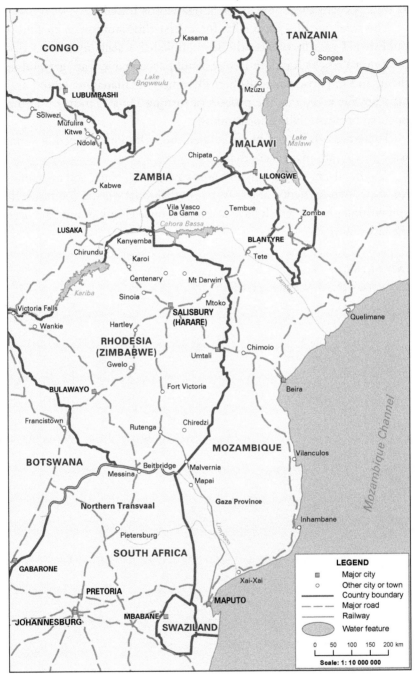

CONGO

Kasama

TANZANIA

Songea

Lake Bngweulu

LUBUMBASHI

Mzuzu

Solwezi
Mufulira
Kitwe
Ndola

MALAWI

Lake Malawi

Chipata

ZAMBIA

LILONGWE

Kabwe

Vila Vasco
Da Gama

Tembue

Zomba

LUSAKA

Cahora Bassa

Kanyemba

BLANTYRE

Chirundu

Karoi

Tete

Centenary

Mt Darwin

Kariba

Sinoia

Mtoko

Quelimane

Victoria Falls

SALISBURY
(HARARE)

Wankie

Hartley

RHODESIA
(ZIMBABWE)

Chimoio

Umtali

Gwelo

BULAWAYO

Fort Victoria

Beira

Francistown

Chiredzi

Rutenga

MOZAMBIQUE

Vilanculos

BOTSWANA

Beitbridge

Malvernia

Messina

Mapai

Gaza Province

Northern Transvaal

Inhambane

Pietersburg

SOUTH AFRICA

GABARONE

Xai-Xai

PRETORIA

MAPUTO

JOHANNESBURG

MBABANE

SWAZILAND

Mozambique Channel

Zambezi

Limpopo

LEGEND

- ▣ Major city
- ○ Other city or town
- ─── Country boundary
- ─ ─ ─ Major road
- ──── Railway
- ⬭ Water feature

0   50   100   150   200 km

Scale: 1: 10 000 000

Helicopter routes to Chimoio and Tembue

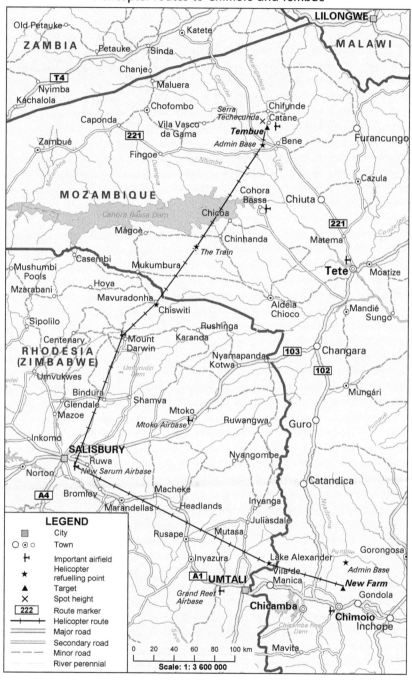

The attack on New Farm, Chimoio

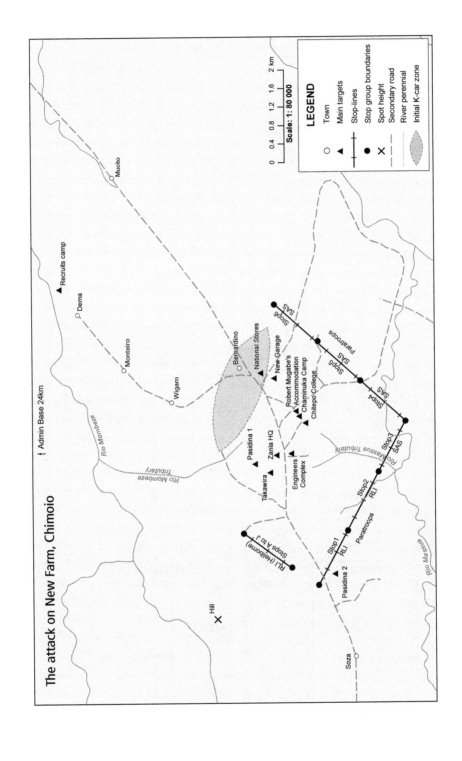

LEGEND

○	Town
▲	Main targets
┼	Stop-lines
●	Stop group boundaries
✕	Spot height
	Secondary road
	River perennial
(shaded)	Initial K-car zone

Scale: 1: 80 000

0 0.4 0.8 1.2 1.6 2 km

Mucito

Recruits camp

Dema

Monteiro

Wigam

Bernardino

National Stores

New Garage

Robert Mugabe's Accommodation

Chaminuka Camp

Chitepo College

Pasidina 1

Zanla HQ

Engineers Complex

Takawira

Admin Base 24km

Rio Mombeze

Rio Mombeze Tributary

Stop6 SAS

Paratroops

Stop5 SAS

Stop4 SAS

Rio Massua Tributary

Stop3 SAS

Stop2 RLI

Stop1 RLI

Paratroops

RLI (Heliborne) Stops A to J

Pasidina 2

Hill

Soza

Rio Massua

The attack on Tembue

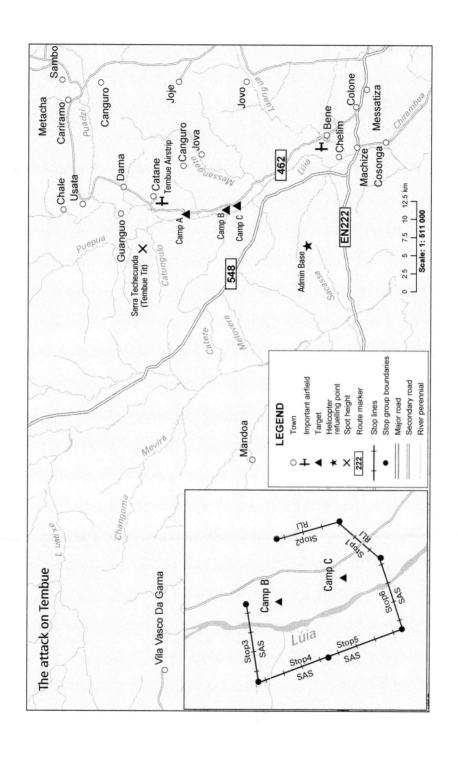

Prologue

Mozambique, 23 November 1977, 07:42

Lines of white vapour streamed off the wing tips of the speeding Hawker Hunter jet as it turned tightly in the moist, early-morning air. An eerie, haunting howl from the Hunter's four gaping cannon ports preceded the war machine, shattering the morning calm. Fishermen on the banks of the Pungwe River fled in panic as the jet screeched over their heads at treetop height. The pilot rolled the wings level on a southerly heading, breaking radio silence with a terse transmission: 'Red 1 at initial point.'

As the jet sped south, the pilot's eyes darted constantly from the ground to his stopwatch and back to the ever-present ground. As the second hand of the stopwatch touched 17 seconds, the pilot pulled back on the stick and the camouflaged war machine rose majestically into the Mozambican sky, white vapour now pouring off the whole upper-wing area.

The pilot's vista changed dramatically – he could suddenly see for miles, and there it was, on his left, exactly where he expected it to be: a whitewashed building with a rusty-red roof. He pushed the radio button again and uttered four electrifying words: 'Red 1 target visual.'

He rolled the jet to his left, almost inverted, not losing sight of the building for an instant. At precisely the right moment, he rolled the Hunter the right way up, the machine now in a perfect 30-degree dive towards the target. As the rusty-red roof started filling the sights, the pilot's right index finger instinctively found the trigger on the stick – he squeezed it firmly. The jet shuddered violently and slowed as all four cannons fired, sending a hail of deadly 30-mm cannon shells towards the target.

He saw glints of light and dust being kicked up as cannon shells struck the earth right in front of the house. 'Perfect,' he said to himself as he released the trigger and pulled back on the stick, feeling a force five times that of gravity tugging at his body as the Rhodesian warplane pulled out of its deadly dive.

Below, cannon shells slammed through the roof of Robert Mugabe's headquarters in Mozambique. The Battle of Chimoio, the first phase of Operation Dingo, had begun.

Part 1

THE GATHERING STORM

1

Stirrings at home

Modern black political consciousness was fairly slow to develop in Southern Rhodesia compared with other parts of the continent. It was not until 1957 that the first mass political movement came into being there. It was named the African National Congress (ANC) after its counterpart in neighbouring South Africa, formed 45 years earlier. The ANC projected a moderate image and chose a moderate leader, an Ndebele called Joshua Nkomo. It filled a political vacuum and quickly grew into a large organisation.

This was at a time when the independence drum was reverberating across Africa. The self-governing colony of Southern Rhodesia and the British protectorates of Northern Rhodesia (to become Zambia) and Nyasaland (later Malawi) were joined in the Federation of Rhodesia and Nyasaland under the Crown. The federation, an awkward grouping of countries, was Britain's counterweight to South Africa, where Britain's influence had suddenly diminished when the Afrikaner-dominated National Party won the general election in the self-governing territory in 1948.

With the black nationalist tide rising fast both in the federation and in Britain, the Southern Rhodesian government banned Nkomo's ANC, which responded by forming a new party: the National Democratic Party (NDP). Nkomo was elected party president.

The NDP platform was more radical than the ANC and made no bones about what its mission would be: to establish black majority rule. One of the senior NDP members, Leopold Takawira, a former teacher turned politician, addressed the party's inaugural meeting, telling the delegates that the issue was no longer asking the white establishment to rule the black majority well; it was about the majority ruling itself.

The agenda was set; the call for majority black rule, one man, one vote, had been made. A clash of some kind was inevitable.

On 19 July 1960, Takawira and other NDP leaders were arrested under the new Unlawful Organisation Act. The arrests sparked a protest march of some 7 000 people from the black township of Highfield to the centre of Salisbury (now Harare), a distance of 12 kilometres, to discuss matters with Prime Minister Sir Edgar Whitehead. Police stopped the march before it could reach the city centre and defused the situation by promising the marchers that Whitehead would meet a delegation the following morning. As the next day broke, the crowd quickly swelled to over 40 000, draining the black labour pool and virtually paralysing Salisbury.

In the crowd was a teacher, on leave in Rhodesia from his teaching job in Ghana, an introvert called Robert Mugabe.

Whitehead reacted angrily. Refusing to meet the NDP delegation, he instead went on state radio to call up army reservists and warn that political meetings in the townships would be banned. On the third day, the police moved decisively to break up the crowd, scattering it and chasing people back to the townships. More than 100 protestors were arrested. The government's action came as a rude shock to the nationalists.

It was also a watershed in Robert Mugabe's life. It drew a line under Mugabe the teacher and ushered in Mugabe the politician. He resigned from his job at the Takoradi Teacher Training College in Ghana and joined the NDP as publicity secretary.

Using the political skills that his partner and future wife, Sally Heyfron, had taught him in newly independent Ghana, Mugabe promptly formed a youth wing, modelled on Kwame Nkrumah's Ghana Youth League. He mobilised the youth to knock on every door in the townships the night before an NDP meeting, reminding residents to attend. The youth would again remind – and sometimes coerce – the residents on the day of a meeting, beating drums and singing to get them motivated.

This method of literally drumming up support worked well then, and would serve Mugabe well for decades to come, although it would become a lot more sinister and brutal.

Anxious to withdraw from the federation, the British government called an all-party constitutional conference in 1961, known as the Salisbury Conference. Joshua Nkomo led the NDP delegation and eventually agreed to accept the 1961 Constitution, which included a qualified all-race voting franchise. Duncan Sandys for Britain, Edgar Whitehead for Southern Rhodesia and Joshua Nkomo for the nationalists signed the 1961 Constitutional Agreement.

The more radical members of the NDP, realising that their quest for power might be delayed for decades, challenged Nkomo behind the scenes. Sensing his party was in danger of splitting, Nkomo suddenly made a U-turn and disowned the deal. But it was too late. The 1961 Constitution soon became law, and Nkomo had seriously compromised his political standing on both sides of the fence.

The legislation called for a new voters' roll and a general election in 1962. The process set in train events that would show the dark side of African politics – intimidation and violence. The nationalists boycotted anything to do with the Constitution and used violence to prevent eligible black people from registering to vote. The intimidation intensified; those siding with the government and failing to carry a party card were dealt with harshly. Gangs roamed the streets, dispensing violent discipline as they saw fit. Mugabe and most of the NDP leadership called for a widening of the conflict to disrupt civil life and force the white people to realise that the Constitution was not viable.

The Whitehead government reacted by banning the NDP, but the nationalists just as quickly formed a new party to replace it, the Zimbabwe African People's Union (ZAPU).

This time the government moved faster. It banned ZAPU, rounded up the leadership and restricted them to their rural-home areas for three months. The restriction order ended just 10 days before the qualified voters went to the polls in the general election of December 1962. By now the federation was doomed and the three countries were going their own separate ways.

The predominantly white electorate in Southern Rhodesia had already been scared by the mayhem elsewhere in Africa. But it was an event two years earlier, in 1960, that had catalysed the hardening of attitudes among white Rhodesians – the collapse of the former Belgian Congo. There, the murder, rape and chaos became especially frightening because the violence was much closer to home.

Television images of violence and destruction in Elizabethville and other cities in the Congo dominated the news. Soon, thousands of white refugees were fleeing the Congo for their lives in cars, with all their possessions loaded on the vehicles. They poured over the border into Northern Rhodesia, but there were no facilities to cope with the exodus. So the Royal Rhodesian Air Force (RRAF) stepped in, transporting blankets, medicine and emergency food supplies to refugee points at Fort Rosebery, Mufulira, Solwesi and Mwinilunga, and flying refugees out.

7

Soon, over 1 500 refugees had been flown into Salisbury. The sight of these families who had lost everything and the horror stories they told made a deep and lasting impression on white Rhodesians. They feared the same would happen at home; they feared being put in a similar predicament by Rhodesian politicians.

The memories of the Congo burnt bright in the minds of the Rhodesian electorate. Then, just 10 days before the 1962 general election, the ZAPU leaders were set free. This was too much for many white people and rang like a death knell for the Whitehead government. A new right-wing party, the Rhodesian Front (RF), launched by Ian Smith and 'Boss' Lilford, won the election. Winston Field became the new prime minister. Field did not last long. The new government's lurch to the right and his failure to secure early independence cost him his job. He resigned as prime minister in 1963 to be succeeded by the first Rhodesian-born prime minister, Ian Smith.

Smith, a BCom graduate from Rhodes University in Grahamstown, South Africa, was a different type of leader. When World War II broke out, he volunteered for service. After his pilot training in Southern Rhodesia, he was seconded to the Royal Air Force (RAF). Smith was badly injured when his Hawker Hurricane fighter plane crashed in Egypt in 1943. As soon as he was fit again, he returned to flying until his Spitfire was shot down by German anti-aircraft fire over Italy in 1944. He bailed out and spent months with partisans before reaching Allied lines. Although he had shown a strong loyalty to the Crown by volunteering to fight for Britain, he would take a much firmer line with Britain over independence.

The RF victory and Field's demise shocked the ZAPU leadership and put paid to any lingering hopes they may have had that the 1961 Constitution could be amended. The nationalists concluded that as a political party, ZAPU was wasting its time pursuing a negotiated settlement. This is when the majority of the executive decided that an armed insurrection was the only way to bring about change.

However, cracks in the party leadership showed again when Nkomo, opposed to a violent uprising, went against the majority. He strongly believed that diplomatic pressure would win the day. More leadership divisions started appearing, this time of a tribal nature: not all the Shona members of the executive took kindly to being led by an

Ndebele. This tribal animosity was deeply ingrained in Rhodesia, and a Shona-dominated party was beginning to take shape.

The Ndebele, a name originating from *maTebele* in Sotho or *ama-Ndebele* in Nguni, meaning 'nomads', were an offshoot of King Shaka's Zulu nation. They had settled in Bulawayo, in the south of present-day Zimbabwe, after being defeated in 1836 by white Dutch-speaking pioneers, the Voortrekkers, in the Transvaal province of neighbouring South Africa.

At the time the Ndebele arrived, the country was a federation of chiefdoms controlled by a *changamire*, a king or general of the Rozwi dynasty. These chiefdoms, which spoke different dialects, were given a collective name by outsiders – the Shona people.

Once Mzilikazi, the Ndebele king, had settled in his new land, he set his sights on the north and soon went on the rampage, killing the ruling *changamire* and forcing most of the Shona, who outnumbered the Ndebele, to flee to the north and east to escape his raiding impis. For protection, the Shona built small stone fortifications in the granite hills, thousands of which are still standing today, especially in Mashona-land and Manicaland.

Nkomo would have to contend with this historical baggage as he grappled to hold together his Ndebele and Shona party.

2

The birth of ZANU and UDI

As disenchantment set in with Nkomo's leadership, it came as no surprise when a group of rebel nationalists met in Salisbury, at the Highfield home of Enos Nkala. The rebels publicly announced their launch of a new party, the Zimbabwe African National Union (ZANU). The same day, Nkomo announced the formation of the People's Caretaker Council, which was essentially a structure formed above ZAPU. In the first demonstration of inter-party political violence, People's Caretaker Council members marched into Highfield, attacking the houses of the three main rebels, Nkala, Takawira and Mugabe.

These attacks did not deter ZANU's leaders, who quickly organised the party's inaugural congress in May 1964 in Gwelo, a town in Rhodesia's Midlands province. The congress elected Ndabaningi Sithole as president, Leopold Takawira as vice-president, Robert Mugabe as secretary general and Herbert Chitepo as national chairman. In addition to being the party leader, Sithole was appointed military commander of an army that did not yet exist. ZANU resolved at the inaugural congress to take over the government from the white minority by force if necessary.

ZANU soon showed its hand. Less than two months after the Gwelo conference, in July 1964, a ZANU group known as the Crocodile Gang, led by William Ndangana, set up a crude roadblock on the main road near Chimanimani, in eastern Rhodesia. A white farmer of Afrikaner descent, Petrus Oberholzer, his wife and four-year-old daughter were travelling along the main road in their Volkswagen Kombi when they came upon the roadblock near the Skyline Junction.

As Oberholzer stepped out of his vehicle to clear the obstacles, Ndangana and his gang set upon him, stoning him and stabbing him repeatedly. Bleeding profusely, the fatally wounded farmer mustered enough strength to fight off the gang with his bare hands and stagger back into the driver's seat, start the vehicle and drive past the roadblock. The car did not get far before overturning in a ditch. The dying man and his traumatised wife locked the Kombi's doors and watched in horror as the gang caught up with them. The ZANU men threw petrol over the Kombi, trying to set the vehicle alight, but in the nick of time, the headlights of an oncoming car scared off Ndangana and his gang.

Oberholzer became the first white Rhodesian to die in a terror attack since the Mashona Uprising, or First Chimurenga, 68 years earlier. Although Ndangana escaped the resulting manhunt, three gang members were apprehended and tried for murder. Two of them were hanged in Salisbury Prison; the third, who was too young for the death sentence, was spared.

Ironically, Oberholzer had bought Curzon Farm from Paul Petter-Bowyer, whose son, Peter, was an air force officer who would play a key role in the first Rhodesian–ZANLA battle and the ensuing war itself.

The amateurish but brutal murder of Petrus Oberholzer under the ZANU banner put the party on a collision course with the Rhodesian government. This murder and the terrible black-on-black political violence provoked the RF government to ban both ZANU and ZAPU and to detain their leaders. Sithole, Nkomo, Mugabe, Takawira, Tekere and the rest of the senior leadership of both parties would spend the next decade in detention.

The one outstanding issue was independence from Britain. That year, 1964, Britain granted independence to Northern Rhodesia, which became Zambia, and to Nyasaland, which became Malawi. However, the self-governing colony of Southern Rhodesia was having no such luck. Talks about independence became mired and patience was running out. This was vividly expressed by the governor of Rhodesia, Sir Humphrey Gibbs, the queen's resident representative, in his address at the opening of Parliament in 1964:

> It is now plain to see that the British government are not prepared to be brought to any conclusion on the question of independence except on the most extravagant terms, not because of misgivings about my government's competence and ability to govern in the interests of the country, or the logic or rightness of my minister's case, but because they wish to placate at all costs members of the Commonwealth who have declared openly their hostility to my government and country.

Smith's popularity had grown dramatically among the white electorate. He needed a stronger parliamentary base and called a general election in May 1965, and won a resounding majority. The die had been cast.

The Unilateral Declaration of Independence (UDI) read as follows:

... We the Government of Rhodesia, in humble submission to Almighty God who controls the destinies of nations, conscious that the people of Rhodesia have always shown unswerving loyalty and devotion to Her Majesty the Queen and earnestly praying that we and the people of Rhodesia will not be hindered in our determination to continue exercising our undoubted right to demonstrate the same loyalty and devotion, and seeking to promote the common good so that the dignity and freedom of all men may be assured, Do, By This Proclamation, adopt, enact and give the people of Rhodesia the Constitution annexed hereto.

God Save the Queen

Given under Our Hand at Salisbury this eleventh day of November in the Year of Our Lord one thousand nine hundred and sixty-five.

Prime Minister	Ian Douglas Smith
Deputy Prime Minister	Clifford DuPont
Ministers	John Wrathall, Desmond Lardner-Burke, Jack Howman, James Graham, George Rudland, William Harper, Philip Smith, Jack Mussett, Philip van Heerden

All across Rhodesia, people listened anxiously to their radios as Prime Minister Ian Smith read out the proclamation. He continued: 'We Rhodesians have rejected the doctrinaire philosophy of appeasement and surrender ... We have struck a blow for the preservation of justice, civilization, and Christianity – and in the spirit of this believe we have thus assumed our sovereign independence. God bless you all.'

The *Rhodesia Herald* summed it up with the headline 'UDI – Rhodesia goes it alone'.

UDI was a very high-risk strategy; some even called it suicidal. Why, they asked, would Smith's cabinet take such a gamble? The context of the time provides clues. The prelude to UDI was a time of great change and turmoil in Africa. As some saw it, if the scramble for

Africa by European powers in the nineteenth century was wrong, the desperate scramble to get out of Africa was immoral.

There was a headlong rush to grant independence to the former colonies. Ghana was the first, in 1957, and then they went quickly – eight French colonies were granted independence in August 1960, starting with Benin on 1 August and ending with Gabon on 17 August. By 1961 no fewer than 28 African countries had been granted independence. Some were nowhere near ready.

Ghana was regarded as the model for African independence. Yet only one year after independence, the Ghanaian leader, Kwame Nkrumah, introduced detention without trial, which he used to crush the opposition. Two years later, he introduced a new Constitution that enabled him to rule by decree, bypassing Parliament and making his rule absolute. He spent money with gay abandon on poorly thought-out, massive industrial projects and set the moral tone by raking off money from these projects into his own private companies. At the same time, Ghana neglected its main source of wealth, namely agriculture.

Investment dried up as corruption set in. Things got worse, and by 1965, the year of UDI, and after only eight years of independence, Nkrumah had taken Ghana from being one the most prosperous developing economies in the world to bankruptcy. The country had achieved the unenviable record of becoming the fastest-declining economy in Africa's history, a record that would only be beaten some 40 years later by an African country led by an ardent Nkrumah admirer: Robert Mugabe.

Nkrumah blamed Britain and the West for his woes and decided to look east for new friends. While visiting one of his new associates in Hanoi, North Vietnam, he was ousted in a *coup d'état*, a method of grabbing power that became fashionable in parts of Africa.

And it wasn't just in Ghana. Brutally repressive and corrupt regimes trampled democracy in many states north of the Zambezi. Even just across the mighty river, in Zambia, formerly Northern Rhodesia, President Kenneth Kaunda was paving the way for a one-party state. Kaunda's rallying cry of 'One Man, One Vote' was humorously modified to 'One Man, One Vote, One Time'. A joke, perhaps, but all too often that was what happened.

With no success stories to build on among the newly independent states, the Rhodesians had no appetite to follow suit by embracing unchecked majority rule. The country had been self-governing for over 40 years, yet the British government insisted that Rhodesia should drop its all-race, but qualified, voting franchise in favour of one man, one vote.

Ironically, neighbouring South Africa had become a republic following a referendum of white voters there in 1961, but with no provision for black people to vote. The Rhodesian government struggled to understand the rules of the game.

The final nail in the coffin was when Britain's Labour Party under Harold Wilson came to power in October 1964, demanding that there would be no independence without majority rule. A clear line was drawn in the sand, which brought about UDI, international sanctions, hardship and war. It laid the foundations for the largest conflict of that war: Operation Dingo.

3

The Silver Queen sows a seed

It was a clear day in late summer 1920, and a palpable air of expectation hung over Southern Rhodesia's second city, Bulawayo. The Silver Queen II, a twin-engined Vickers Vimy World War I bomber aircraft converted for commercial use, was expected to land on the city's main horse racecourse. This would be the first aeroplane ever to land on Rhodesian soil.

Just after 10:00 on 5 March, Bulawayo's warning guns sounded. The ultra-wide streets of the city, built to accommodate the turning circle of an ox wagon, suddenly thronged with people as shops, offices, factories and homesteads were vacated and everyone joined a disorganised charge of humanity to the racecourse. The huge biplane eventually came into view from the north. Clearly visible were the 12 long wooden struts and a network of cables anchoring the two wings and framing the two square engines either side of the big spruce plywood fuselage.

The cheering was so wild that it drowned out the sound of the band playing the welcoming piece. Officials struggled to keep the crowd off the racetrack to allow the Vimy to land safely. At the controls were Quintin Brand and Pierre van Ryneveld, the first men to attempt to fly from London to Cape Town.

The flight to Bulawayo had not been without incident. A radiator problem ended the flight when the aircraft had to make a forced landing in southern Egypt (present-day Sudan), which damaged the Vimy beyond repair. The aviators were loaned another Vimy, hence the name Silver Queen II, and continued south.

After the pilots' mayoral lunch in the town hall and a festive night in Bulawayo, the adoring crowds returned to the racecourse at dawn to witness the departure of the Silver Queen II. The Vimy taxied out to enthusiastic cheering, turned and the pilots gunned the engines. But the cheers turned to groans as the aircraft struggled to get airborne in the thin air, clipped some trees at the boundary of the racecourse and crashed with a tearing thump.

Both pilots and both engineers survived, sustaining minor injuries, but the Silver Queen II followed its predecessor to the scrapyard. Brand

and Van Ryneveld were determined, however, to be the first men to complete the London–Cape Town route by air. They were lucky: South African premier Jan Smuts loaned them a de Havilland DH9, enabling them to continue to Cape Town, where they landed in Wynberg on 20 March 1920. Both men were knighted for their efforts.

Sir Quintin Brand, who had fought with distinction in World War I as a fighter pilot with No. 1 Squadron, Royal Flying Corps (which became the Royal Air Force), went on to the rank of air vice-marshal with the RAF during World War II, commanding the South-Western Sector during the Battle of Britain. Five years after the war, he left Britain to settle on a farm in Southern Rhodesia. Sir Quintin's nephew, Richard 'Rich' Brand, would later also command No. 1 Squadron, but in a different air force: the Rhodesian Air Force. Rich Brand opened the air attack in a Hawker Hunter at Chimoio to start Operation Dingo.

The arrival of Brand and Van Ryneveld in Bulawayo in the Silver Queen firmly planted the aviation seed in Southern Rhodesia. Civil aviation expanded exponentially after this event. In the 1930s, there were calls to establish an air force in Southern Rhodesia, but in peacetime they fell on deaf ears. It took the rise of German National Socialism and aggressive rearmament to rekindle the air force debate.

Despite strong opposition, an air section was established in November 1935 as part of Southern Rhodesia's Territorial Army. Soon training for military pilots started at the civil airport at Belvedere, barely three kilometres west of the junction of First Street and Jameson Avenue in the heart of Salisbury. Instructors from the de Havilland Aircraft Company in Britain began training pupils in the Tiger Moth two-seat trainer aircraft.

There was, nevertheless, still considerable opposition to the establishment of an air force. Politicians simply didn't see the need. Sentiment changed quickly, however, when Germany started suggesting that its former colony Tanganyika should be returned.

'If that happens,' said Prime Minister Godfrey Huggins, 'we might very well have an enemy on our doorstep.'

On 17 July 1936, the embryonic air force, known as the Air Section, Southern Rhodesian Defence Force, was officially gazetted. A dedicated military airbase was established in Cranborne, a suburb four kilometres south of the city. Hawker Hart fighter planes were soon added to the air section as advanced training aircraft. The sight of these powerful, fast, noisy twin-seaters flying over Salisbury's south-eastern suburbs brought much excitement, but also some resentment from those who used to picnic in the quiet, tranquil Cranborne woodlands. In May 1938, the first six trainee pilots graduated when Governor Sir Herbert Stanley awarded them their wings at Cranborne.

As the drums of war reverberated across Europe, the need to train pilots to defend the empire became increasingly apparent. To speed things up, the air section established a travelling flying school, which flew to selected centres outside of Salisbury to train pilots.

When war was declared on 3 September 1939, it took only three days for the Southern Rhodesian government to decide that a dedicated air force was paramount. The Southern Rhodesia Air Unit was renamed No. 1 Squadron, Southern Rhodesian Air Force, and an extensive recruitment campaign for pilots and ground crew followed. The Rhodesian Air Force (RhAF) was born.

Many Rhodesian airmen – a disproportionate number given the small colonial population – would serve with distinction under the RAF in the North African campaign and Europe. More than 100 Rhodesian airmen were awarded the Distinguished Flying Cross. Inevitably, many would make the supreme sacrifice. The worst-hit squadron was No. 44 (Rhodesia), which suffered one of the highest number of Lancaster Bomber losses of all 59 Lancaster squadrons. The losses in World War II were felt all the more acutely in the tiny colonial community back home in Africa.

Training continued at Cranborne after the war, by which time noisy American Harvard trainer aircraft had replaced the Harts. A combination of the noise generated by these machines and the odd crash in the Salisbury suburbs brought pressure to bear on the air force planners to find a new base. In 1952 the air force moved from Cranborne to Kentucky Farm Airfield, a site 12 kilometres south of Salisbury and away from built-up areas. Purpose-built hangars, a control tower and other facilities were constructed on the south side of the main runway.

The new base was later named New Sarum, after Old Sarum, an aerodrome near the English town of Salisbury. The Old Sarum aerodrome was built during World War I. Old Sarum is an ancient hill fort established during the Iron Age and later used by the Romans. The hill fort serves as an excellent landmark for the airfield, lying just 700 metres from the threshold of the east runway.

In July 1953, the new Kentucky Airport staged the Rhodes Centenary Air Rally, the largest air event to be held in the subcontinent at the time. Aircraft from the RAF, Southern Rhodesian Air Force and South African Air Force, as well as privately owned and commercial-airline aircraft, took part. Pylon racing, aerobatic displays and other forms of competition thrilled the crowds during the morning session, and the air forces performed in the afternoon. The final day of the event was marred when two Harvard trainers of the RAF collided during a complex formation manoeuvre, crashing in front of the huge crowd and killing all three on board.

Establishing New Sarum well away from suburbia meant that attention was now drawn to Salisbury's civil airport at Belvedere. Because of Belvedere's suburban location, a new civil air terminal was built on the north side of the main runway at New Sarum and named Salisbury Airport, once again bringing the military and civil operations together with a shared runway. The 2.5-kilometre main runway was just long enough for the typical aircraft of the day, but at 5 000 feet above sea level, it was inevitable that a longer runway would be needed. With good foresight, the planners had set aside land to extend the runway to the south-west when the time came.

The Southern Rhodesian Air Force became the Royal Rhodesian Air Force in 1954 when the queen granted it royal status. The RRAF continued to adapt. It introduced the Hunting Percival Provost as the basic trainer and the DC-3 Dakota as the transporter. Vampire fighters signalled the arrival of the age of jet power, replacing the Spitfire as the main fighter and ground-attack aircraft. In 1959 English Electric Canberra jet bombers were added to the fleet, followed in 1962 by the impressive Hawker Hunter fighter and ground-attack jets.

The RRAF's final major acquisition was the Alouette III helicopter in 1962.

The little lark

The French had built a new, highly versatile light-utility helicopter, the Alouette (lark). Conventional helicopters at the time used heavy piston engines, and they struggled to fly at high altitudes. The French designers chose a different type of engine, one that was not just lighter and smaller, but could also perform at high altitude. They used a jet engine.

The shaft gas turbine engine enabled the Alouette to achieve impressive altitude records with a heavy cargo. In 1961 the third marque, the Alouette III, capable of carrying seven people, entered production. This helicopter was exactly what the Rhodesian Air Force needed, and the first Alouettes were acquired in 1962. These deft little machines would form the backbone of Rhodesia's counter-insurgency operations for years to come.

The Alouettes, Hunters, Canberras, Vampires and Dakotas were the main attacking force in the Rhodesian Bush War.

4

ZANU starts the Second Chimurenga

UDI dealt a blow to the jailed nationalist leaders and any hope of their early release. They knew that they would have to direct events from behind bars – which was not difficult, as there was always a friendly warden or sympathiser willing to act as a messenger. Astonishingly, the jailers were unaware of this. Sithole's jailed executives were able to smuggle documents and letters out of the detention centres almost at will.

One of the most important documents to be smuggled out was the Sikombela Declaration, which authorised Herbert Chitepo, a lawyer who had fled to Lusaka in neighbouring Zambia, to organise the external wing of ZANU. Chitepo would head up what was to be known as the Dare reChimurenga (war council). Chitepo was given full accountability for conducting the war and running the affairs of ZANU from Zambia, at least while the executive remained in prison.

Chitepo and his fellow ZANU exiles organised the war; their new army was known as the Zimbabwe African National Liberation Army (ZANLA). Although Chitepo had only a handful of trained guerrillas at his disposal in 1966, he was keen to start hostilities, particularly in response to UDI, but also to steal a march on ZANU's other enemy, Joshua Nkomo, and his ZAPU army, the Zimbabwe People's Revolutionary Army (ZIPRA).

Chitepo's strategy was simple – to mount attacks inside Rhodesia to scare the white people and ignite a popular rebellion. In April 1966, Chitepo dispatched the first group of 21 ZANLA insurgents from Zambia to Rhodesia. Their objective was to sabotage major electric power lines, blow up the Beira–Salisbury oil pipeline and murder a few white farmers along the way.

The fully armed insurgents boarded a truck in Lusaka for the 90-minute drive to the outskirts of Chirundu, the border town linking Zambia and Rhodesia via a road bridge. After dark, the truck continued down a bumpy sand road to a point near the banks of the Zambezi. From here they were ferried across the crocodile- and hippopotamus-infested river to the Rhodesian side. They then split into three groups of seven men. These were the first insurgents to enter Rhodesia; they were about to start the Second Chimurenga (uprising), 70 years after the Mashona Uprising, or First Chimurenga, against Cecil Rhodes's British South Africa Company pioneers in 1896–97.

While Chitepo had been readying his insurgents to cross the Zambezi in early 1966, Flight Lieutenant Peter Petter-Bowyer was about to become the first locally trained RhAF helicopter pilot. Those before him had learnt to fly the French-made Alouette helicopter in France or South Africa. As No. 7 (Alouette) Squadron expanded, however, training pilots externally was proving costly with scarce foreign currency. PB, as he is known, an experienced and qualified fixed-wing flying instructor, joined No. 7 Squadron to establish whether local training were possible and, if so, to become a qualified helicopter instructor.

He soon graduated, which brought the dubious honour of serving an immediate seven-day stint as the squadron's standby pilot at the New Sarum Airbase on the outskirts of Salisbury. Being duty pilot usually meant hanging around the crew room all day reading books and hoping for a flying task. It was peacetime, so a typical call-out duty might be to airlift a seriously injured road-accident victim to hospital or help round up escaped convicts. It didn't get more exciting than that, but then, being stationed in the delightful city of Salisbury made up for the boredom.

It was a pleasant Wednesday afternoon in late April 1966. PB had no idea that his inaugural duty as standby pilot would be fateful; he was about to make history.

In times of peace, Wednesday was a half-day for most air force personnel. Around noon, the bulk of normal activity at the base ground to a halt as people dashed off to change into sports gear. Wednesday afternoon was time for sport – cricket in summer, rugby in winter, with tennis, golf, bowls, squash and other activities played all year round. This enjoyable sporting ritual naturally excluded those on essential duty. All PB could do was watch with envy.

But then things started looking up. The phone in the crew room jangled. 'Petter-Bowyer, there has been a sabotage attempt on the power lines near Sinoia. Fly to the police station in the town immediately,' said the duty officer.

A farming town 100 kilometres north-west of Salisbury, Sinoia is an anglicised version of Chinhoyi, the town's name derived from the local chief who used to take refuge in the famous and beautiful Sinoia

Caves whenever the fierce Ndebele from the south raided the area for cattle and women.

PB guessed that a gang of saboteurs had attempted to cut the main electricity lines supplying Salisbury from the hydroelectric generators deep in the bowels of the Kariba Dam wall, where the waters of the mighty Zambezi River are harnessed to produce clean power. PB and his flight technician, Ewett Sorrell, strode briskly to the Alouette helicopter standing on the apron, its three rotor blades drooping forlornly.

After checking the Alouette, PB strapped himself into the right-hand seat while Sorrell checked the start process from the outside. PB flicked the fuel booster switch to 'on' and lifted the red safety cover housing the engine selector switch – the starter button. As he flicked the starter, the characteristic high-pitched whine of the Turbomeca gas turbine engine broke the silence. The sound grew louder and more intense as the kerosene fuel ignited with a deep whoosh. The scream became shriller until the little turbine settled at its idling speed of 17 000 rpm.

PB advanced the fuel-control lever steadily, increasing the turbine speed until the centrifugal clutch started taking, transmitting power from the engine to the gearbox and driving the main rotors, which, in turn, drove the tail rotor. The three drooping rotor blades lazily started rotating clockwise, but quickly became a flat, blurred disc as the engine and rotors reached their operating speed. The wind-up was complete; the Alouette was ready to fly.

'Cyclone 7, you are clear to lift off, cross runway zero six and route direct destination low level, call leaving the control zone.' PB replied to Salisbury air-traffic control with a crisp 'Roger, Cyclone 7 clear lift and cross'.

PB lifted the collective pitch lever, increasing the rotor pitch, and soon the Alouette eased effortlessly off the ground into a hover. After a few more checks, he edged the cyclic stick forward to achieve forward flight, pulling gently on the collective lever to establish a climb into the prevailing north-easterly breeze. Once at a safe height and speed, PB banked the helicopter left onto a westerly heading, passing near the civilian airport complex.

Soon they were flying over the southern suburbs and industrial areas of Salisbury, which gave way to the fairly flat but productive commercial farmland of the Mount Hampden area. To the right of track stood Mount Hampden – a koppie that had been the intended location of Fort Salisbury when pioneers first arrived in 1890. They found a better supply of water near another koppie, however, 20 kilometres south-east of Mount Hampden.

The Alouette continued across farmland rimmed to the west by the Great Dyke, a band of narrow ridges and hills running north–south for about 500 kilometres through Rhodesia. Visible from space, this feature was formed 2.5 billion years ago when molten rock forced its way through the original surface strata, later eroding and leaving behind this unique, dyke-like structure rich in minerals, including chromate, nickel, cobalt, gold, silver and platinum. PB started a gentle climb to crest the top of the Dyke, and descended on the other side.

'That's Trelawney on the nose; we are spot on track with 13 minutes to run,' PB said to Sorrell over the intercom. At their two o'clock position, the imposing grain silos of Banket stood out – 20 massive concrete storage bins in a long row. It was late April, and harvesting was in full swing. The bins were being filled, a process that would continue until June.

Banket is a town at the centre of the Lomagundi area, one of the most fertile farming regions in the world. Enormous quantities of maize, cotton, tobacco and beef were produced there. Much of the produce from Lomagundi, and Rhodesia's other farming areas, was for export, earning the bulk of the nation's foreign currency.

Although he didn't know it at the time, PB was flying to Sinoia to engage ZANLA insurgents bent on destroying the commercial farming sector in this land of plenty. They would eventually succeed, but it would take them about 40 years to smash the breadbasket and precipitate one of the fastest economic declines in world history.

Sinoia loomed large as the Alouette crossed the Hunyani River to the south of the town to set up an approach into the Lomagundi Police HQ. After landing in the police station car park, PB began reversing the helicopter starting process, winding the machine down. After the urgent scramble from Salisbury, the apparent lack of urgency in Sinoia seemed a bit odd.

The officer in charge of Lomagundi District, Police Superintendent John Cannon, met the crew and invited them to join him and his wife for a leisurely lunch. After a pleasant meal, Cannon, a former Lancaster Bomber pilot during World War II and holder of the Distinguished

Flying Cross, got down to business and briefed the helicopter crew about the situation.

An armed group of ZANLA insurgents had botched an attempt to blow up a main-line electricity pylon near Sinoia. Cannon explained that field intelligence revealed that 21 ZANLA insurgents had crossed the Zambezi from Zambia near the border town of Chirundu and split into three groups of seven. Cannon was most anxious to apprehend the group that had tried to blow up the power pylons. He called this group the Armageddon Gang. Cannon was candid with the helicopter crew. 'I have no idea where to start looking,' he said. 'But it seems a good place to start would be at the site of the sabotage attempt.'

They flew there in the Alouette. The inspection revealed the saboteurs had a poor understanding of explosives and demolition techniques; the damage was only superficial. Other than the evidence at the base of the pylon, there were no obvious signs pointing to where the saboteurs had gone. Cannon assumed they would not be far, so he asked PB to deploy sticks of his regular and reserve police force by helicopter so that they could sweep the area and flush out the gang.

With Sorrell left on the ground to make room for the rather large police reservists, mostly farmers, PB's first human deployment nearly ended ignominiously. Although he had been well trained to fly the Alouette safely and accurately, little of PB's training time had been devoted to landing at maximum weight in a tight landing zone (LZ).

Landing a lightly laden helicopter is a fairly straightforward process. The pilot slows the machine down, aiming for an upwind landing spot. As the machine gets closer to the spot and the ground, the pilot slows both the forward and downward speeds until both are effectively zero, ideally entering a stable hover a few feet above the spot on the ground. When the machine is heavily loaded, however, a lot more power is required to arrest the descent and hold the hover. If a heavy machine is allowed to descend too fast, the power available is insufficient to stop the descent, and it will bang to the ground – a bad outcome euphemistically known as 'settling with power'. Once committed to a landing, or, in other words, past the point of no return, all the pilot can do to cushion the impact is pull the last trace of power from the rotors. But there's one problem: the gearbox can only take so much strain, or torque, after which it will start shearing itself to bits.

PB was committed to the landing. All he could do was pull collective power past the torque limit of 1.0 and brace himself for the inevitable hard landing. The Alouette landed heavily, its tough undercarriage flexing to absorb much of the shock. The machine seemed to have survived intact, though. That 'arrival' – in air force speak, anything other than a gentle touchdown is denied the dignity of the word 'landing' – taught PB a poignant lesson. From that day forward, all new helicopter pilots would, as a matter of routine, learn to operate at the extremes of the helicopter's performance envelope.

The police swept through the bush but found nothing, not even a trace of the insurgents. With ideas running out, PB and Sorrell flew off to try to spot the gang from the air. They flew low and slow, searching various likely hiding places – a very dangerous way to look for the enemy, as it presented the unarmed helicopter as a big, fat sitting duck. But the air force men knew no better; there was no precedent. Luckily for them, but frustratingly, there seemed to be no trace of the Armageddon Gang. The mood back at the police complex was sombre. The question on everyone's mind was, how are we going to find these bastards? Then the phone rang.

The call was from the Police Special Branch (SB), a unit of dedicated detectives, who would be integral to the Bush War. The SB had an undercover agent working within ZANU, and this man happened to be the Armageddon Gang's main contact in Rhodesia. Even better news was that he was due to meet with the gang the next morning just outside Sinoia. This intelligence simplified things for Cannon. Once the undercover agent had ended his meeting with the insurgents, Cannon's force of regular and reserve policemen would pounce and engage the enemy in a classic police cordon-and-search operation.

But as they gave it more thought, Cannon and PB became worried that a vehicle seen tailing the spy's car might scare off the gang. Always the solutions man, PB had an idea: 'Sir, may I recommend we use a high-flying helicopter to track the agent's car all the way from Salisbury? I am certain that a chopper at great height will not upset the contact man or the terrorist group.' Cannon liked the idea.

PB called his HQ in Salisbury. He received not only the tailing helicopter, but also three additional Alouettes. PB's common sense, and his experiences from the previous day, told him that a single helicopter and a bunch of policemen were not enough. They were about to confront a fully armed insurgent group, not a few escaped prisoners.

Sinoia Police Station was bristling with activity that late April morning in 1966. Police reservists arrived from their farms in their typical gear – short-sleeved shirts, shorts, floppy hats and *veldskoens* with no socks. Meanwhile, Air Lieutenant Murray Hofmeyer was tailing the undercover agent's Ford Anglia in his helicopter at 6 000 feet. Once the Anglia passed Banket, three other Alouettes, flown by Squadron Leader John Rogers (officer commanding of 7 Squadron), Gordon Nettleton and Dave Becks, landed there to await a call to move forward.

Superintendent John Cannon commanded absolute attention as he briefed his force of regular policemen and reservists, the latter now dressed in their dark-blue riot-control uniforms. He told them that a gang of seven insurgents was hiding in the bush across the nearby Hunyani River. The plan was simple: the reservists would be dropped by trucks on two sides of the insurgents in a V-shape and would sweep towards the insurgents, driving them into a stop line at the top of the 'V'.

The plan seemed perfect, until Hofmeyer's call from his 6 000-foot perch interrupted proceedings: 'The occupants of the vehicle have gone into the bush on the south side, repeat south side, not north, as expected.' The original plan and briefing were now redundant. Time was running out. But being a sceptic, PB had already worked out alternative deployment plans. The best option was a mirror image of the original plan. However, the snag was that one side of the V-formation could not be reached by road, so PB suggested helicopter deployment.

Cannon quickly ordered one of the road groups to get over to the sports field on the double. For many it would be their first helicopter flip. By now the three Alouettes from Banket had landed and were ready. Paradoxically, PB, the newest helicopter pilot, was now in charge of the airborne operation, which meant even giving instructions to his boss, Squadron Leader John Rogers. But the pilots were unfazed by this and accepted PB's leadership.

Hofmeyer called with the news that the undercover agent and his Anglia were now leaving the area; the Battle of Sinoia was about to begin. The impending confrontation on Thursday 28 April 1966 would mark for ZANU the official beginning of the Second Chimurenga.

Although 70 years had passed, it was again the British South Africa Police (BSAP) who would respond to the threat. In 1896 the BSAP had been the only military force in Rhodesia; by 1966 there was both an established army and air force. This mattered little to Police Commissioner Frank 'Slash' Barfoot, however, who insisted that the insurgents were criminals, and, therefore, 'this [was] a matter for the police'. He reminded everyone that the BSAP, which was descended directly from Rhodes's British South Africa Company Police, was, after all, the 'senior service'.

Although John Cannon and PB knew that these regular policemen and reservists were not properly trained to fight an armed gang in thick bush, Barfoot remained unmoved. By pure coincidence, however, and without Barfoot's knowledge, the army did get involved.

Major Billy Conn, a Rhodesian Light Infantry (RLI) officer, and his quartermaster, Sergeant Moore, just happened to be driving through Sinoia en route to Kariba when they popped in to say hello to John Cannon. Seeing all the activity, Conn pulled his Land Rover up next to PB's helicopter and asked, 'What the hell's going on?' A highly experienced infantry officer, Conn quickly persuaded Cannon to let him join in. His participation would make a difference.

The operation began as the first helicopter, flown by PB, lifted off to deploy a stick of six excited policemen, soon followed by the other helicopters, with Hofmeyer also joining in. While PB was shuttling additional police reservists into position, he spotted a lone man standing under a tree. Without warning, one of the reservists suddenly opened fire from his seat in the helicopter; fortunately, the bullets missed the whirling rotors. PB was so incensed that he unceremoniously dumped the stick on the first LZ he could see – the bridge over the Hunyani River.

Shortly afterwards, a member of the gang broke cover and opened fire on PB's helicopter. The unarmed Alouette could not respond, but, fortunately, Hofmeyer's helicopter was armed with a crudely mounted infantry machine gun that his technician, George Carmichael, could fire from the left-rear doorway. When a helicopter is moving forward, direct aiming with a conventional sight is useless. What is needed is an offset sight that in fact aims behind the target. Even then, the altitude of the helicopter and its speed have to be taken into account or at least standardised – but such refinements were not to come until later. After many bursts from the helicopter, Carmichael used the position of the dust caused by the bullets striking the ground to adjust his aim and eventually bring down his quarry. Godwin Manyerenyere became the first ZANLA casualty of the war and the air force's first kill. There were to be many more.

A major problem soon became apparent: the helicopter radio frequencies were incompatible with the police sets on the ground. At one stage, two police groups were unwittingly converging on each another, and police-on-police fire was imminent. Dave Becks took the initiative by hovering his Alouette close enough to the policemen to enable his technician to use hand signals, thereby preventing a clash. It was a miracle that nobody was shot by friendly fire that day.

In another incident, a stick of reservists shot and killed a member of the gang, and in their excitement went to inspect the body in a group, breaking one of the most fundamental infantry rules. Observing them from the bush were two insurgents, one about to toss a grenade into their midst. The reservists were unaware of the danger, and, luckily for them, Major Billy Conn shot the grenade thrower just in time. The Russian grenade fell to the ground and exploded, finishing off both the ZANLA men. Without Conn's intervention, there would certainly have been Rhodesian casualties that day. The police muddled through and, slowly but surely, managed to flush out and eliminate the entire Armageddon Gang.

The jubilant policemen returned to the HQ complex to celebrate their victory over ZANLA. Although the operation had clearly been a success for the former Lancaster Bomber pilot Superintendent John Cannon and his untried police force, there were many who didn't see it that way. The army was particularly incensed that it had not been kept in the loop, and the air force castigated Hofmeyer and Carmichael for using far too much ammunition (147 rounds) to bring down one enemy.

Nevertheless, plenty of useful lessons were learnt. First, good intelligence proved to be vital. Second, the advantage of the helicopter as both a troop carrier and a gunship was demonstrated. Good and compatible communications were also shown to be essential.

Although none of the participants realised it then or later, this engagement laid the foundation for counter-insurgency operations. Over the next eight years, the concept of heli-borne troops and helicopter gunships would be refined and honed to form the most lethal weapon in the Rhodesian arsenal, and one that would be used on a grand scale in Operation Dingo: the Fireforce.

5

New strategy for ZANLA

After the Battle of Sinoia and further costly encounters with the Rhodesian forces, the mood at the ZANU headquarters was dark. Herbert Chitepo was licking his wounds and pondering the consequences of sending his forces across the Zambezi to certain death. He needed material and political support, especially as the Organisation of African Unity (OAU) and the host country, Zambia, officially supported Joshua Nkomo's ZAPU.

Chitepo gambled that if ZANU started the war they would steal a march on ZAPU and sway opinion within the OAU. Therefore, the Armageddon Gang and other insurgent groups had been rushed prematurely into Rhodesia in 1966. The result was the loss of their best-trained men, which seemed in vain, as neither the OAU nor Zambia budged, and they made it clear they wanted a single, unified liberation movement. The Soviet Union, a key backer of liberation movements, supported ZAPU and did not recognise ZANU. The party had a choice – merge with ZAPU or seek help elsewhere.

ZANU was fortunate because the Chinese government was keen to assist, but there were difficulties. China and the USSR were competing for influence in Africa, and Zambia was wedded to the Soviets, rendering China unwelcome there. ZANU would have to find a host country where China did hold sway. That country was Tanzania.

Chitepo established a training base in south-west Tanzania at Itumbi, an abandoned farm and gold mine dating from German colonial times. Chitepo simultaneously sent small groups to China for training. The first group went in 1963, led by Emmerson Mnangagwa, who would later become one of the most powerful and feared men in Zimbabwe. The initial training in China focused on teaching the trainer the skills of military instruction. Little time was spent on military strategy.

But that changed when a group known as the Nanking Eleven returned from China shortly after the Battle of Sinoia in 1966. This group had just completed training at the Nanking Military Academy in Peking, where they were taught the critical elements that contributed to Mao Zedong's communist victory in China – mass mobilisation, guerrilla warfare, military intelligence and control of the mass media.

Leading the Nanking Eleven to Peking was a tall and charismatic Shona military instructor by the name of Josiah Tongogara, who grew up on a farm near Selukwe in Rhodesia's Midlands. In one of those amazing ironies of history, Tongogara's parents worked for a farmer called John Smith, the father of future prime minister Ian Smith. To earn pocket money, the young Josiah would retrieve tennis balls when Ian played matches on the farm court during his school holidays. Little did Ian Smith suspect that one day this polite ballboy would become his arch-enemy and the prime target of one of the biggest battles of the war: Operation Dingo. The two would not meet again until many years later in 1979, when they faced each other across the negotiating table in Lancaster House in London. Despite the history and animosity, Tongogara never showed any personal hostility to Smith. In fact, he would often embrace Smith as a friend at the start of the day's negotiations in London, to the intense irritation of Robert Mugabe.

In 1963 Tongogara joined ZANU and started recruiting young black Rhodesians, mainly from his Karanga clan, for military training. Tongogara also underwent military training in Tanzania before his stint at the academy in Nanking. With his newfound knowledge, Tongogara could see that the tactics employed by Chitepo were wrong: there was no point fighting the enemy entirely on his own terms.

Tongogara passionately believed in the Chinese strategy of first winning the hearts and minds of the people, and then – and only then – escalating the war. But first he had to persuade Chitepo and the ZANU leadership to accept the strategy. The problem for Tongogara was that the Dare reChimurenga (ZANU's war council) was made up entirely of politicians with no military skills or experience whatsoever.

He presented his new three-pronged strategy to the Dare. The first strategic goal was for the ZANLA forces to merge seamlessly with the rural peasantry – 'like fish in water', as Chairman Mao had put it. Tongogara used a Shona phrase to describe the same concept: *simba rehove riri mumvura* (a fish is strong when it is in water).

This initial phase would be entirely political. Confrontation with the Rhodesian security forces was to be avoided at all costs. This crucial phase could, and would, take years to prepare for and implement. Once implemented, the second prong of the strategy would begin: hit-and-run attacks on a very wide front to stretch the Rhodesian forces. The third and final phase of Tongogara's plan would be more conventional, namely engaging the Rhodesian forces directly.

Tongogara put his strategy forcefully to the Dare, arguing that Mao's way offered the best chance of success. But the majority of the politicians on the Dare were not listening. They were impatient to resume the war, especially as the rival guerrilla movement, ZIPRA, had by now sent large groups into south-west Rhodesia.

Ignoring Tongogara's advice, in July 1968 Chitepo sent 50 men through the Mpata Gorge into Rhodesia, the largest ZANLA group yet to be deployed. But there was a subtle difference in strategy. This time, they avoided the main towns and moved instead in a south-easterly direction into the Dande area, in the heart of the old Monomotapa kingdom.

Eight days after the group had crossed the border, their spoor (tracks) were picked up by a Rhodesian border patrol. ZANLA had made a mistake: they chose to enter Rhodesia at the height of the dry season when the bush is sparse and water scarce. Even with these handicaps, however, they were still eight days ahead of the RLI, which could mean a gap of 160 kilometres or more.

But help for the RLI was at hand. ZANLA's nemesis from the Battle of Sinoia, Peter Petter-Bowyer, was on his way with four Alouette helicopters. Using them to cover ground quickly, the pursuers soon caught up with tracks that were just 24 hours old, meaning they were very close to their quarry. By then, the ZANLA gang had realised that they were being followed and split up into smaller groups.

The largest ZANLA group, with more than 15 men, was pursued by Lieutenant Jerry Strong, a Sandhurst Royal Military Academy Sword of Honour recipient, who would become one of the most effective counter-insurgency leaders in the war and would play an important role in Operation Dingo nine years later. As Strong closed in, it became apparent that the insurgents were heading for Mozambique.

'We needed diplomatic clearance from the Portuguese to enter Mozambique in hot pursuit,' recalls PB. This gave the gang a little time, but not enough, as the helicopter again proved its worth as a key counter-insurgency weapon. Diplomatic permission eventually came through, and early the next morning, the battle cry 'contact' came over the airwaves. Strong was engaging ZANLA. In a series of firefights over a wide area, most of the group were eventually killed or captured. ZANLA had failed again.

Tongogara was pretty upset about these latest losses, but not as angry as his forces, who were becoming disillusioned about being sent to Rhodesia as cannon fodder. Nevertheless, it took another two years before Chitepo slowly started accepting that there was some sense in the strategy Tongogara was proposing. Chitepo finally gave the new plan his full support, and even gave the impression that it was all his idea. 'It is useless to engage in conventional warfare with well-equipped Rhodesian and South African troops along the Zambezi,' said Chitepo in a news interview published in the *Rhodesia Herald* in August 1971. Chitepo's interview publicly signalled the switch of strategy.

The new strategy was sound in principle, but the hot valley of the Zambezi with its sparse population did not provide Tongogara's fish with much water. An added complication was that the Zambezi Valley was a long way from ZANLA's training base at Itumbi. Despite the distance, however, Tongogara managed to smuggle a reconnaissance group through Zambia into the Zambezi Valley to observe the Rhodesians and establish links with friendly peasants. The group returned to Itumbi with discouraging news. Not only was the valley a physically hostile environment, but the local people were distinctly unfriendly to ZANLA and had no desire to be 'liberated'. They also had a nasty habit of reporting the presence of insurgents to the Rhodesian authorities.

A new plan was needed, one that would completely bypass Zambia. Tongogara realised that the best chance of success would be to abandon Zambia and instead send his forces into Rhodesia's north-east through Tete Province in Mozambique.

6

Lessons from Sinoia

In the wake of the Battle of Sinoia in 1966, a troubled Flight Lieutenant Peter Petter-Bowyer started applying his entrepreneurial mind to improving helicopter performance.

'I took it on myself to design, build and test a decent mounting for a 7.62-mm MAG machine gun and to fit a gun sight suited to side firing in forward flight,' recalls PB.

PB had good hands and a natural gift for making things. At home, he made curtains and clothing for the kids, and even tailored dresses for his wife, Beryl. Born in Salisbury in 1936 to Paul and Shirley Petter-Bowyer, PB had aviation in his blood. On his father's side there was an established tradition of naval pilots, and his great-uncle, the famous William Petter (the maiden name of Paul's mother), had helped design the short-field Lysander aircraft of World War II fame, and later the English Electric Canberra, an aircraft that would play a key role in Rhodesia. William Petter was also a principal designer of the famous supersonic English Electric Lightning interceptor and the Folland Gnat jet trainer.

From early boyhood, PB had wanted to become a surgeon. At the appropriate age, his parents put his name down for a place at Edinburgh University to study medicine. It was not to be, however. PB's dream of being a surgeon started falling apart when his parents suddenly separated and divorced. Ensuing financial pressure meant that PB and his brother were transferred from a top private school to a state school, albeit a good one, in the beautiful Eastern Highlands town of Umtali.

PB settled quickly into Umtali High and made good progress, until one day his father dropped a bombshell: 'I am pulling you out of school.' Without a matric exemption, PB knew he could not go to university. His dream was shattered. Deep down, he suspected his stepmother was behind it, but he had no choice in the matter. After PB had been working on a farm for a while, his father told him, 'I have found a job for you as an apprentice carpenter and joiner based in Umtali.' Yet again, PB had to comply; it hurt deeply. Nevertheless, he applied himself to his new craft and progressed well.

Then one day in 1956, everything changed when the RAF paid Umtali a flying visit. Four Venom jets came screaming through the valley and passed over Umtali. PB stood mesmerised as the jets shrieked past; he had never seen anything like it.

'That's it, I want to be a pilot with the Royal Rhodesian Air Force.' PB was taking charge of his own life for the first time. His first task was to tell his boss that he was leaving to become a pilot. But he had a problem – joining the air force required a matric exemption. His boss, Mr Burford, disappointed as he was about the prospect of losing this talented apprentice, could sense PB's enthusiasm, so he decided to help. Burford called PB's old headmaster from Umtali High, who offered to vouch for PB's academic ability. 'Great,' thought PB. 'All I need to do now is get Dad's signature.'

An excited PB grabbed the RRAF forms, hopped onto his motorbike and went to see his father and stepmother. However, it was a bitterly disappointing trip; someone was trying to prevent him from doing well in life. When PB arrived at his father's house, his stepmother coldly hissed to his father: 'Not over my dead body will you sign that application form.' PB left the house in a daze, holding back tears as he kicked the motorbike into action and roared away from the source of his pain.

PB broke the news to Burford, but instead of being pleased that his gifted apprentice would after all be staying in the business, he called his lawyer. The law provided that PB's mother, Shirley, who had also remarried, could sign the form as a parent. Shirley agreed to sign, even though she had lost both her brothers as pilots in World War II. Out of 350 applicants, PB was shortlisted along with 34 others to do further aptitude tests and interviews in Salisbury. He became one of only 18 candidates selected to join No. 10 Short Service Unit (SSU), and started training on 3 January 1957.

Before he knew it, PB was sitting at the controls of a Percival Provost trainer. Teaching him to fly was much-feared instructor Flight Lieutenant Mick McLaren, who would go on to become the air force commander. PB was a diligent pilot. After 13 hours of training, McLaren opened the hatch after a particular landing and, as he hopped out, said, 'Well done, Petter-Bowyer. You are on your own. Fly a circuit and land.'

Without the authoritative presence of McLaren in the right-hand seat, it felt very different, but soon the task absorbed all his attention. He took off, revelling in the feeling of being alone in the cockpit, but all too soon it was time to land – a sobering thought, with nobody to help. PB need not have worried. He executed a perfect landing, thereby completing that unforgettable aviation milestone, the first solo.

PB sailed through instrument flying, night flying and precision navigation, and then graduated to jets, flying the Vampire T11 twin-seater and FB9 single-seater variants, an experience he loved.

PB married Beryl in 1958. A few weeks later, he achieved another aviation milestone. Sir Roy Welensky, the prime minister of the Federation of Rhodesia and Nyasaland, gave a set of wings to each successful No. 10 SSU pilot, the proudest moment for an air force pilot. PB went on to learn about weapons – cannons, rockets and bombs – a discipline he mastered well, and, when combined with his entrepreneurial flair, one that would make him, years later, the top counter-insurgency air-weapon developer in an air force that was crippled by sanctions. His inventions would play an important role in Operation Dingo and many others in this war.

After finishing a spell as an instructor flying Provosts at Thornhill Airbase, PB became the station admin officer, but his real job was testing locally made weapons. One of the first weapons he tested contained a locally manufactured version of napalm. These fuel-gel incendiary devices were known as frangible tanks, or frantan.

On one testing sortie, PB nearly became a fried victim of frantan. He experienced what every bomber pilot dreads: a bomb that will not release, known as a hang-up. The armed and primed device would not release from the Provost, despite his trying to dislodge it by means of high-G manoeuvres (increasing the effective weight of the bomb through acceleration forces) and severe yawing to shake it off. PB had no choice but to land with the hung-up frantan. During the landing roll, the frantan released and ignited near the aircraft's tail. Fortunately for PB, the Provost was still travelling quite fast when this occurred – any slower and the aircraft could have been incinerated. PB got away with nothing more than a badly 'sunburnt' neck, and the Provost with severely blistered paint.

In early 1966, PB joined No. 7 Squadron to start his helicopter training, which soon saw him involved in the Battle of Sinoia. After this, he determined to design a suitable gun platform with an appropriate aiming sight to enable a helicopter's side-firing machine gun to be operated safely and accurately. He also took it upon himself to design a refuelling system that was better than the one used at the time – the *kamina-kawena* (mine-yours) handpump, which usually involved two people rocking a handle backwards and forwards to pump fuel from a 210-litre drum – a slow and laborious process.

Operational flying also occupied PB's time. Four weeks after the Battle of Sinoia, he saw victims of terror for the first time when he was called out to respond to a ZANLA attack, this time by the Zvimba Group, a sister group of the Armageddon Gang, which had been wiped out in the Sinoia encounter. This attack took place near Hartley, not coincidentally in the area where, 70 years earlier, Gumboreshumba, also known by his spirit-medium name, Kaguvi, had been instrumental in organising the First Chimurenga.

The leader of the Zvimba Group was a BSAP deserter, who had taken on the *nom de guerre* Gumboreshumba. Two weeks after the Battle of Sinoia in April 1966, the Zvimba Group attacked Nevada Farm and gunned down Hendrik Viljoen and his wife, Barbara, in cold blood. Four helicopters led by John Rogers, with PB, Ian Harvey and Gordon Nettleton piloting the others, flew to the farm.

PB remembers the awful sight: 'Mr Viljoen was naked and lying dead on the floor, and his wife, who had clearly tried to assist him, was gunned down next to him. Miraculously, their baby, in a cot alongside the main bed, was unscathed, although there were bullet holes in the wall inches from where the baby lay.'

Although Petrus Oberholzer, the farmer who bought his farm from Petter-Bowyer's father, had been the first white person killed by ZANU, the Nevada incident was the first armed attack on a farm for 70 years.

Rhodesian forces eventually hunted down the Zvimba Gang and accounted for six of the seven. The sole survivor of the original 21 insurgents was Gumboreshumba, the former police officer, who managed to escape along the Hunyani River to Mozambique and ultimately Zambia. Edmond Nyandoro was less fortunate. Captured alive, he faced trial for the murder of the Viljoens. He was found guilty and sentenced to death. Before his hanging, Nyandoro revealed that he had received training at the Nanking Military Academy in China. This was the first tangible proof the Rhodesians had of Chinese involvement with ZANLA.

Meanwhile, PB continued working on the helicopter machine-gun mount and refuelling system. Together with ever-helpful technicians, he developed a robust, highly effective mounting for the machine gun, which incorporated a container for catching expended cartridges and links, thereby protecting the fast-spinning tail rotor and those on board from red-hot cartridges.

Now he needed to incorporate a sight. PB discovered a French-made reflector sight that improved accuracy dramatically. The Alouette could now double as an effective gunship and troop carrier. With only minor modifications, PB's system rendered useful service throughout the war and played a key role in heli-borne operations.

PB also cracked the refuelling device, despite strong opposition from some senior air force officers who believed the manual system did not need to be changed. 'We fuelled Spitfires in the Western Desert from jerrycans – a pump is a luxury' was the cry from the old guard. However, they failed to appreciate that the Alouette's short range meant that a cumbersome and slow handpump seriously compromised the helicopter's main potential – rapid response.

PB was convinced that the aircraft 'should be a slave unto itself' and, undeterred, he worked on secretly. His invention utilised the Alouette's engine as a substitute for human muscle. Powered refuelling was now possible with the engine running at idling speed and the rotor blades stationary. By taking a tapping from the compressor phase of the Alouette's jet turbine engine, air pressure forced fuel from the drum through a hose into the helicopter's fuel tanks. This invention proved to be significantly faster, cleaner and easier than the *kamina-kawena* handpump. It worked like a dream and became the standard until some years later, when small petrol-driven pumps became fashionable.

7

Tete Province

On a map, Tete Province in Mozambique looks like the head of a mouse in cartoon-character form. On the mouse's nose is Zambia, its hat is Malawi and below its chin lies Rhodesia.

In the days of the Monomotapa and Rozwi kingdoms, Tete, or more particularly the Zambezi River, was a highway for trade. Gold, slaves, ivory and other tradable items were transported along the river to the Indian Ocean and on to Arabia.

This all started changing when the Portuguese mariner Bartholomew Dias landed at the mouth of the Gouritz River near present-day Mossel Bay in his caravel, the *São Cristóvão*, in 1498. He was the first European to see the shores of South Africa. Now that Dias had discovered that there was a sea route around the foot of Africa to the east, Portugal could challenge the Muslims in their domination of trade in the Indian Ocean. Dias's discovery eventually led the Portuguese to what they called the Estado de Africa Oriental – the State of East Africa – and in particular to a land named after the local sultan: Mozambique.

The Portuguese started pushing the Muslims out of Mozambique and wrested control of Mozambique Island from them in 1505. In 1522 they built a chapel on the island, which they named the Capela de Nossa Senhora do Baluarte (Chapel of Our Lady of the Rampart), the oldest European building in the southern hemisphere, which is still standing today. When trade started drying up in the sixteenth century, the Portuguese lost interest in the interior and Tete Province.

Centuries later, in the late 1960s, operating from Zambia, an anti-Portuguese liberation group, FRELIMO (an acronym for Frente de Libertação de Moçambique – 'Freedom Front of Mozambique'), had penetrated deep into Tete Province and consolidated their position. This did not seem to bother the Portuguese, who were content with merely protecting the Cahora Bassa hydroelectric facility on the Zambezi. With Tete forming a 350-kilometre border with Rhodesia, from Kanyemba in the west to just south of Nyamapanda in the east, the Rhodesian government was very uncomfortable about the idea of FRELIMO running free in the province.

The Rhodesian Central Intelligence Organisation (CIO) was also concerned about a change in FRELIMO's modus operandi. 'FRELIMO had switched from their prime objective of attacking Cahora Bassa to politicising the population and they were systematically eliminating all the tribal chiefs north of the Zambezi,' recalled CIO head Ken Flower in his memoirs.

It became obvious that if the Portuguese failed to contain FRELIMO in Tete, ZANU and ZAPU would move in, perhaps even threatening Manica Province to the south. This concern led to high-level talks between the two governments and set in train a Rhodesian military involvement in Mozambique that would last for the rest of the war.

In December 1968, under strict secrecy, four Alouette helicopters of the RhAF led by Norman Walsh landed in the small hamlet of Bene on the Luangua Grande River, just off the main road linking Tete town with Zambia. Bene is very close to Tembue, the site of a ZANLA camp that would be the second target – known as Zulu 2 – during Operation Dingo, nine years later. Peter Petter-Bowyer, flying one of the Alouettes, remembers Bene only for its stench. The camp 'architect' had done one thing properly: he put the communal toilet downwind of the camp, but, unfortunately, it was right next to the helicopter LZ.

'The latrine arrangement,' recalls PB, 'was one single trench line about 45 metres in length, over which a continuous wooden seat was set with at least 30 holes for users, who were afforded no privacy.' It was so bad that the Rhodesians arranged daily 'toilet flights' in an Alouette to a nearby bald granite dome. The rock is part of the Granitos Castanhos range, which aptly translates as 'brown granite'. The Portuguese were shocked at the eccentricity of these strange Anglo-Saxon types who used an expensive helicopter to go for a crap.

Nothing they saw in Bene impressed the Rhodesians much, except for one piece of military kit: a 20-mm light cannon fitted to a Portuguese Alouette helicopter. The reason the cannon attracted such interest was that shooting a moving target from a moving platform with a machine gun is very difficult. But a cannon firing high-explosive shells that explode on impact and deliver shrapnel over a good radius reduces the need for pinpoint accuracy. This weapon was truly impressive, but it would take another four years for Rhodesia to circumvent the arms embargo and acquire the French-made weapon. This cannon turned the Alouette into one of the deadliest air-to-ground weapons of the war.

The objective of the operation, codenamed Operation Natal, was for the Rhodesians to help the Portuguese reverse FRELIMO's gains in Tete. An RLI captain, Ron Reid-Daly, who had served with Peter Walls in the Rhodesian Special Air Service (SAS) in Malaya and would later command the Selous Scouts, was one of the first infantry officers to work closely with the Portuguese in Tete. The Portuguese army serving in Mozambique were mainly conscripts from Portugal, whereas most of the Rhodesian servicemen were born in Africa and believed their future lay in the continent. Despite cultural differences, well illustrated by the daily toilet trips to the Granitos Castanhos, and very different ways of seeing and doing things, the Rhodesians were determined to make it work.

And they did. Clandestine Rhodesian military involvement in Mozambique began in 1968. Sometimes the Rhodesians combined with the Portuguese, but often they were on their own. The SAS were the first troops deployed in Mozambique, initially to help the Portuguese track FRELIMO, and later to attack FRELIMO directly.

The Rhodesians would make life a lot tougher for FRELIMO.

8

Tongogara's Phase 1

It had taken Josiah Tongogara years to persuade Herbert Chitepo and the ZANU politicians of the need to wage war in three distinct and sequential phases – firstly, politicising the peasants, then engaging in hit-and-run battles to stretch the Rhodesians, before finally moving to conventional battles. The Dare reChimurenga eventually endorsed Tongogara's plan in 1971, allowing him to begin Phase 1, which involved covertly infiltrating ZANLA insurgents into north-eastern Rhodesia through Mozambique's Tete Province.

Before Tongogara could dispatch his men into Tete, he first needed permission from FRELIMO, who were fighting an escalating battle with the Portuguese. FRELIMO had consolidated their position in Tete to the point that they were agreeable to the idea of Rhodesian guerrilla forces using Tete to enter north-eastern Rhodesia.

Much to Tongogara's frustration, however, FRELIMO invited its natural ally, ZAPU, to open a new front in the north-east. Meanwhile, the ZAPU war council was paralysed by a rift, with politician James Chikerema on one side, and military leader Jason Moyo on the other. Preoccupied with this power struggle, ZAPU ignored the offer of a new front in Mozambique, a move that would prove to be a massive strategic error. Zimbabwean history might have been very different had ZAPU accepted FRELIMO's offer.

Reluctantly, FRELIMO allowed ZANU to use Tete and work with them to gain war experience and learn how to organise the peasant population.

By late 1971, Tongogara was ready to begin Phase 1. On the night of 4 December 1971, Amon Zindoga and Justin Chauke were the first ZANLA commissars to cross the Rhodesian border in the north-east, near Mukumbura, beating a pathway that thousands would follow in the years to come.

Politicising large groups of people without attracting the attention of the Rhodesians would be a challenge, but for ZANLA there was a very effective way around this problem – the *pungwe*.

For centuries, the *pungwe*, a gathering of people at night, was a time of spiritual encounter between families and clans, on the one hand, and on the other, it provided contact with the spiritual ancestors, who offer security, guidance, healing and renewal. The *pungwe* became especially significant during times of strife and hardship.

Titus Presler, a scholar of Shona customs and culture, writes in his book *Transfigured Night: Mission and Culture in Zimbabwe's Vigil Movement*: 'The pungwe is a flexible but formative ritual phenomenon in Shona life. It is a movement of wilderness nights during which the people engage the major spiritual struggles of their lives, gain victory and so make of the wilderness a garden.'

The guerrillas exploited the *pungwe* to great effect, using this age-old ritual as a means to preach the politics of ZANU while promising to restore the 'wilderness' of their overcrowded and overgrazed farm plots to a vast 'garden' of fertile land taken back from the white people.

Usually, the *pungwe* consisted of an all-night vigil of drumming and singing liberation songs, interspersed with breaks for political speeches. The singing and drumming would usually last until first light. By combining spiritual, political and military concerns, ZANU had tapped the mother lode.

The Rhodesians struggled to come to grips with Tongogara's strategy, and it would eventually pave the way for a landslide election victory for Robert Mugabe and his ZANU party in 1980. The *pungwe* would be resurrected in a sinister form, but to great effect, long after the war was over to keep Mugabe in power for decades to come.

ZANLA copied many of FRELIMO's politicisation methods, and a number of Portuguese words entered the Shona language, such as *povo* (the populace/peasants) and *parara* (go to). Every encounter with peasants started with the chanting of simple slogans extolling the ideals of the struggle and condemning the enemy. The slogans would soon become a greeting ritual. Typically, the guerrilla commander or commissar would chant *pamberi nehondo* (long live the war of liberation). The peasants would respond *pamberi* (long live). After a host of *pamberi* chants, it was time to focus on the enemy: *pasi nevatengesi* (down with sell-outs).

Pasi, chanted the peasants.

Pasi nemabhunu. (*Mabhunu* is a derogatory word for 'white people'.)

Pasi.

Pasi naSmith.

Pasi.

And so the chants would continue, accompanied by clenched fists for emphasis.

The peasants in the north-eastern border area were descendants of the old kingdoms of the Monomotapa and Rozwi, and shared the same culture and language. To these people, the border between Rhodesia and Mozambique was of little consequence. FRELIMO were able to cross the border into Rhodesia to obtain supplies and avoid detection by the Portuguese. FRELIMO slowly garnered sympathy for their cause among the peasants in Rhodesia. By the time ZANLA arrived in the area years later, they pushed at an open door.

Building on FRELIMO's contacts, many of whom were schoolteachers and sympathetic local chiefs and headmen, ZANLA found a receptive audience for their propaganda. The FRELIMO support enabled the guerrillas to spread their message quickly and effectively across a sizable area of the north-east. Simultaneously, ZANLA was able to bring large quantities of war materials across the border and cache them in Rhodesia.

ZANLA named this new war zone the Nehanda Sector, after the spirit medium who was a catalyst in the Mashona Uprising, or First Chimurenga, in 1896. The adjacent sectors east of Nehanda were named Chaminuka, after the most famous Shona spirit, and Takawira, after Leopold Takawira, ZANU's vice-chairman, who died of diabetes in Salisbury Prison in 1970.

The Rhodesian CIO soon got a whiff of Tongogara's new strategy. 'The lull in the war showed signs of being over in the latter half of 1971,' recalled Ken Flower. 'Intelligence reports coming from the north-eastern districts indicated a guerilla presence in the border regions and fleeting contact was made with columns of porters passing southwards through the Mazarabani and surrounding areas ... More and more frequently the words Chaminuka and Nehanda appeared in reports.'

The risk was perceived to be low, which gave ZANLA the best part of a year to politicise the peasants. Flower recalled: 'The guerilla presence and activity were not defined clearly enough for the Security Forces to react militarily.'

9

Phase 2: The hit-and-run war begins

Within a year of the first ZANU commissars beating a path into Rhodesia, ZANU had managed to politicise pockets of peasants across a vast area stretching from Sipolilo in the north-west to Mtoko in the east, a distance of 170 kilometres.

Making up a large chunk of this area was fertile commercial farmland along the Zambezi escarpment. Here, the Rukowakuona and Mavuradonha mountain ranges rise sharply above the Zambezi Valley, creating ideal conditions for summer rain, essential for growing tobacco and maize. The summer rains also filled the rivers and greened the bush, providing cover for Tongogara's forces.

Tongogara told the Dare in November 1972 that it was time to start the war in north-eastern Rhodesia. He chose one of his best commanders to organise the first attack, Soviet-trained Rex Nhongo, who was by now totally converted to the Chinese military way of doing things. Nhongo (real name Solomon Mujuru) slipped into Rhodesia in late November 1972 and blended into the Chiweshe Tribal Trust Land (TTL), ready to strike when the time was right. By that stage, the Chiweshe population had been well politicised by ZANLA, with the blessing of its most senior citizen, Chief Chiweshe.

The TTL nestled in the centre of the major commercial farming areas of Centenary, Mount Darwin, Bindura and Umvukwes. From this ideal vantage point, Nhongo studied the lay of the land and in particular the commercial farms. Tongogara wanted multiple attacks on farms to take place between Christmas and New Year, when the Rhodesians would be enjoying the holiday and least expect an attack.

Meanwhile, the Rhodesian SB was gaining ground in the intelligence field. The SB had pieced together information that would confirm the ZANLA presence in the north-eastern border area. Detective Inspector Winston Hart based himself in Bindura, a farming and mining town 70 kilometres north of Salisbury, and kicked off intelligence-gathering operations in the north-east and Tete. It soon became apparent to the SB, by working with the Portuguese military and intelligence services, that FRELIMO had firmly established itself along the Rhodesian border.

More alarming was the discovery of ZANLA reconnaissance groups in the same area.

Detective Section Officer Peter Stanton, who was seconded to help Hart, recalls: 'One of the most important features of the ZANLA reconnaissance missions was to establish contact with the local Rhodesian border populace and gauge its standing and reception.'

Stanton soon learnt of a FRELIMO camp at Matimbe, just across the Rhodesian border, and strongly suspected that ZANLA would be there too. The Portuguese, still sceptical about a ZANLA presence in Tete, reluctantly allowed the Rhodesians to recce and then attack the camp. In March 1972, the SAS, under Lieutenant Bert Sachse, attacked Matimbe and killed a number of defenders, but it was impossible to establish whether the dead were from FRELIMO or ZANLA. The SAS brought all the documents they could find for Stanton and his SB colleagues to sift through, but most of them were written in Portuguese or the local border dialect. Nevertheless, Stanton managed to find something: 'I came across a small note written in English indicating that the "comrades" had arrived. The message was for a local inhabitant in Rhodesia.'

This was the first documented evidence of a ZANLA presence in the north-east border area. That single note galvanised the intelligence-gathering process, which became more intensive. It soon became apparent that ZANLA had already politicised vast numbers of local peasants, yet no hard evidence emerged of a ZANLA presence within Rhodesia. The cat-and-mouse game continued until three black members of the uniformed BSAP arrested three trained ZANLA insurgents in the Kotwa area, 20 kilometres west of Nyamapanda, a town on the border with Mozambique.

Stanton, described by fellow SB officer Keith Samler as a 'walking memory with an incredible knack for remembering names, places and circumstances', interrogated the three and they were soon singing like canaries.

They told him about a large arms cache north-east of Mtoko. Stanton took one of the captives with him and after much tramping about in the bush, they came to some small koppies on the edge of the Nyangwa mountain range on the border. 'We found plaited bark and vine straps that had been made to carry weapons of war,' recalls Stanton.

The ZANLA captive also spoke about a ZANLA 'letter box' in a prominent tree. Stanton found the tree, and copied and replaced the letters before setting up an ambush. In the night, an unknown number of ZANLA walked into the trap and one perished. The next day, a wide search of the area revealed a massive cache of weapons, landmines and ammunition, which Stanton describes as 'one of the largest arms caches of the war'. As Flight Lieutenant Dick Paxton recalled: 'I flew heavy loads of war material in my helicopter to Mtoko.'

Stanton's efforts led to Operation Tempest, the precursor to Operation Hurricane. News of the setbacks to the ZANLA effort in the far north-east as a result of Tempest reached Nhongo at his secret base near St Albert's Mission, and he decided he could wait no longer. He quickly chose targets, the first being Altena Farm in the Centenary area, owned by a 37-year-old tobacco farmer, Marc de Borchgrave. Nhongo's primary objective of the first attacks was to study the reaction of the Rhodesian security forces. He delegated the initial attack to his deputy, who used the *nom de guerre* Jairos.

The group of eight left Chiweshe under cover of darkness, marching in the night for 16 kilometres from the sparse TTL to the heavily cropped commercial farmlands of Centenary. Nhongo split from the group to observe the reaction of the Rhodesian forces. The main group arrived at Altena farmstead at midnight, cut the phone wires and laid a Soviet TM-46 landmine in the entrance road. In the early hours of 21 December 1972, Jairos fired the opening rounds of what white Rhodesians would mark as the beginning of the Bush War.

The attack with rocket-propelled grenades (RPGs) and AK-47 automatic weapons was brief. But De Borchgrave, fearing another attack, stole out into the night on foot to get help. For those in the house, the long wait for De Borchgrave's return became unbearable. Eventually, a house guest spirited the kids into the car and, without turning on the headlights, they fled the farm in the dark, narrowly missing the landmine outside the farm gate. The De Borchgrave family were given refuge on a neighbouring farm, Whistlefield, owned by Archie Dalgleish.

It was a bad choice: Whistlefield was attacked 48 hours later. This time, the hapless Marc de Borchgrave and his young daughter, Anne, were injured by shrapnel from an RPG that slammed into a window near where they were sleeping. Once again, the insurgents laid a landmine on the road to the farm.

A massive explosion rocked the early-morning air when a truck carrying the RLI reaction force detonated the TM-46 mine. Corporal Norman Moore, riding on the tailgate, was flung high into the air and fatally wounded.

The RLI immediately started looking for spoor so that they could mount a follow-up. However, unlike in previous encounters with ZANLA, the spoor was very difficult to follow, a sure sign that ZANLA had learnt from their earlier setbacks.

The attacks on Altena and Whistlefield shocked Rhodesians, just as the attacks on the Norton family had shocked the pioneers nearly 80 years earlier at the start of the First Chimurenga. Prime Minister Ian Smith had warned in a radio interview two weeks earlier that 'if the man in the street could have access to the same information which I and my colleagues have, then I think he would be a lot more worried than he is today'. Despite the warning, the attacks still came as a shock.

The intelligence services now understood why weapons were being brought into the country via Mukumbura, Mzarabani and as far as the Nyapakwe Mountains further east. And they had also learnt that many young people were leaving north-east Rhodesia to join ZANLA in Mozambique. The threat had indeed been underestimated.

Stanton's ultimate boss, Chief Superintendent Mike Edden, would later tell journalist David Martin in an interview: 'We didn't expect the ZANLA guerrillas to come through Tete and we didn't know about ZANU's new policy. If we had we might have taken FRELIMO and the threat from Tete more seriously.'

Yet there were other powerful clues of this threat; they were provided by the RhAF. Peter Petter-Bowyer, who by now was commanding No. 4 Squadron, was not one to sit back and enjoy the trappings of the new rank. The new squadron leader got stuck in to developing visual reconnaissance, or recce.

PB had become adept at studying human and animal pathways from the air, differentiating between what is normal activity and what is not. Flying at 1 500 feet between 10:00 and 15:00, when the sun cast the least shadow and the ground reflected light well, he was able to quickly spot unusual pathway patterns that indicated a temporary guerrilla campsite. These camps would usually be in bush cover and not far from a village, where the guerrillas would obtain food and female company.

Together with his trainee recce pilots, PB was busy meticulously plotting pathways over a large area between Centenary and the Zambezi River in Mozambique. It was long, tedious work and tough on the bladder, but once the pathways were plotted, any changes to established patterns were relatively easy to see. Besides spotting numerous temporary camps, PB identified a single well-trodden route from Mozambique south along the Musengezi River and up the escarpment near St Albert's Mission.

'I was convinced ZANLA terrorists were active right there,' he recalls. 'I went to Air HQ to make a presentation of 4 Squadron's findings. I stressed that terrorists were active in the St Albert's Mission area of the Kandeya TTL and this posed an immediate and serious threat to Centenary farmers bordering on the area.'

Nevertheless, just as Rhodes's officials had preferred to listen to the Native Commissioners, who failed to see the Chimurenga threat 76 years earlier, the Rhodesian government seemed to do the same again. When PB's disturbing findings were presented to Prime Minister Ian Smith, he asked why the Department of Internal Affairs had not reported this before.

The Department of Internal Affairs took umbrage at PB's assertions, assuring the prime minister that there were definitely no terrorists in the Kandeya area. PB was horrified. Not only was his intelligence ignored, but a superior officer ticked him off for 'causing unnecessary alarm and despondency'. PB was joylessly vindicated four months later when Altena Farm was attacked. 'It was maddening,' he recalled.

But the damage was done. ZANLA was by now well established in the north-east. Ken Flower wrote in his diary that the failure to spot ZANLA was 'a dismal failure of our much vaunted "ground coverage" and our previously successful techniques of counter-insurgency'.

Things had indeed changed dramatically. The previously successful techniques Flower referred to had relied on the peasants compromising the insurgents. But ZANLA was now, as Chairman Mao put it, like fish in water: they were living among the peasants.

The army commander, Lieutenant General Peter Walls, would later recall: 'Had the police commissioner and CIO been good enough to tell us the intelligence they had at the time, we would have been even more prepared. I can't help feeling a bit bitter about the lack of cooperation there.'

10

Hurricane and Tete

Attacks came thick and fast in the wake of ZANLA's opening attack on Altena Farm. Ida Kleynhans became the first farmer to die in the north-east when ZANLA attacked Ellan Vannin Farm near Centenary. The attacks spread further east to Mount Darwin. Then came a report that some land inspectors were missing in the far north-east. Flight Lieutenant Dick Paxton, an RhAF helicopter pilot based in Rushinga, was tasked with searching for their missing Land Rover. He soon spotted a vehicle parked by the side of the road. Not expecting foul play, Paxton landed his Alouette on the road behind the vehicle and shut down the engine. Paxton recalls:

> As I approached the vehicle on foot, I saw a tarpaulin draped over the back of the Land Rover. As I got closer the hairs on my back started standing on end. I had an eerie feeling something was awfully wrong. I peered in through the driver's window and saw an AK rifle magazine and a bush hat lying on the front seat. I went cold, cursing myself about how daft I had been to land the heli, and worse still shut it down. I was sure the terrs were watching me as I gingerly retraced my steps back to the helicopter. It was the longest Alouette start-up I have ever experienced.

A much-relieved Paxton was soon airborne, and he raised the alarm. Later, the bullet-riddled bodies of two land inspectors, Robert Bland and Edward Sanderson, were found under the tarpaulin. A third man, Gerald Hawkesworth, had been taken prisoner by the ZANLA attackers.

The scale and spread of the attacks in the north-east brought home to Rhodesians the realisation that ZANLA had managed to infiltrate a vast area. The conflict had now become serious.

Although a year behind the curve, the Rhodesian response was swift. The Joint Operations Command was set up in Centenary in late 1972 to bring together the army, air force, police and SB; these corps worked together to plan operations. The military response to ZANLA

49

in the north-east would be known as Operation Hurricane. The kill rate increased dramatically as many of the original ZANLA attackers were apprehended by the army and the SAS.

Unlike the Altena Farm attackers, the gang that attacked Whistlefield Farm left spoor, which the SAS picked up and followed relentlessly. With a brilliant mix of soldier's intuition and a good understanding of counter-insurgency techniques used in Borneo, Major Brian Robinson, the new SAS officer commanding, decided to place ambush positions on the Musengezi River, along a route he was sure the ZANLA gang would follow. His intuition paid off – the ZANLA group walked right into the trap; three were killed and two captured.

Free-falling into Tete

Robinson, the man who, five years later, would command the ground forces during Operation Dingo, was delighted with the result. However, he also knew that regular infantry operations were not the domain of the SAS. He was keen to get the SAS back to what they should be doing – disrupting the enemy behind the lines in Mozambique.

The target he had been pursuing in Mozambique had shifted from FRELIMO and the odd ZANLA guerrilla to ZANLA itself. He was anxious to take the war straight to ZANLA, disrupting its supply lines and transit routes from Zambia and Tete into the Nehanda, Chaminuka and Takawira sectors. Intelligence indicated that the kidnapped land inspector, Gerald Hawkesworth, had already been marched into Mozambique. This gave Robinson the opportunity and excuse to enter Mozambique to try to free him.

Robinson organised the first ever Rhodesian night-time free-fall deployment into enemy territory, some 40 kilometres inside Mozambique. He had been working with Flight Lieutenant Frank Hales of the Parachute Training School (PTS) to train his men in free-fall parachuting, and in particular high altitude low opening (HALO) techniques. The advantage of HALO was the silent deployment it afforded. The aircraft would fly high, ideally at 18 000 feet, to reduce the likelihood of alerting the enemy. The paratroopers would then free-fall to 2 500 feet, open their chutes and drift silently to earth. On a very still night, anyone near the drop zone might hear the rumbling of a parachute opening in the violent terminal-velocity wind, but at night it would be difficult to know what the sound meant.

Two teams of four pathfinders, the first led by Lieutenant Chris 'Schulie' Schulenburg and the second by Captain Garth Barratt, weighed down by their heavy kit, clambered aboard a World War II–vintage Dakota aircraft at New Sarum Airbase near Salisbury for the hour-long flight to their drop zone in Mozambique. It was late afternoon when the Dakota's wheels left Runway 06. The men near the Dakota's open door saw the bright-orange late-afternoon sun reflecting magnificently off Lake McIlwaine in the distance. The Dakota climbed slowly to 11 000 feet, the height extending the daylight. The cold intensified. Although it was high summer and the temperature was 24 °C on the ground, the laws of nature meant the temperature dropped by about 2 °C for every 1 000 feet the aircraft climbed. By the time the doorless Dakota had levelled off, the blast of air whipping around the cabin was close to freezing, with a wind-chill factor well below that.

The SAS men sat in silence, lost in their own apprehensive thoughts, some rubbing their hands, some pretending to sleep and others incessantly tapping their altimeters to make sure the devices were working. In daylight it is difficult to judge accurately one's height above ground in free fall; at night it is impossible, hence the 'alti' is the free-faller's best friend.

As the Dakota crossed the border, the pathfinders stood up to check their equipment. It was cold. The twilight was still quite bright at this altitude, but the SAS men knew that as they fell through the air things would get darker quickly. The red light blinked on and Schulie moved into the doorway, ready to fling himself out into the slipstream.

The green light signalled 'go', and Schulie leapt from the door sill into the powerful slipstream of the Dakota's prop wash, which snatched at him and tossed him about. Just as suddenly, it was quiet and he was falling in undisturbed air, keeping stable by arching his back and controlling his direction with outstretched arms, legs and hands. It took 12 seconds for Schulie to reach terminal velocity, the equilibrium free-fall speed of about 200 km/h, when the wind resistance on your body equals the force of gravity pulling you to the ground.

An amazing feature of free fall is that there is no sensation of falling whatsoever. The feeling is one of floating – floating in a very powerful wind. The only time a feeling of speed is experienced is when the free-faller passes something static, hopefully nothing firmer than a cloud.

Schulie fell for another 40 long seconds, during which he looked up, his face distorted by the powerful wind, to see his three team members free-falling above him, and he could just make out Barratt's men in the rapidly fading distance. Schulie saw his altimeter go through 3 000 feet as it approached the red zone of 2 000 feet, at which height the free-faller is only 11 short seconds from impacting the ground. Schulie waved his arms to signal to his team that he was going to open his chute, reached in with his right hand and tugged the metal ripcord from its housing. The sudden deceleration from 200 to just 20 km/h made him dangle like a rag doll for a brief moment and then there was absolute silence. The contrast between falling in a super-hurricane and floating quietly under the canopy is dramatic.

Then Schulie saw one of his men, Sergeant Frank Wilmot, plummet past him in full free fall. Sadly, Frank's parachute did not open and he fell to his death in a deserted gully near the Musengezi River. The SAS would never know precisely why Wilmot failed to open his chute, but he was in a spin as he plummeted earthwards. In the fading light, it may well have been that Wilmot was focusing so hard on stopping the spin that he lost awareness of his altitude. Frank Wilmot's death on 19 January 1973 was 'the worst possible birthday gift I could ever have received,' recalled Brian Robinson.

After Wilmot's body had been recovered by helicopter, Schulie and Barratt picked themselves up and continued the mission. Although the SAS never found Hawkesworth, they managed to ambush quite a few ZANLA forces, who had no idea any Rhodesians were in Tete.

This set the tone for operations in Mozambique over the next few years, when the SAS, operating by parachute, canoe, foot and from a fixed base in Tete, would inflict serious damage on ZANLA's war effort in the province.

While the SAS were upsetting things for ZANLA in Mozambique, Operation Hurricane was making life very tough for ZANLA within Rhodesia. The Selous Scouts were mastering 'pseudo', the art of decep-tion, in the targeted area. Using black and white soldiers, and captured ZANLA guerrillas whom they had turned, the Selous Scouts were able to impersonate real ZANLA groups and cause mayhem. The main objective of the pseudo operation was to infiltrate areas where real ZANLA groups were known to be by asking the locals to guide them to their 'comrades'. Once the scouts had located a group, they would call in heli-borne troops and direct them to the target by radio.

The Alouette helicopter was again proving its worth by carrying troops quickly to ZANLA positions. Although the number of contacts and the kill rate increased, too many were getting away. Once the guerrillas heard the sound of approaching helicopters, they would bombshell in all directions; the optimum time to hit them was when they were still grouped together.

If the fixed-wing Provost managed to attack guerrillas while they were bunched, the kill rate was good. But more often than not, they were already legging it by the time the strike aircraft arrived, making things much more difficult. Also, after each attack, the Provost had to reposition itself for subsequent dive attacks, losing yet more time.

The side-firing machine guns on the Alouette troop carriers did account for a number of enemy kills, but hitting a moving target from a moving platform with ordinary bullets was difficult. The sights were calibrated at a given airspeed (easy to replicate) and at a given height above the ground (hard to replicate over hilly terrain). More firepower with a greater spread was needed. Ideally, a helicopter that could lob bomblets among the enemy quickly and continuously, without having to reposition, would have been best.

The K-car

The answer was the Matra 20-mm cannon, which some Rhodesian pilots had first seen mounted in a Portuguese Alouette helicopter at Bene, Mozambique, six years earlier. Rhodesian procurement agents eventually managed to secure a supply of the weapons and ammunition, and a few helicopters were fitted with the cannons for trials. This newly fitted Alouette gunship was called the K-car (command car, also known as the killer car). The size of the cannon, firing from the left doorway, meant that no troops could be carried; the K-car was a dedicated gunship.

Soon a place was made on the floor in the left bubble of the Alouette for the infantry commander, who sat in an armoured seat facing backwards. A force of one K-car, three G-cars (Alouette troop carriers with machine guns) and an armed Provost made up a highly effective new counter-insurgency unit, which soon took on the name 'Fireforce', or, in radio speak, 'Foxtrot-Foxtrot'.

The first major K-car action took place in June 1974 from Mount Darwin, when a group of 35 ZANLA guerrillas were spotted by a Selous

Scouts ground observation post. Flight Lieutenant John Annan, piloting the K-car, and his technician, Gary Whittal, operating the Matra cannon, accounted for a large portion of the 20 killed and five wounded. A number of things went right that day, but by any measure it was a spectacular success, proving the effectiveness of the K-car and setting the tone for things to come.

So effective was the 20-mm cannon that captured guerrillas would often recall their fear of the K-car, describing it as 'the helicopter that throws down grenades'.

Flight Lieutenant Mark McLean, a K-car pilot, described the role of the Fireforce pilots:

> The K-car pilot has the advantage of having an overall picture of the contact and you're directly involved with the airborne army commander. You carry out his wishes in directing the G-cars to their drop points. At the same time, you are watching the ground for gooks, watching own forces, talking on the radio, looking out for other choppers, and so on. When you have a target you need to get the gun to bear and give the gunner a decent platform, regardless of where you may be in either height or pattern.
>
> The great thing was that when you saw the enemy, you put down some 20-mm high explosive and you would get them.
>
> The G-car pilot drops the boys wherever he is directed. So he has to be slick in finding an LZ, sussing it out at a glance and sliding his machine in fast and efficiently. Most times the boys go out from a low hover – that reduces the risk of a tail strike or damage to the belly from stumps or rocks. And then, as soon as they're out, you scoot via the 'safest' departure route. No guarantee that it's safe, as many pilots either landed near gooks or flew over them.

What were the elements that made for a successful Fireforce deployment? McLean believed it was down to a combination of the variables:

> If the topography is good for Selous Scout observation – koppies and river lines – chances are that the action will go well because the enemy are enveloped by the attackers. But even then, they might slip past the end of a sweep line or you run out of daylight before you can make the kill. If the countryside is flat and a callsign has

made contact and called for back-up, the enemy could be long gone before the Fireforce arrives. A frightened man can run a long way in 30 minutes, so your area of uncertainty enlarges with every minute of response time.

The combination of the Selous Scouts and the Fireforce was proving to be a deadly weapon. Kill rates soared in the Chiweshe and nearby Madziwa TTLs, and two of the most sought-after ZANLA commanders, going by the *noms de guerre* James Bond and Mao, were eliminated. Their bodies, and those of hundreds of other ZANLA guerrillas killed in the area, were taken to the Mount Darwin police station for identification by SB. Thereafter, a uniformed police detail would take the bodies on the back of a Land Rover to an old disused mineshaft, known as the Monkey William Mine, and tip them in. The duty became known as the 'Mashfords run', named after a local firm of undertakers. The remains of these dead guerrillas (and probably some post-war additions) were only discovered in 2011, which caused quite a stir.

These heavy losses put ZANLA squarely on the back foot in the Hurricane arena.

The Fireforce deployment evolved and improved with experience. A key change was made – instead of the Alouettes picking up the nearest available troops, dedicated RLI or Rhodesian African Rifles troops were used, based permanently near the helicopters.

Later, the ageing Provosts were replaced by the French-built Cessna 337 or Lynx attack aircraft fitted with machine guns, rockets and frantan. But there was a limitation – the Alouette could carry only four troops. The Fireforce commander would have his four-man sticks dropped in strategic places, either in the likely line of enemy escape (known as a stop group) or to sweep towards the enemy to flush them towards a stop group. As the ZANLA groups grew bigger, it was not uncommon for a four-man Fireforce stick to find itself in a firefight with a much larger enemy force.

The limitation of the Alouette helicopter's carrying capacity was overcome a few years later when a World War II–vintage Dakota aircraft was added to complement each Fireforce unit. The Dakotas carried some 20 paratroopers, which instantly more than doubled the available ground troop numbers.

The success of the Fireforce in the Hurricane arena swung the momentum right back to the Rhodesian forces. ZANLA admitted that half of its forces had been killed. Even so, the insurgents were staying ahead in one crucial part of their strategy – recruitment.

Mujibha

Through encouragement and often by force, ZANLA ensured that a steady stream of young peasants flowed into Mozambique's Tete Province for training. As the influence of the guerrillas spread, local chiefs, headmen and sometimes schoolteachers became a key part of the recruitment chain. And to bolster its numbers in Mozambique, ZANLA trained people locally, known to the security forces as LTTs (locally trained terrorists). However, even with the addition of the LTTs, the task of spreading the ZANU message across the vast Hurricane area was time-consuming and difficult.

ZANLA addressed this shortcoming by co-opting a massive number of impressionable rural children, instilling in them an unquestioning idealism with a ruthless streak. The chosen youngsters, known as *mujibha* (boys) or *chimbwido* (girls), would act as the eyes and ears for the guerrillas. They were their messengers. The most effective task these kids performed was reporting the presence of Rhodesian forces.

But there was a sinister side to the role of the *mujibha* and *chimbwido*: reporting traitors, or sell-outs. The youngsters were encouraged to report anyone who was 'betraying the struggle'. They did this to a degree. Reporting traitors, however, also allowed the young recruits to exact revenge as it suited them, on somebody who had been unkind to them, such as an overly strict schoolteacher, for instance.

A culture of spying on neighbours and even relatives was developed, much like the systems Stalin and Hitler used to great effect to neutralise opposition. There was no appeal process – once a youngster had identified a *mutengesi* (sell-out) to a ZANLA commander, no further investigation was done and no other witnesses were called to substantiate the allegation. The victim was executed on the word of a young boy or girl. Therefore, these youngsters became very powerful people in their villages; they wielded power over life and death.

The worst possible fate that could befall a person in the rural areas was to be labelled a *mutengesi*. Once identified as such, the guerrillas would choose the right moment to make a public example of him, and it was always brutal. The victim would be summoned, accused of being a sell-out, usually beaten and then summarily executed in front of family and friends, normally by a single shot to the head.

To add to the family's misery, the guerrilla leader would often order that the body was to be left where it fell, usually outside the victim's house, for days or even weeks. The sight and smell of a decomposing body was a forceful deterrent to anyone who contemplated dissent.

Mourning a *mutengesi* was forbidden, which violated the deep-rooted Shona custom of mourning their dead and burying them after proper funeral rites had been performed. Thousands of rural people, including schoolteachers, administrators and businesspeople, would be branded as sell-outs and executed by ZANLA during the Rhodesian War. Whether the victims were innocent or guilty, it was a highly effective way of forcing total loyalty. Indeed, so effective that ZANU would use this system of rooting out and punishing sell-outs long after the war was over.

11

Détente and the Carnation Revolution

The intensification of Operation Hurricane and increased SAS incursions into Mozambique worried Rhodesia's neighbour, South Africa. John Vorster, the South African prime minister, was concerned that his country was gradually being sucked deeper into the Rhodesian War. South Africa had already dispatched a police force with helicopters to Rhodesia in response to the South African ANC joining their traditional allies, ZAPU, in combined excursions into western Rhodesia.

What worried Vorster most was that South Africa's involvement in Rhodesia was giving political ammunition to the global anti-apartheid lobby. To reduce this political pressure on South Africa, Vorster started an exercise he called 'détente' – engaging in dialogue with friendly anti-communist African leaders. On his way to his first meeting with a black African leader, President Hastings Banda of Malawi, Vorster spent a night at the Rhodesian prime minister's residence. Vorster explained his ambitions to Smith, who thought it all sounded quite reasonable. Little did Smith suspect that Vorster's new policy would prove to be more of a threat to Rhodesia than the combined menace of ZANLA and ZIPRA.

The first inkling Smith had of the issue was the sudden shift in the Afrikaans press in South Africa from a very pro-Rhodesian stance to one of hostility. Smith recalled:

> They [the Afrikaans press] were now indicating in no uncertain manner, as part of what was clearly an orchestrated campaign, that Rhodesia was not doing enough to settle the constitutional problem. At the same time they started reminding us that we were leaning heavily on South Africa for support, and that this was becoming an embarrassment.

While a rift was developing between the South African and Rhodesian governments, the Fireforce was mauling ZANLA in the Hurricane area, and the SAS and air force were hitting them hard in Tete. Then, in April 1974, an event thousands of miles away dealt a savage blow to the Rhodesian strategic military effort: the Carnation Revolution in Portugal.

After decades of authoritarian rule and costly wars in their African colonies, the Portuguese were impoverished and wanted change. Events came to a head on 25 April 1974 with a *coup d'état* that overthrew Prime Minister Marcelo Caetano's government. The coup became known as the Carnation Revolution, as supporters of the revolution in Lisbon wore red carnations.

The new left-wing leadership was anxious to end Portugal's five-century-old African colonial hegemony as soon as possible. The Lisbon government entered into dialogues with its former enemies, the guerrilla groups in Mozambique, Angola and Portuguese Guinea. The objective was to hand power over to them as quickly as possible.

Rhodesia and South Africa suddenly had to face up to the fact that soon there would no longer be a friendly Portuguese power along their vast eastern borders with Mozambique. Instead, the unfriendly Marxist guerrilla movement FRELIMO, under their commander, Samora Machel, would take over. The Rhodesians knew full well that ZANU and FRELIMO were allies. ZANLA would now be free to move about Mozambique, enjoying moral and material support from the new FRELIMO government. In a stroke, the strategic advantage swung from the Rhodesians to ZANLA.

With the collapse of the Caetano government and the need to deal with new Marxist neighbours in Mozambique and Angola, Vorster's mind shifted to one objective – protecting South Africa's interests. So he accelerated his strategic gamble of détente and stepped up the dialogue with selected African leaders. To gain credibility with his new-found friends and to shift the international focus away from South Africa, Vorster had to offer something in return.

Rhodesia would be that something – the sacrificial lamb.

Vorster's plan was simple: he would pressurise Ian Smith into engaging in dialogue with the nationalists, while President Kenneth Kaunda of Zambia and Tanzanian president Julius Nyerere would bring pressure to bear on ZAPU (Nkomo) and ZANU (Sithole) to sit around a negotiating table with Smith.

The South Africans held all the cards, their ace being Rhodesia's vital supply lines through their country. What Smith did not know was that Vorster had already indicated to Kaunda that he would secure both a ceasefire and the release of the key political prisoners in Rhodesia. After a tense meeting in Pretoria, an unhappy and cynical Smith went back to Rhodesia to announce a ceasefire on 11 December 1974, just two years after the Altena Farm attack.

Smith ordered the release of Mugabe, Nkomo and all the nationalist political prisoners, who had spent the last 11 years in detention. Rhodesian forces could only sit and watch as the badly mauled and demoralised guerrilla forces picked themselves up and headed to Mozambique and Zambia to regroup and rearm.

At the time, ZANLA were down to less than 100 trained men in Rhodesia. But probably more significant was the loss of face for the Rhodesian government in the eyes of the peasants, many of whom saw the release of the political leaders as a sign of weakness. Serious damage was done to the Rhodesian cause.

12

ZANU falls apart

Despite the unexpected gift of a ceasefire, ZANU was falling apart. The problems began four years before the ceasefire, in 1970. First, the ZANU vice-president, Leopold Takawira, died in prison of diabetes, which shocked the jailed ZANU leadership badly. Takawira's death and the strain of six years in prison took their toll on Ndabaningi Sithole, the ZANU president. His erratic behaviour prompted a coup by his fellow inmates in Que Que Prison. They met secretly in a cell and voted to sack him. Had Takawira still been alive, he would have automatically succeeded Sithole as leader. So the next man in line, the party's secretary general, was appointed interim leader until the party held its next conference. That man was Robert Mugabe.

Meanwhile, on the front, the Rhodesian CIO was sowing mayhem among the guerrillas. By interviewing numerous ZANLA captives, the CIO became aware that the front-line guerrillas were badly demoralised from the pounding they had taken in Rhodesia, and by a serious lack of fighting equipment. They were also disillusioned with their leaders, whom they hardly ever saw anywhere near the front.

The CIO also learnt of serious tribal differences pulling ZANU apart. Two rival Shona clans, the Karanga and Manyika, were battling for supremacy in ZANU. The Karanga had provided the bulk of recruits for ZANLA, and they had fought more battles and lost more fighters than any other group. Consequently, they felt that their clan should carry most weight on the Dare reChimurenga.

ZANU reorganised the external wing of the party in 1973, with the lion's share of posts going to the Karanga, leaving the scraps of power to the Manyikas. The exception was Herbert Chitepo, a Manyika, who remained leader of the external ZANU organisation. However, his post had become largely symbolic. The real power lay with Josiah Tongogara, a Karanga, who controlled all the key levers of power.

In a brilliant piece of counter-espionage, the CIO managed to meet discreetly with the ZANLA commander of the Nehanda Sector, a Manyika, Thomas Nhari, near Mukumbura. By feeding him information about the lavish lifestyles enjoyed by the Karanga leadership, the advent of détente and jobs for the Karanga, Nhari was provoked to rebel.

Nhari and his rebels planned to muster support from the large ZANLA training and transit base at Chifombo, on Zambia's border with Mozambique. They would then march to Lusaka in a show of force. Not all those at Chifombo, however, supported the rebellion and some refused to join. Nhari's response was brutal: he rounded up his main opponents and executed them. A few days later, on 9 December 1974, Nhari and his band of rebels arrived in Lusaka to air their grievances, embarrassing Kaunda, who was in the middle of the détente dialogue.

Chitepo was willing to hear the rebels' grievances, but Tongogara saw them as traitors and was dead against negotiating with them. To show they were serious, the rebels kidnapped a number of ZANU leaders, including Kumbirai Kangai and Tongogara's wife, and took them back to the Chifombo camp as hostages.

Fearing the hostages would be executed, Chitepo quickly changed his mind and supported a plan by Tongogara to retake Chifombo by force, without delay. Tongogara quickly raised a force of 300 guerrillas from ZANLA's Mgagao camp in Tanzania. Led by Rex Nhongo, they attacked Chifombo and quickly defeated the unsuspecting Manyika rebels, killing nearly 50 of them and capturing many more. A tribunal, headed by Chitepo, was convened on 22 January 1975 to try the captured rebels.

It was a trial of vengeance. Many of the officers were found guilty within minutes and executed outside, including the rebel leader, Thomas Nhari, who had been one of Tongogara's most successful commanders. The executions were carried out in full view of the remaining camp inhabitants, including women and children. It didn't end there. A wave of reprisals aimed at rooting out any potential Manyika rebels left many more dead.

As a Manyika, Chitepo became the meat in a very hostile sandwich. The Karanga blamed him for sparking the uprising in the first place, whereas his fellow Manyika felt he had betrayed them. His position as ZANU's external leader had become untenable.

Neither Chitepo nor Kaunda realised that the real threat was the Rhodesian CIO. On the morning of 18 March 1975, barely two days after meeting with Kaunda, Chitepo got into his blue Volkswagen Beetle parked outside his house in Lusaka. When he turned the ignition, the car exploded. The car bomb was so powerful that it uprooted a tree next door and threw parts of the Beetle onto the roof of his house. Chitepo died instantly.

Kenneth Kaunda was incensed by the assassination. He believed Chitepo was an essential ingredient in the détente initiative. Kaunda immediately set up a commission of inquiry consisting of officials from 14 African countries. Tongogara, meanwhile, fearing that he would be blamed for Chitepo's death, fled to Mozambique with many of his leading commanders. Immediately after Chitepo's funeral, Kaunda's men rounded up senior ZANU personnel and demanded that FRELIMO send Tongogara and others back to face the music. When they arrived in Lusaka, Kaunda jailed them.

With Chitepo dead and Tongogara in a Zambian jail, ZANU was decapitated. Ken Flower recalled: 'The extent of the reaction in Zambia to the death of Herbert Chitepo astounded even the CIO.' The guerrilla movement was at war with itself, while its most effective leader and military strategist languished behind bars.

The timing of Chitepo's assassination made it hard to believe that it was a Rhodesian plot. The popular perception was that it was an all-ZANU conspiracy, directly related to the Nhari rebellion. Hence the rebellion, the executions and the assassination of Chitepo left a deep and permanent scar on ZANU. These events would shape the politics of Zimbabwe well into the twenty-first century.

Another significant, but unintended, consequence of the Chitepo assassination was that it opened the leadership door to Robert Mugabe. A further consequence was the ascendancy of Mugabe's fellow Zezuru-clan comrade, Rex Nhongo, who stepped into Tongogara's shoes after his arrest.

13

Mugabe heads east

When Mugabe heard the news of Chitepo's assassination, he believed the external leader had paid the price for standing in the way of Kaunda's détente plans, and that the Zambian government was behind Chitepo's assassination.

The ZANU executive quickly convened a meeting at a hotel in the Highfield township of Salisbury and resolved that Mugabe, as the party's secretary general, should leave for Mozambique to take over the reins until a new leader could be elected. Another member of the executive, his fellow prison inmate Edgar Tekere, would accompany him.

Mugabe and Tekere were spirited out of Salisbury, changing cars at Cold Comfort Farm in Ruwa. Their Volkswagen Beetle spluttered along the main road east towards Rusape, a small farming town 135 kilometres from Salisbury, where they stopped to refuel and buy snacks and refreshments.

Mugabe wasn't known in these parts and went by unnoticed; Tekere, however, kept a low profile, as this was his backyard. From Rusape, they took the road east towards the Inyanga Mountains. The topography changed quickly to reveal spectacular, massive granite hills weathered over millions of years into amazing shapes. The hills gradually became mountains, and the flora thickened – a sign of regular rainfall. They were entering the beautiful Eastern Highlands, a part of the country that looks more like Scotland than Africa, where many Rhodesians had holiday cabins to escape from the summer heat.

Finally, they passed Troutbeck Inn, a delightful hotel boasting one of the prettiest mountain golf courses in the world. Shortly after Troutbeck and after passing World's View, which affords a magnificent vista over Mozambique some 5 000 feet below, Mugabe and Tekere were dropped off and walked the rest of the way to Nyafaro, where they were fed and sheltered by a community of tribespeople led by Chief Rekayi Tangwena. Mugabe and Tekere spent a number of weeks there before crossing the Karezi River into Mozambique in early April 1975.

Mozambique had been in a state of flux since the coup in Lisbon a year earlier. The war between the Portuguese and FRELIMO was over, and by the time Mugabe and Tekere crossed the border, the Portuguese forces had already pulled out of much of rural Mozambique. Samora Machel and his FRELIMO guerrilla party would assume power two months later, on 25 June 1975.

ZANU was quick to use its new strategic advantage by going on a massive recruitment drive in the areas of Manicaland adjacent to the Mozambican border. Young men and women were encouraged to cross the border into Mozambique to join the struggle; they were promised quick training and a rapid return to Rhodesia, armed with the best weapons. But there was no planning, and soon vast numbers of recruits were pouring haphazardly over Rhodesia's porous eastern border.

The sudden arrival of recruits worried FRELIMO, who were pre-occupied with figuring out how they were going to govern their own country. Trying to bring some control over the situation, FRELIMO herded the recruits into abandoned Portuguese military camps at various locations along Highway 102, the main north–south road in Mozambique's Manica Province.

This turbulent situation is what Mugabe and Tekere encountered when they entered Mozambique. After crossing the border, they were taken to a small FRELIMO camp in the Choa area. FRELIMO were quite unsure what to do with their new visitors, who, in turn, were miffed about not being given a hero's welcome by their new comrades. Eventually, Mugabe and Tekere were taken on a long walk around the imposing Serra Nhatoa mountain to the nearest holding camp for recruits at Vila Gouveia on Highway 102. They were met by 400 hundred recruits.

'The new recruits were all boys, who expected to immediately be given guns and go off to fight; they wanted to go off and kill all the whites,' wrote Edgar Tekere in his autobiography, *A Lifetime of Struggle*.

Tekere knew that the recruits needed to be kept occupied, so he introduced physical exercise and drills. 'Many were disappointed and frustrated and this led to insubordination.'

FRELIMO, playing pass the hot potato, moved the entire group to an old FRELIMO camp further north, where another 600 recruits had been herded together. Eventually it was decided that the safest option was to bring together the recruits and politicians in one place. They chose the provincial capital of Manica Province, Vila Pery, named after

João Pery de Lind, governor of Mozambique, who turned the fertile Chimoio area into Mozambique's top agricultural centre in the early 1900s.

Before the Portuguese arrived centuries before, the area was known as Chimoio, after the slain son of a paramount chief of the Moyo clan. With the rise of the Monomotapa kingdom in the Zambezi Valley, Arab traders began sailing their dhows up the Buzi and Revue rivers from Beira to trade gold, slaves and other merchandise with the Mono-motapa people. They marked their routes by planting non-indigenous Palmyra palms along the way as navigation beacons. Many are still visible in the area, notably on Monte Zembe, a mountain landmark 24 kilometres south of Vila Pery. Samora Machel renamed the town Chimoio shortly after coming to power in 1975.

FRELIMO managed with difficulty to transport 1 000 ZANU recruits 115 kilometres south to Chimoio. As the trucks neared the town, Mugabe and Tekere would have noticed many empty farmsteads, recently abandoned by white farmers in their panic to flee Mozambique ahead of the FRELIMO takeover. Machel would later publicly rue scaring the white people away with his threats to nationalise every-thing, including domestic houses. The sudden vacuum created by the exodus quickly turned Mozambique into a basket case.

Ironically, it was Machel who, five years later, would pressurise Robert Mugabe and ZANU to delete the heady socialist clauses from their election manifesto to avoid the mistakes he had made himself. As it turned out, Mugabe did largely heed Machel's advice for nearly 20 years before he purged Zimbabwe of not only most of its white citizens, but also vast numbers of black people who fled the eco-nomic and political mayhem and one of the world's fastest economic collapses.

In another twist of irony, white Zimbabwean commercial farmers thrown off their land by Mugabe would be invited by the Mozambican government to resuscitate and farm the fertile Chimoio area.

Tekere describes what he and Mugabe saw when they arrived at Chimoio: 'There we found about 3 000 more recruits. And for the first time we encountered females.' The recruits were completely un-trained; the only thing binding them together was a romantic ideal to join the Chimurenga. The FRELIMO area commander, a man called Jehovah, was nervous about the ever-expanding recruit population in

Chimoio Town, all needing to be fed, cared for and kept out of trouble. FRELIMO decided it was best to get them out of the town, so the commander took Tekere on a real-estate tour of abandoned Portuguese farms and small army camps between the Mombezi and Massua rivers about 20 kilometres north of Chimoio, offering this prime land and infrastructure to ZANU on a plate. The area selected stretched nine kilometres from the abandoned De Sousa family farm in the west to the Monteiro farm in the north-east.

Tekere centred the new ZANLA complex on three old farms: the Adriano Antonio farmstead in the middle, flanked by the De Sousa farm, just under two kilometres to the west, and the Graça farm, lying the same distance to the east. The modest Antonio farmhouse and out-buildings were surrounded by lush trees, orderly palms and a pleasant garden, with its front gate right on the dirt road to Chimoio Town, only 17 kilometres away. The old Graça farm was also very pleasant, with big tobacco barns and several outbuildings. Tekere was spoilt for choice, but he made a decision: the old Antonio farmhouse would be the new ZANLA headquarters in Mozambique. The Graça farmstead would form the main storage complex, known as the national stores, and the De Sousa farm would be turned into the main convalescence centre. These three farms and the surrounding buildings became known collectively as New Farm, but many just called it Chimoio. It became the nerve centre of ZANLA, from where Mugabe, Tongogara and Nhongo would direct the war.

Over the next year, the complex grew exponentially and soon in-corporated a registry; a holding camp for recruits due to be trained abroad and another for housing fully trained guerrillas bound for Rhodesia; vehicle-repair garages; massive ammunition stores; a college for training political commissars; a school for the children of those based permanently at the camp; and other support structures. The recruits undergoing training were housed in a large camp just over six kilometres to the north-east of the HQ building.

Given the sheer length of the border with Rhodesia, it was difficult to channel all the new recruits to New Farm, so Tekere was taken on another real-estate tour to the Monte Nhamapaco area, 50 kilometres north, where he was offered more land. Tekere chose a picturesque spot in a horseshoe bend of the Rio Nhazonia, also known as the Nyadzonia River. He would later deeply regret this choice of location for a recruit camp, calling it a 'death trap' after the Selous Scouts attacked the camp in a daring vehicle-borne daylight raid.

The new Chimoio HQ complex acted like a magnet attracting not only increasing numbers of new recruits and their families and hangers-on, but also trained, experienced ZANLA guerrillas from the north-east theatre. According to Tekere, future Zimbabwean vice-president and wife of Solomon Mujuru, Joice Mujuru, using the *nom de guerre* Teurai Ropa Nhongo, gave the first military instruction at Chimoio. Teurai Ropa ('Spill Blood') taught Tekere how to handle a gun.

FRELIMO were wary, however, about too many armed people running around, so they restricted the distribution of weapons to ZANLA. Trainees used drill sticks, pick handles and shovels as gun substitutes.

While Tekere organised logistics, Mugabe focused on delivering political lectures to the recruits, subtly raising his profile within the military wing of the party. Then one day, out of the blue, FRELIMO arrived with orders to remove the two ZANU leaders from the Chimoio area.

Samora Machel was deeply preoccupied with trying to run his new government. The OAU, however, was pressing him to support ZAPU. So instead of welcoming Mugabe and Tekere as friends, Machel had them trucked off to the small coastal town of Quelimane in central Mozambique, a serene but sweltering settlement on the banks of a picturesque lagoon that empties into the warm Indian Ocean. They were effectively under house arrest.

Mugabe was deeply unhappy. He knew that while he lingered in Quelimane, time was slipping by and there was the risk that Sithole would make a comeback as ZANU's leader. Some 16 months had passed since Mugabe and Tekere had entered Mozambique, when, in August 1976, a respected senior ZANLA commander, Wilfred Mhanda, whose *nom de guerre* was Dzinashe Machingura, arranged to quietly slip Tekere, and later Mugabe, back to New Farm for military briefings.

He did not think much of Mugabe, and later publicly criticised him as being 'too conservative'. Mugabe reacted by having Machingura and his allies jailed in Mozambique for the rest of the war.

Machingura would later tell the BBC in an interview: 'When Mugabe takes a dislike to someone, he becomes vindictive and never changes his mind.' Tekere would learn the same lesson a few years later when he too fell foul of Mugabe.

14

Mosi-oa-Tunya

With Chitepo dead, Tongogara in jail and Mugabe confined to Queli-mane, Vorster's détente initiatives were going ahead at full steam. Ian Smith recalled a meeting with Vorster at Libertas, the South African prime minister's official residence, in which Vorster described the warm reception he was receiving from black leaders in Africa.

'I've got them eating out of my hands. They have promised that if I can help them solve the Rhodesian problem they will acknowledge South Africa as we are today,' he said.

Smith asked, 'With your apartheid intact?'

'Certainly,' replied Vorster.

'But you don't believe them?' Smith asked.

'My dear friend,' said Vorster, 'you've been out of touch with the world around you for so long that you are unaware of the changes which have taken place.'

Smith could hardly believe the man's naivety, but he knew Vorster was deadly serious.

To show how serious he was, Vorster started to hint that he was about to pull the South African Police (SAP) out of Rhodesia, even though just two days before Christmas in 1974, four SAP men had been gunned down in cold blood in a ZANLA con trick on the Mazoe high-level bridge. This murder had taken place two weeks after the ceasefire agreed by Vorster and Kaunda.

Ignoring his men's bitterness towards ZANLA, and to make sure Smith would be cooperative, Vorster slowed down ammunition and fuel supplies to Rhodesia. Ken Flower wrote in a memorandum in November 1974: 'Since [October] there have been two meetings of the Rhodesian and South African Prime Ministers ... Prime Minister Vorster made it clear to Mr Ian Smith that he must get a settlement, and get it quickly, or South Africa would cut off our water ...'

According to Flower, the relationship between Smith and Vorster finally broke down irreparably in early 1975. Then, in August of that year, without even telling Smith, Vorster ordered the SAP to pull out of Rhodesia during the hours of darkness.

'I received an early-morning phone call,' recalled Smith, 'informing me that the South Africans were pulling out.' By the time Smith got to his office, the vanguard of the massive convoy of SAP trucks had already reached the border at Beitbridge.

The gloves were off. Vorster had withdrawn his policemen and then he told Smith that he would soon be attending a conference with the black nationalists to solve the Rhodesian problem.

Vorster and Kaunda had been working hard behind the scenes to lay the ground for a conference to settle the Rhodesian issue. In August 1975, Smith, Nkomo and Sithole were ordered to show up. In the hope of gaining wider support within Rhodesia, they also invited Bishop Abel Muzorewa, who had formed a new party in Rhodesia, the United African National Congress, to lead the delegation.

Mosi-oa-Tunya, or the 'Smoke that Thunders', is the traditional name of the world's largest waterfall. This is where the mighty Zambezi River, dividing Rhodesia and Zambia, tumbles into a deep, time-eroded geological fault at a rate of more than a million litres per second. This was the conference venue.

A luxury South African Railways coach, parked on the middle of the Victoria Falls Bridge, which straddles the Zambezi Gorge and the two countries, formed what surely must have been the most spectacular conference setting ever. The massive plume of spray from the great waterfall provided relief against the flat landscape of bush and baobab. At either end of the conference coach was a buffet car.

Vorster, relishing what he thought would be his moment of African political glory, inspected the conference facility, and then walked across to Zambia for a meeting with President Kenneth Kaunda. Later the black delegates walked on foot to the coach from the Zambian side as the white Smith delegation approached from the Rhodesian side. After a brief opening ceremony, Vorster and Kaunda retired to another coach to await developments. The delegates were left to get on with negotiating a settlement.

In their naivety, the two leaders failed to take heed that most of the delegates were at the Victoria Falls conference simply because they had been ordered to attend. Muzorewa opened the contest by claiming one man, one vote was the central issue and then he went on to list a series of demands.

Smith was flabbergasted. He had been categorically assured by

Vorster that Kaunda and Nyerere had agreed there would be no pre-conditions. He made it clear that the Rhodesians would not accept one man, one vote, and would fight an all-out war to prevent it.

The talks never got beyond the procedural stage. Smith called a recess; he told Vorster what had happened and left the way open to resume talks. Vorster's massive public relations stunt had failed, and the dejected South African prime minister left Victoria Falls for Pretoria, while Kaunda felt humiliated by Vorster's inability to get Smith to bend.

On the way to the airport to board Air Force One, a World War II-vintage Dakota, Smith stopped at the bridge to see if there was a chance of talking any further. He commented: 'Apart from the train crew and the security personnel, the place was deserted. We were informed that within about an hour our "friends" had drained their saloon dry of its contents, and had weaved their way across the bridge to their cars on the north bank.'

Soon after the failed talks, the front-line presidents (Nyerere of Tanzania, Machel of Mozambique, Kaunda of Zambia and Masire of Botswana) met in the Mozambican coastal town of Quelimane to discuss the way forward. Kaunda, who feared a Marxist government in Rhodesia – hence his energetic efforts at détente – told the meeting that his patience with Smith was exhausted and he also believed that 'majority rule must now be decided on the battlefield'.

Vorster's détente exercise with Kaunda was not only futile, but also seriously damaging for the Rhodesians. The ceasefire had given ZANLA and ZIPRA precious time to regroup and the failed Victoria Falls conference inadvertently opened another door for Robert Mugabe to become ZANU's party leader.

Mugabe was still confined in Quelimane when the front-line leaders met there, and he was allowed to hover in the background. This lifted his profile somewhat, although the presidents regarded Sithole as the ZANU leader.

After the leaders had departed, Mugabe leveraged the failed Victoria Falls conference to full effect. He spent hours on his typewriter in his room in Quelimane tapping out letters to the guerrilla leaders in the camps, sending them a simple, but effective, message denouncing Sithole, Muzorewa and Nkomo as 'negotiators with the enemy' and 'sell-outs'. Mugabe's prime target was Ndabaningi Sithole, the man stubbornly getting in his way to become the undisputed leader of ZANU.

Pasi naSithole. Pasi nevatengesi (Down with Sithole, down with sell-outs) was Mugabe's war cry.

Slowly, his message got through to some of the key ZANLA commanders in Mozambique and Tanzania.

Another big factor in Mugabe's favour was that he was from neither the Karanga nor Manyika clans: he was a Zezuru, which allowed him to adopt a middleman position in the Karanga–Manyika power struggle. In October 1975, Mugabe's first big break came. The officers of the largest ZANLA guerrilla camp, at Mgagao in Tanzania, issued a declaration that they sent to the OAU. The declaration supported the 'struggle', condemned the negotiators and declared that the officers believed Mugabe should lead the party, as he was 'the only person who can act as a middleman'.

It would take Mugabe two more years and then a marathon meeting of the entire ZANU leadership at the ZANLA HQ at New Farm near Chimoio to realise his quest for power.

15

Meat-axe diplomacy

Despite his setback with Zambian president Kenneth Kaunda following the collapse of the Victoria Falls conference, the South African prime minister, John Vorster, was still firmly wedded to his strategy of facilitating the creation of friendly, non-communist, black governments in Rhodesia and Angola. Vorster still believed this would be a good political heat shield for South Africa.

Mozambique already had a Marxist party in power. In Angola, however, three rival former anti-Portuguese guerrilla forces were fighting each other for power, with the Soviets and Cubans supporting one, the Chinese another and South Africa, with covert backing from the US, a third.

In August 1975, at the time the Victoria Falls conference was convened, Vorster sent South African forces into Angola to seize and protect the South African–funded hydroelectric complex on the Cunene River. The Americans and President Kaunda were anxious to prevent the Marxist MPLA (the Movimento Popular de Libertação de Angola, or Popular Movement for the Liberation of Angola) from securing power in Luanda. Even so, the political world at large strongly condemned South Africa's presence in Angola. The US responded by suddenly withdrawing its covert support for South Africa.

According to Ian Smith, the US was keen to make amends to South Africa for its about-face in Angola and also to reinstate South Africa's standing in the OAU. Solving the Rhodesian problem would enhance the standing of both countries. So the Americans became directly involved in the Rhodesian issue. US president Gerald Ford's fix-it man, Henry Kissinger, was called in.

Kissinger, under his previous boss, Richard Nixon, had brokered the Paris Peace Accords in 1973, which were supposed to end the conflict in Vietnam. Like Vorster's détente-inspired ceasefire in Rhodesia, the Vietnam ceasefire gave North Vietnam and their communist allies in the south time to regroup and rearm. When North Vietnam was ready, the Paris ceasefire agreement was torn up and the north invaded the south, finally taking Saigon in April 1975. The rapid communist victory in Vietnam achieved what more than 50 000 Americans and a lot more Vietnamese died trying to prevent.

In classic Kissinger deal-making style, known in America as 'meat-axe diplomacy', Kissinger promised Vorster important incentives on condition he made the Rhodesian prime minister, Ian Smith, fall on his sword.

While Kissinger was touring the region to get an understanding of the issues, the Rhodesian forces were planning an audacious raid on a prime ZANLA camp in Mozambique.

Nyadzonia, August 1976

The Selous Scouts, operating in the Holdenby TTL near Inyanga, had a lucky break. They captured Morrison Nyathi, a senior ZANLA sectoral commander (equivalent to a brigadier), who had recently crossed into Rhodesia from Mozambique.

Chief Superintendent 'Mac' McGuiness of the Special Branch interrogated Nyathi, who revealed there was a massive ZANLA transit camp north of Chimoio, called Pungwe. Nyathi even described the position of the huts housing the senior camp commanders. The Selous Scouts officer commanding, Lieutenant Colonel Ron Reid-Daly, was keen to attack the base, but he needed more than Nyathi's description – he needed an aerial photograph of the camp.

Try as they may, the air force's high-flying Canberra jets could not find the Pungwe camp. They were looking for the camp – quite logically – on the banks of the Pungwe River, but there was nothing. Then, in a stroke of luck, a Canberra flown by Squadron Leader Randy du Rand flew over a gap in the thick cloud cover. Suddenly, there it was: Tekere's camp. It was not on the banks of the Pungwe River, however, but eight kilometres up a tributary called the Rio Nhazonia, or Nyadzonia River. The navigator managed to set the camera rolling before the cloud closed over again. The photographs revealed a large camp with a parade square, on which an estimated 5 000 personnel were clustered.

Reid-Daly was delighted. He took the pictures and McGuiness's dossier to his commander, an old colleague from the Malaya campaign days, Lieutenant General Peter Walls. Reid-Daly outlined his plan for 60 men to go into Mozambique by vehicle, disguised as FRELIMO, and then attack the camp. The element of surprise, backed up by

20-mm Hispano cannons mounted on Unimog trucks and armoured cars, meant the risky plan should be achievable.

'Peter Walls tends to whistle through his teeth when he is anxious,' recalled Reid-Daly. 'Jesus, Ron, this is a hell of a risk' was his response. 'Peter Walls was supportive, but he had to go to South Africa the next day on urgent government business, so he asked me to brief the heads of the army, air force, CIO, SB and Foreign Affairs.

'I was called to Milton Building by Walls's second in command, General John Hickman. I told the assembled gathering that trying to stop the gooks in Rhodesia was like emptying a bath with a teacup with both taps fully open. What is needed is to tackle the problem at its source,' said Reid-Daly. 'John Hickman and Archie Wilson (former air force commander) were supportive, but the CIO, SB and Foreign Affairs weren't.'

There was serious concern that the political fallout from the raid might exceed the gains. If no trace of a Rhodesian presence was left, however, maybe it could work. Hickman dismissed Reid-Daly and had a private discussion with the chiefs about the audacious plan.

When Reid-Daly got back to his HQ at Inkomo Barracks, the phone rang. It was Hickman: 'It's a go, Ron, you owe me a beer, good luck!'

There was one condition: no air support would be provided, so Reid-Daly's men would have to fight their way out of trouble.

The Unimog trucks were painted in FRELIMO camouflage and the men kitted in FRELIMO uniforms, manufactured in the tailor shop at Inkomo Barracks. Captain Rob Warraker, formerly with the RLI and SAS, would lead the raid.

'After I bade my men farewell, I was very anxious,' recalled Reid-Daly. 'I slept on a hard bench near the radio, only leaving for a pee or a crap.'

Keeping away from main roads as much as possible, Warraker's convoy of 10 Unimogs and four armoured cars threaded its way across the border into Mozambique. They drove into the camp in the early morning, singing a FRELIMO song. The inhabitants, assembled on the parade square, welcomed them enthusiastically. The Scouts opened up, wreaking death and destruction. Only four Selous Scouts were injured when fire was eventually returned.

Reid-Daly's radio receiver remained silent until later that morning.

'The first news I heard was when one of my men manning an OP [observation post] on Mount Inyangombe radioed to report a massive explosion in Mozambique. I knew then that Robbie Warraker and the team had blown the Pungwe River bridge to prevent a FRELIMO follow-up. They were on their way home.'

As it turned out, the column did get air support as they were threading their way out of the now well-alerted Mozambican countryside. Two Hawker Hunter jets blasted a troublesome FRELIMO mortar position.

'Rob Warraker's callsign was Zero Whisky, so I made sure I had plenty of Bell's Scotch whisky waiting for him and his men when they eventually got back to Inkomo,' said Reid-Daly. But the men were so dog-tired that only superficial damage was done to the whisky stocks.

A FRELIMO board-of-inquiry document, found a year later at the ZANLA HQ at Chimoio by Detective Superintendent Keith Samler, confirmed 1 026 had been killed. It also confirmed that Nyadzonia was indeed a camp for combatants and recruits.

Nevertheless, Reid-Daly was castigated by some senior military figures for engaging in an external operation, which was the domain of the SAS. 'I said to them, "Listen, we can do things externally that you can never do because you haven't got black troops."'

The man who had chosen the Nyadzonia site for ZANLA regretted his choice: 'We lost more than 700 people,' wrote Edgar Tekere in his memoirs. 'What had attracted me was the Nyadzonia River, which flowed in a horseshoe shape around the camp. The Rhodesian forces attacked from the west, at the narrow entrance, forcing our soldiers into the deep river where they were either drowned or eaten by crocodiles.'

Vorster fumes

The political fallout after the Nyadzonia raid was serious. Much of the world press took the ZANU line and instantly judged that Nyadzonia was a refugee camp. John Vorster was extremely embarrassed and let Ian Smith know in no uncertain manner how angry he was. Vorster made sure Smith understood his anger by sending his air force commander, Lieutenant General Bob Rogers, to Salisbury to tell the Rhodesians that all helicopter crews and signals technicians would be withdrawn immediately. The South African pilots flying on Fireforce duties around Rhodesia were astounded when they were told to pack up and leave immediately for home.

The Nyadzonia raid took place while Kissinger, Vorster, Kaunda,

Nyerere and the British government were finalising a new Rhodesian settlement deal. That explained, in part, Vorster's anger. He soon summoned Smith to South Africa to tell him about a 'reasonable plan' the South Africans and Henry Kissinger had worked out for Rhodesia. Vorster let Smith know early on that the stakes were high.

Smith recalled Vorster's warning to him: 'If we were not prepared to accept this offer of the hand of friendship from our only friends in this world, then we would be on our own, with sanctions tightening, terrorism increasing and finally the Russians coming in.'

Vorster explained the plan, which, in a nutshell, meant full majority rule in two years, with various guarantees, including a $2 billion trust fund to secure pensions and foreign exchange for those who wished to leave Rhodesia.

'After lunch,' recalled Smith, 'we came to the conclusion that it would probably be a good thing to bring the Americans in, since this might have a stabilising effect on the South Africans.' The scene was set for Smith to meet Kissinger a week later.

Smith arrived for the meeting in Pretoria a day early, on 18 September 1976, to watch the Springbok rugby team play the New Zealand All Blacks at Ellis Park. The home side prevailed by one point, winning 15–14. The celebration of the victory was brief; Ian Smith's mind was on the next day.

While the rugby game was being played and to demonstrate his determination and the gravity of the situation, Vorster closed the rail bridge over the Limpopo River at the Rhodesian–South African border town of Beitbridge. With Mozambique's ports closed to Rhodesia, the landlocked country's main supply line was suddenly throttled.

Sunday 19 September 1976 was a warm, dry, hazy day in Pretoria. Smith turned up at the US ambassador's house in the pleasant suburb of Waterkloof for his fateful meeting with Kissinger.

'On the Sunday morning, after the introductions, Kissinger suggested that he and I go into a small adjoining room,' recalled Smith. 'He told me that, as he saw it, he was being asked to participate in the demise of Rhodesia.' After the one-to-one meeting, and then a joint meeting, Kissinger made Smith walk the plank.

A dejected Ian Smith and his team flew back to Salisbury to explain the deal to cabinet, discuss it and then make the toughest television announcement of his life. The man who had proclaimed that one-man-one-vote majority rule would not happen in Rhodesia 'for a thousand years' had to announce to his people that he now accepted the very principle of majority rule.

In that historic broadcast on Friday 24 September 1976, Smith made it quite clear he had been told what to do: 'The American and British governments, together with major Western powers, have made up their minds as to the kind of solution they wish to see in Rhodesia, and they are determined to bring it about.'

The fact that Smith made no secret of the fact that this plan had been imposed by external parties made it all the more shocking to Rhodesians. Many people's conclusion was that their friends had all deserted them, including South Africa.

Wing Commander Prop Geldenhuys, then forward airfield (FAF) commander of the Buffalo Range (FAF 7) base in the south-east, summed up the feelings of many military personnel in his book *Rhodesian Air Force Operations*: 'General Walls briefed us, psychologically persuading the field commanders while Ian Smith was meeting with his full cabinet. I can unashamedly record that the tears ran down my cheeks – the end was in sight – it was capitulation.'

The Kissinger plan called for a conference in Geneva between leaders of both sides.

16

Geneva

With all the bravado of his 'meat-axe diplomacy', Kissinger had simply not grasped the fundamental issue: the serious divisions within the black nationalist movement. Who would represent them in Geneva?

The front-line states (Mozambique, Tanzania, Zambia and Botswana), countries that were suffering terribly from the effects of the Rhodesian War, desperately wanted a settlement, so it fell to them to galvanise an effective alliance to negotiate with Smith in Geneva.

The front-line leaders tried a number of combinations, but eventually decided to summon Nkomo and Mugabe to Dar es Salaam and bang their heads together, forcing them to negotiate as one, as the Patriotic Front. This was a bittersweet turning point for Mugabe. Although he would have to sit at the negotiating table with his archenemy, Nkomo, he was for the first time being recognised as a leader. Not *the* ZANU leader, but at least *a* leader. The front-line leaders invited Sithole too, so ZANU would be a two-headed beast.

When Mugabe left for the meeting in Dar es Salaam, ZANU divisions were opening up again. This time it was a clash between the new educated and old uneducated classes. A group of young Marxist–Leninist idealists called the *vashandi*, or workers' group, publicly rejected Mugabe's leadership. Mugabe was deeply worried that his quest would be derailed. So he reacted to this challenge in a way that would become his hallmark – first outsmart and then snuff out his opponents.

With very few cards to play, Mugabe then produced his ace. His main military colleague, Rex Nhongo, sympathised with the *vashandi*, so Mugabe demanded the release of Josiah Tongogara as a precondition to attending Geneva. Kaunda could hardly refuse, so after 18 months in a Zambian jail, Tongogara and his colleagues were set free.

Mugabe got ZANU's most effective military leader on his side in return for allowing him to resume his role as supreme military commander of ZANLA, and Tongogara now supported Mugabe's bid as party leader. Samora Machel, a great fan of Tongogara, accepted this alliance, which gave Mugabe at least some recognition.

Mugabe knew that he had to be seriously radical if he were to win over the *vashandi* and keep the party together. He wasted no time letting everyone know, not least his own party, that he was in no mood to compromise. Soon after arriving in Switzerland, a journalist asked Mugabe what sort of Rhodesia he wanted. 'What I am saying is that we are socialists and we shall draw on the socialist systems [state control of the economy] of Tanzania and Mozambique' was his reply.

These socialist policies had ruined both countries, and so, once again, Ian Smith was being coerced into accepting a solution guaranteed to fail.

To stir things further, Mugabe told the journalist: 'None of the white exploiters will be allowed to keep an acre of their land.'

Mugabe's demands were absolute blockers for Ian Smith and his delegation. And another factor was working against Mugabe. This was 1976, the height of the Cold War, and the American and British governments had no wish to see pro-communist nationalists come to power in Rhodesia.

But the main stumbling block for Smith was that Vorster and Kissinger had categorically assured him that once he accepted Kissinger's proposals, Kaunda and Nyerere would ensure that the nationalists fell in line and accept them too. In spite of these hurdles, the conference dragged on for weeks before eventually running out of steam just before Christmas 1976.

Discipline issues at New Farm

While the ZANU leaders were negotiating in Switzerland, discipline in the guerrilla camps was falling apart. The worst case was the ZANLA HQ complex at New Farm, Chimoio. Rugare Gumbo, a member of the ZANU high command, spoke of a breakdown of strategy, discipline and organisation at the camps.

He told journalist David Martin in an interview that 'camp life had broken down at Chimoio. It was like a village. We had to reshape it and return discipline and structure ... you don't wander about doing as you please. It's a military camp.'

And ZANLA had another headache – too many people were pouring in from Rhodesia to join the struggle. Many were too old or too young for training, and, in any event, there wasn't enough capacity to train even the suitable ones. ZANLA tried sending them back, but with little effect. By 1977, the numbers, excluding those selected for training, had swelled to 30 000. These surplus people, often with families in tow, were moved out of the ZANLA Chimoio complex and squeezed into three makeshift refugee camps at Gondola, Chibabawa and Mavudzi, where living conditions were bad.

Samora Machel also criticised the poor ZANLA discipline. The Mozambican president frequently received reports of heavy boozing and womanising in the nightclubs of Maputo. In the camps, senior commanders were known to arrive at night and demand 'warm blankets', meaning females for sex. This had a demoralising effect on the guerrillas.

When Tongogara, Mugabe and the rest of the huge delegation returned from Geneva, they started re-establishing discipline. First they arrested Mhanda and the *vashandi* leaders, who would spend the rest of the war in jail near Nampula. Then Mugabe used the poor discipline to make his mark. The teetotaller introduced a strict new disciplinary code that forbade drinking and loose living. Disciplined life slowly returned to the Chimoio base at New Farm. Parade-ground drills, physical exercise, lectures, rifle-range practice and the usual military activities replaced the unrestrained behaviour. Mugabe and his senior commanders started spending more time at Chimoio to show presence and to direct the war.

But Mugabe and Tongogara were naively taking a huge risk. New Farm was barely 70 kilometres from the Rhodesian border. Nevertheless, they believed that with civilians and their children dotted all over the complex and a large FRELIMO force with Russian tanks and Strela anti-aircraft missiles at Chimoio, only 17 kilometres away, they were safe from a Rhodesian attack. In fact, they felt so secure that they brought the entire ZANU and ZANLA hierarchy to New Farm for nearly two weeks in late August 1977 for a marathon meeting.

The objective of this meeting was to hammer out a new organisational structure and elect a supreme leader. The military members of ZANU wanted a military man in charge; the politicians thought that political acumen was paramount. Over and above these considerations, there were tribal issues, particularly between the Manyika and Karanga clans. After nine days of intense debate and much lobbying, the leaders opted for compromise by electing a clan-neutral Zezuru politician they had grudgingly come to trust, Robert Mugabe.

Mugabe's triumph as leader of both party and army was acclaimed by the entire leadership organisation under the lush trees planted many years before by the Antonio family to provide a shady garden around the farmstead. This man, who, as a shy and awkward boy, stood up at his primary-school graduation at Kutama Mission, saying, 'When I am a man, I'll be a teacher, if I can', was now leader of both ZANU and ZANLA. Little did the cheering party executive know that Mugabe would cling to that position for more than three decades. He would also ostracise many of those supporters in that garden.

As Mugabe celebrated, he would have seen the blue-tinged mountains to the west, Rhodesia's Eastern Highlands, unaware that across those beautiful mountains, a plan had long since been hatched to wipe out his headquarters at New Farm. It was a daring plan, codenamed after the free-roaming wild dog of Australia, the dingo.

17

Finding Chimoio

There is little doubt that the unsung heroes of the Rhodesian War were the small band of police detectives known as the SB (Special Branch). This group worked tirelessly, gleaning pieces of intelligence, or 'int', from the field, which eventually formed a mosaic that would shape the strategy and tactics of most military operations in the war, not least Operation Dingo.

Int was gathered in two basic ways – urgent field intelligence for immediate follow-up and strategic intelligence gained over the longer term. The data came from a wide variety of sources – captured documents and aerial pictures; from sources in other countries and sources at home.

But without a doubt, the best int came from captured guerrillas; dead ones were not of much use. Gathering and processing intelligence requires patience, persistence and the ability to persuade people to disclose truthful information. The SB operative must use psychological techniques to get captives to speak willingly.

Detective Inspector Peter Stanton describes the art of getting int simply as 'knowing where to get it. Information comes in dribs and drabs, and over time a picture starts emerging; that's when it becomes intelligence.'

Stanton does not believe in the word 'interrogation' because 'it denotes cruelty or using force, whereas the true art of getting information is interviewing a person in such a way that he relates a story to you in the correct order. For example, if the captive has just been in battle and is full of adrenalin, the objective is to bring him down gently, because if you don't, he will tell you anything. So you look after his wounds and give him a bit of assurance, no matter who he is.'

Detective Superintendent Keith Samler, the SB officer attached permanently to the Selous Scouts in the Thrasher operational area at the time of Operation Dingo, explains it further:

As policemen and criminal detectives, all SB personnel have received training in the technique of interrogation. Here's a simple example:

I can quickly tell if someone is lying by looking at their carotid artery. A sudden, pronounced pulsing indicates the person is undergoing mental stress, probably caused by lying or covering something up. However, soldiers do not have this training, so it was very important that SB did the initial interrogation of captures.

Samler preferred wounded captives because they were generally easier to 'turn', a term used when a guerrilla would willingly switch sides, usually after a short period of acclimatisation. Whenever possible, Samler would move the wounded captives to his Selous Scouts' 'fort', at the end of the airstrip at Rusape:

> Wounded captures would be taken to the medical tent and attended to by a 'doctor', actually an army medic with a stethoscope, and given an immediate injection of saline. They loved injections – the instant cure for all ills. I would give the capture a cigarette. His eyeballs would pop out, and you could almost hear him thinking 'where is the noose and the firing squad?' If he could eat, a white waiter would appear with the biggest plate of food imaginable and a Coke; questioning would begin a few minutes later. The answers flowed like a torrent.

Usually, the captured guerrilla would be met by turned comrades, who would accuse him of being a *skuze a' po* (Selous Scout). This was a dreadful accusation, implying he was the worst possible type of traitor, and in most cases it motivated the captive to assert his true credentials by revealing as much as he could about his life with ZANLA. This subtle double-crossing worked extremely well.

Samler tells a story of a brilliant sting operation in his area:

> After a contact near the Mozambique border, a Selous Scout callsign 'recovered' a ZANLA cadre who had become detached from his comrades during a contact and was disorientated. He was blindfolded and brought back to the fort at Rusape by truck and put into a tent with no other outside contact. Waiting to meet him in the tent were former ZANLA comrades who had been through the 'turning' process and were now members of the Selous Scouts.
> While he was receiving over-the-top medical treatment, I was

lighting his cigarette and holding it for him to puff on. I was wearing East German rice-fleck camouflage kit with a Cuban-style military forage cap, as were my colleagues. After the cigarette, Coke and sticky-bun treatment, we debriefed him over four days. The whole time, the ZANLA man believed friendly forces had taken him back to Mozambique.

The intelligence we obtained had a significant bearing on subsequent contacts with the remainder of his group. It also provided information which assisted in formulating plans to attack terr bases in Mozambique, especially Chimoio.

When the capture discovered he had been duped, apart from being somewhat shell-shocked, he was thoroughly impressed and his induction into the Selous Scouts had begun.

It was during this time, in 1976, that Samler started hearing about a major base in Mozambique called Chimoio, sometimes referred to as Vanduzi East or New Farm. Captured political commissars often revealed they had attended Chitepo College at the base. Samler fed this information back to his HQ. There were similar reports coming in from the Repulse (south-east) and Hurricane (north-east) operational areas. All the signs pointed to a large and very important camp in, or near to, the town of Chimoio.

Peter Stanton was attached to the SAS and worked closely with Major Brian Robinson, the SAS commanding officer, and Captain Scotty McCormack, Robinson's SAS intelligence officer. Robinson was itching to continue neutralising ZANLA camps in Mozambique, building on his success in Tete Province. 'Find the camp, quickly' was Robinson's simple request.

McCormack engaged high gear, often accompanying Stanton and other SB officers to interrogate captures, particularly if a link to Chimoio was suspected. The information they were gathering was slowly turning into real int. Now all they needed to do was find this camp.

Stanton explains how there were three ways to locate the camp: 'We could take a captured gook with us to show us the camp, but managing the gook in the field has all sorts of risks. Another way would be to send in our own recce team to find the camp, but the chances of being compromised in a heavily populated area were high. The third method is to fly it, take aerial shots.'

Stanton and McCormack went to meet Bill Buckle of the Joint

Services Photographic Interpretation Staff to put in a bid for photographic support, competing with many other requests. McCormack and Stanton told a compelling story, with the result that soon a Canberra jet bomber from No. 5 Squadron was on its way to photograph the area the captives had indicated. When flying very high, a Canberra is virtually invisible to the naked eye and barely audible. Stanton hoped that No. 5 Squadron would hit the jackpot, as they had for the Selous Scouts over Nyadzonia.

And they did. The Canberra returned with lots of good pictures. When the photographs were developed, they shocked everyone. The camp complex was far bigger than the intelligence had suggested. It was occupied by thousands of personnel.

The pictures debunked the belief that ZANLA was cohabiting with FRELIMO at their brigade HQ in Chimoio Town. Instead, they revealed the autonomous, integrated complex that Edgar Tekere had started developing 18 months earlier. There were parade grounds, rifle ranges, admin buildings, hospitals, facilities for vehicle servicing and repair, and a host of support structures linked by roads and well-maintained pathways. There were hundreds of mud-and-thatch huts used for sleeping accommodation and bigger ones used as support infrastructure, which were supplemented by canvas marquees. Defence trenches and anti-aircraft pits criss-crossed the area. It was pretty obvious this was the New Farm or Chimoio that ZANLA captives had been telling SB about.

The SAS now had high-resolution pictures of the ZANLA nerve centre in Mozambique. This was the largest staging post in Mozambique for trained guerrillas arriving from China, Ethiopia and Tanzania before entering Rhodesia. It was also the main reception centre for new recruits heading the other way for training.

The astonishing fact was that ZANLA was brazenly running its main HQ barely 70 kilometres from the Rhodesian border. The HQ was fully staffed. Mugabe, Tongogara, Tekere and Nhongo spent much time there. Oppah Muchinguri, who survived the war to become one of Mugabe's most loyal ministers, was a secretary there. 'I was a member of the general staff,' she told the Zimbabwe Broadcasting Corporation (ZBC) in November 2010, 'where I worked as secretary of the high command. We had several bases at Chimoio – farming, medicine, commissariat, etc.... Chimoio was the headquarters.'

Chimoio was without any doubt *the* ZANLA target in Mozambique, and where the most damage could be inflicted on the guerrilla movement. Brian Robinson wasted no time. His first port of call was the office of his good air force friend, Group Captain Norman Walsh.

Walsh had long seen the big picture, realising early on that simply waiting for ever-increasing numbers of enemy to enter the country was the wrong strategy. As air staff director of operations, Walsh had the ear of the Operations Coordinating Committee (OCC), essentially a high command made up of the commanders of the army, air force and police, and the heads of Internal Affairs and the CIO.

He argued passionately for the need to attack ZANLA and its supply lines in Mozambique using a two-pronged strategy. This comprised, firstly, slowing the movement of the enemy and disrupting his supply lines by systematically destroying bridges, railways, roads and other infrastructure in Mozambique and Zambia, and, secondly, reducing the enemy numbers able to infiltrate Rhodesia by taking the war to them, by attacking the large external camps.

Walsh's plan made perfect strategic sense, yet some senior members of the OCC were dead against external attacks, fearing political backlash and a widening of the war. The choice was stark: attack the enemy in his own backyard or wait for him to come to you. Those opposed to Walsh's strategy, reinforced by Western and South African political pressure, won the day. His plans were shelved for the time being.

Walsh was not one to give up, though. When Brian Robinson visited him in November 1976 to show him pictures of the Chimoio complex, the two men got straight down to planning Rhodesia's largest and most daring air and ground attack of the war.

'Brian Robinson and I had planned several minor operations together in the past,' recalled Walsh. 'We worked well together as a planning team.'

The admiration was mutual. Brian Robinson had immense respect for Walsh as an airman and military thinker. He later paid a great tribute to Walsh: 'I had a fantastic friendship with him, although he outranked me by miles. He would have made an outstanding SAS officer.'

It was Walsh's ability to see the bigger picture that made him stand out. Peter Petter-Bowyer describes him as 'a battle-experienced pilot with outstanding qualities in leadership and bags of common sense'.

Wing Commander Hugh Slatter, who would later serve as Walsh's chief of air staff, takes it further:

He was a true natural leader, and a quiet man of action. He possessed an extraordinary ability to see through the non-essentials and very quickly arrive at the right solution. While serving on the joint planning staff, Norman would have his instinctive solution to the problem almost immediately, whereas the formal process required the preparation of a service paper, which meticulously considered all relevant facts and aspects of the situation, before coming up with a recommended solution, which took anywhere from three to five days of investigation and writing, and never, in my memory, did it come up with a solution different from Norman's. This almost uncanny ability of his served him well, especially when it came to planning and executing operations.

18

Planning Dingo

'No battle plan ever survives first contact with the enemy.'
– HELMUTH VON MOLTKE, NINETEENTH-CENTURY GENERAL
OF THE PRUSSIAN ARMY

Scotty McCormack was delighted with the photos of New Farm. He chose the best ones and had them enlarged as big as they would go. Then he called in a mapping expert, Captain Jacques du Bois of the Rhodesian Intelligence Corps, who when not in uniform worked for the government mapping department.

Away from prying eyes in the SAS headquarters, Kabrit, in the Salisbury suburb of Cranborne, Du Bois beavered away with maps, photos, papier mâché, ink and paint to produce a professional, large-scale model of the entire ZANLA complex at New Farm, Chimoio.

During their intelligence gathering for Chimoio, SB told McCormack that they had picked up int about another big base deep inside Tete Province, almost on the Malawian border. ZANLA captives in the Op Hurricane area called it Tembue; this was the main ZANLA base in Tete Province.

Tembue operated as a staging point for trained guerrillas before they were deployed into the Hurricane area. It also had a specialist training facility and served as a reception point for new recruits. Tembue was far – 185 kilometres – from the Rhodesian border, nearly three times as far as Chimoio. Nevertheless, McCormack ordered and received aerial photos, then asked Du Bois to make a model of Tembue too.

Now it was time to begin the serious planning. Brian Robinson, the SAS commander, is modest about his role in planning Dingo: 'I can only take credit for the concept of parachute vertical envelopment. This came about because I realised we would never have sufficient helicopters to go around.'

Robinson called on his pal, the commanding officer of the Parachute Training School, Squadron Leader Derek de Kock, to work out the finer detail for the mass paradrop. 'We had learnt that the closest we should drop troops to the target was 1 000 metres,' recalled De Kock, 'mainly because the gooks seemed to be able to run 1 000 metres in a minute and would escape.'

The next challenge was to ensure that the aircraft and paratroopers remained clear of each other. De Kock explained:

> The line-astern formations of the Daks were such that they were staggered slightly vertically and slightly to starboard. The troops were dispatched very slowly, not faster than one man per second, to ensure that each Dak load would cover at least 1 000 metres. Each man out was counted and this was broadcast, so that the pilot of the next Dak in line switched on his green light as the count reached 19.

Robinson went back to his HQ and continued planning. 'The SAS style of planning,' says Robinson, 'was to develop a plan with the officers. That made them part of the planning from the start. They would take immediate exception to be just given a set of orders. This does not mean that the SAS was a Chinese Parliament which put operational matters to the vote. However, freethinkers had to be given the opportunity of contributing to the plan.'

Operation Dingo was no different, he explains: 'The administrative plan was done by my second in command at the time, Mike Graham. All the troop commanders, including Grahame Wilson, assisted him. This was done in minute detail and could serve as a model for any operation of this size in the world.'

The air effort

The whole operation depended on the air force: every soldier would go there and back – alive, dead or injured – by air.

Before the troops arrived, the target had to be softened with a heavy aerial assault, and, vitally, the anti-aircraft sites had to be neutralised to protect the big, slow paratrooper Dakotas and the trooper Alouettes, or G-cars. After the paratroopers had been dropped, the jets would need to provide top cover, which meant remaining above the target ready to strike ground targets to support the troops. Walsh also had to ensure he had at least one fighter jet armed for air-to-air combat in case the Mozambican air force decided to intervene with its Russian-built MiG jet fighters.

The challenge was that there were only eight serviceable Hawker Hunters in the entire air force and one needed to be on standby. All seven would have to fly to the target at low level to avoid enemy radar, which guzzles fuel in a jet. They needed to be over the target almost simultaneously to achieve surprise and neutralise the anti-aircraft weapons quickly. With fuel and ammunition being the constraining factors, there would be times when there was no Hunter top cover, a dangerous situation.

Walsh had to devise a plan to ensure there was uninterrupted top cover. He quickly came to the conclusion that the ancient Vampires of No. 2 Squadron would have to be used to fill the gap while the Hunters returned to base to refuel and rearm.

The de Havilland Vampire, a stubby little jet with a twin tail boom, came into service with the RAF just at the conclusion of World War II. Armed with four 20-mm cannons and rockets, the Vampire packed a punch. But it became dated when better machines, notably the Hawker Hunter, had come into service in the mid-50s, rendering the little jet obsolete. The RAF withdrew it from front-line service in 1955. At the time of Operation Dingo, 22 years later, the Rhodesian Vampires were the only ones still flying combat missions. And they would fill the void perfectly.

Planning a massive airborne assault requires great detail and accuracy. The only given for the planners was the location of the target. As the crow flies, New Farm was 279 kilometres from New Sarum, Salisbury, from where most of the aircraft would depart. The distance for the Hunters leaving from Thornhill, Gwelo, was 388 kilometres.

Norman Walsh had to factor in the range of speeds from the slowest to the fastest aircraft. The difference was 340 knots, from the Alouette helicopter averaging 80 knots to the Hawker Hunter barrelling along at 420 knots.

Using his experience of standard procedures with the squadrons, Walsh worked out the precise strike times, down to the second, and the attack direction. The rest was up to the pilots. 'All individual squadrons were left to plan their own routes, strike plans and recovery,' said Walsh.

This put an enormous burden of responsibility on the squadron leaders. For example, if the Hunters arrived 30 seconds late, they risked shooting down the Canberras and putting the Dakotas at serious risk from anti-aircraft fire. The knock-on effects of getting the timing wrong were huge.

The same issues of precise timing applied to the helicopters. Their task was to deliver 40 men to the target, which required 10 Alouette helicopters. Another 10 would be in the gunship, or K-car, configuration to complete the target envelopment. And Walsh himself needed a command helicopter, necessitating 21 helicopters in all.

The biggest challenge would be recovering a total of 184 paratroopers and returning them to Rhodesia, together with their chutes, prisoners, captured weapons, documents and, of course, any injured personnel. The 10 G-cars would have to fly 46 sorties to the target just to retrieve the men, four at a time. Another 13 sorties were needed to get the parachutes out – with sanctions, nothing was wasted – and probably another 20 sorties for prisoners, documents and weapons. All in all, each G-car would have to do 10 trips to and from the target, assuming no losses. In itself, this was not insurmountable, but the problem was that the extraction phase could only begin once the battle was over, which may well be in the late afternoon, thereby compressing the available time. It was a big task, especially as the RhAF only had 24 serviceable Alouette helicopters at the time.

Another problem was that the Alouette had a very limited range with a full load, which meant that refuelling staging points would be needed – inside enemy territory. Walsh worked out the details down to each helicopter and plotted the staging points on a map. It would be tight.

Armed with the impressive models of the target and a well-thought-through ground and air plan, Robinson and Walsh invited the OCC to a briefing at the SAS HQ. The philosophy behind Dingo was a no-brainer: big camps, like this one, full of ZANLA guerrillas ready to pounce on Rhodesia presented a very clear and present danger. Something had to be done.

Robinson and Walsh outlined their idea. They would surprise the target with a massive air strike and then quickly surround it with paratroopers and helitroopers, a tactic known as vertical envelopment.

Attacking camps in Mozambique wasn't a new concept. The SAS had been wreaking havoc in Tete Province for years; the Selous Scouts had destroyed ZANLA's Nyadzonia camp in Manica Province; and in the south-east, the Scouts, backed up by the RLI and the regular army, had taken on ZANLA in Gaza Province. But an attack on the scale being planned for Chimoio (codenamed Zulu 1) and Tembue (Zulu 2) in some ways resembled an invasion of Mozambique, rather than a series of pre-emptive skirmishes. Nevertheless, Robinson and Walsh hoped the leadership would see beyond the diplomatic hurdles and approve the plan, especially as large numbers of enemy were poised to enter Rhodesia with the imminent summer rains.

They duly briefed the members of the OCC. Norman Walsh's request was quite straightforward, but the scale of what he was presenting could not be hidden. The highlights of the final briefing probably went something like this: 'Sir, may I please requisition the entire Rhodesian Air Force? Yes, all serviceable aircraft. And yes, all our aircraft will need to fly over a foreign country.'

Where will the helicopters land to refuel? 'Inside hostile territory and, yes, the trooper helicopters will all need to refuel near the target at about the same time.'

What losses can we expect? 'We've studied some American operations reports on aircraft losses; we found them surprisingly high by our standards. So we will use our standard procedures based on past experience with the squadrons to keep losses to a minimum.'

Brian Robinson's request was equally straightforward, and would have probably gone along the following lines: 'I need 88 men from the RLI, plus 96 of my own SAS paratroopers. This force will box off three sides of the target.'

How big is the target? 'Eighteen square kilometres; anything outside of that will be attacked by air only.'

How much territory must each man defend? 'On landing, the gap between our paratroopers will be about 47 metres.'

What is the enemy strength? 'We estimate about 2 500, but it could be as high as 8 000.'

So you are saying that the best-case scenario is odds of 14 to 1 in ZANLA's favour – or at the other extreme 44 to 1? 'Yes, but we have air support and the element of surprise.'

How are you going to extract 184 troops and their equipment? 'By using all the available helicopters we have, sir.'

The plan was not just bold, it effectively threw all the air force dice at once. If it went horribly wrong, Rhodesia might no longer have an air force to speak of, and lose its key weapon in the counter-insurgency war.

The OCC was uncomfortable with the plan and refused to sanction it. As Walsh had learnt before, timing was the big issue: it was the right plan at the wrong time. This was late 1976, right at the time Henry Kissinger's Rhodesia peace proposals were about to be debated in Geneva. It also came only a few months after the Selous Scouts had wiped out the ZANLA camp at Nyadzonia, an attack that had seriously irritated South African Prime Minister John Vorster and brought a wave of international condemnation on Rhodesia.

Under the prevailing circumstances and the risk of bringing Mozambique into the war, the Rhodesian government simply could not authorise an attack on this scale.

Norman Walsh later commented: 'The possible overseas reaction delayed the green light. Also, there was considerable opposition to external operations, particularly from one senior Internal Affairs officer.'

Operation Dingo was on the skids, but at least the OCC had not rejected it out of hand. The dynamic duo were not about to give up. Tenacity and Walsh's influence would make a difference: 'We had to convince them,' said Walsh, 'and there were several attempts.'

Brian Robinson had this to say: 'Had it not been for Norman Walsh, the operation would never have got any further than the model stage. Setting up an admin base in the middle of enemy territory was unheard of. Only Walsh could have sold the concept to a gaggle of brass who had never heard a door slam.'

Robinson was right about Walsh, but perhaps a bit disingenuous about the 'gaggle of brass'. The Combined Operations (ComOps) leader, Peter Walls, had heard more than a door slam when he was commanding C Squadron, SAS, against Chinese insurgents in Malaya, and he was very supportive of external operations. He also believed in Walsh's operational planning abilities. 'I trusted Norman Walsh completely,' recalled Walls. 'To me, he is a great, great guy and a great mate of mine.'

But Walls was not in a position to authorise Operation Dingo, although Walsh and Robinson presented the plan several more times. Political attitudes started changing, however, in 1977.

19

The Year of the Fire Snake: 1977

The second moon after the winter solstice in 1977 heralded the Chinese Year of the Fire Snake, a year of many ups and downs, according to Chinese astrologers. Each lunar New Year brings a new animal; there are 12 animals in the cycle. There are also five cosmic elements: wood, fire, earth, metal and water, which, in turn, run in a cycle with the animals, meaning that the same animal and element pair up only once every 60 years.

The previous Year of the Fire Snake, 1917, saw the birth of John F. Kennedy. Also born in the Year of the Snake – but the Water Snake, 24 years earlier, in 1893 – was Chinese leader Mao Zedong, whose revolutionary tactics Josiah Tongogara and ZANLA had adopted in the Rhodesian conflict. Astrology aside, the New Year promised a showdown between the Rhodesian forces and ZANLA.

It was also a year that ushered in change. In 1977, the world's first personal computer, the Commodore, was launched, followed shortly by a rival machine, the Apple. Optical fibre was first used to transmit a telephone call. The bacteria causing legionnaires' disease were isolated, and the movie blockbuster *Star Wars* hit the cinema screens. British Airways launched the first scheduled supersonic flight between London and New York using an elegant new airliner called Concorde. The same year, the music world mourned the death of a man who had grown up in the poor area of Tupelo, Mississippi, and became one of the most popular Americans of all time – the undisputed king of rock 'n' roll, Elvis Presley.

On the political front, Republican Gerald Ford handed over the White House to Democrat Jimmy Carter, who was sworn in as the 39th president of the United States. Henry Kissinger handed his keys over to Cyrus Vance. The new administration had little sympathy for white people in southern Africa and wanted to see majority rule not just in Rhodesia, but in South Africa too.

Schoolchildren rioted in South Africa over being forced to use the Afrikaans language at school. The riots had started in Soweto the previous year and spread across the country, bringing John Vorster under the international media spotlight. His vigorous efforts at détente had come to nil, other than pushing Rhodesia to the brink.

During the first days of 1977, the chairman of the stalled Geneva conference on Rhodesia, Ivor Richard, desperately ploughed on trying to resuscitate the negotiations. In a frantic attempt to bring Mugabe and Nkomo back to the negotiating table, Richard offered to scrap the key concessions Smith had managed to squeeze from Kissinger in return for accepting majority rule.

'We were now confronted, in early 1977, with the dreadful situation that our worst fears had been realised,' observed Ian Smith. 'With Kissinger gone, only Vorster remained as part of the agreement. It left me with a desperately uneasy feeling, because of the clear change in Vorster's character over the last few years, associated with his escapade into détente.'

Smith saw Richard's move as blatant betrayal. Vorster and Kissinger had assured Smith that by accepting majority rule, he would have to bend no further. Now he was being asked to concede much more. Vorster had again misread how much clout, or lack of it, the front-line presidents had over ZANU and ZAPU.

Smith rejected Richard's new proposals outright. He went to the television studios at Pockets Hill and announced to the nation: 'After all our efforts and the sacrifices which have been made, there can be no question of surrender.'

Geneva was dead and Kissinger's proposals were history. Nevertheless, Vorster did not see it that way. He still naively believed he could resuscitate Kissinger's Pretoria Agreement and make friends with the Carter administration. But he was in for a rude shock.

The South African prime minister travelled to Vienna in mid-1977 to meet the US vice-president, Walter Mondale, and was given a taste of his own medicine. Mondale tried to bully him about Rhodesia and South West Africa (Namibia), and demanded political change in South Africa too. He told the press that he wanted to see one man, one vote in South Africa. Vorster was incensed.

But the damage to Rhodesia had been done. When Vorster had forced Smith to declare a ceasefire in late 1974 and told him to attend the Victoria Falls conference, Smith was still 'allowed' to negotiate his own position. But the Kissinger agreement was very different. Vorster and Kissinger forced Smith to accept majority rule, or else. Now, with

Smith having been reluctantly forced to accept majority rule, there was no reciprocation, no settlement. It was no surprise that morale in Rhodesia's white community plummeted. Many people were thinking they had made all these concessions – and for what?

'Regrettably, there were signs that our white community, for the first time, was beginning to have doubts about our future,' observed Ian Smith. He was correct – the Kissinger proposals signalled the beginning of the end of Rhodesia. But giving up was not Smith's style.

For the moment at least, Smith had Vorster off his back and he could start picking up the pieces. He would try to negotiate a settlement internally, without everyone interfering. This impasse also allowed him to continue prosecuting the war, particularly in the south-east.

Repulse in the south-east

Even though the Rhodesian government could not authorise an operation on the scale of Dingo in early 1977, especially in the wake of Vorster's anger over Nyadzonia, the military commanders were prepared to continue hammering ZANLA in the south-east in a series of short, covert external raids.

After his release from jail a year earlier, Tongogara had started forging a strategic advantage, opening up a front along the whole Mozambican–Rhodesian border. He had supplemented his infiltration from Manica Province by sending his forces into the south-east of Rhodesia, from Gaza Province into the Gonarezhou Game Reserve, in the heart of a new military operational area known as Repulse. This was a serious strategic threat.

Ron Reid-Daly, the Selous Scouts officer commanding, explained the problem:

> The south-east of Rhodesia is flat and with no population to speak of. What the Scouts liked was hilly country because there are lots of vantage points. We also liked lots of population so we could swan in amongst them with our black troops as pseudos, get information and bring the Fireforce onto them.
>
> At that time, ZANLA had access to a railway line running right up to Malvernia, so they could run their troops straight up to the border, fit, fat and flourishing, hop off and cross the border. Our strategy was to entice ZANLA to use the tar road running along

the eastern border and to deploy their troops in the Eastern Highlands, rather than into the flat south-east. That is why we started
knocking out Mapai and blowing up the railway lines to slow that
avenue of incursions down, which we did.

But Tongogara was not to be put off. He knew that his forces were
faring better in the south-east, and they were able to attack the crucial
rail and road supply lines to South Africa, which was of great symbolic
value to ZANLA. Tongogara soon had 1 700 guerrillas operating in
the south-east, more than in any other operational area.

Navigating in the south-east wasn't easy. Often the only landmarks
ground forces had were ancient beacons planted by Arab and Persian
traders between the tenth and fifteenth centuries. The traders planted
Palmyra palm trees in the flatlands of the south-east as navigation aids
to guide them from the Mozambican port of Sofala to Mapungubwe,
the region's major trading centre, situated between present-day Beitbridge and the Shashi River. These tall non-indigenous palms, usually
planted at river crossings, had reproduced over the centuries and provided very useful landmarks.

Aircraft down

This new theatre of the war brought some setbacks in early 1977.
It started badly when a Dakota flew into power lines straddling the
Lundi River in the south-east, killing both pilots and destroying the
aircraft. Then came the death of Reid-Daly's daring leader of the
Selous Scouts' raid on the ZANLA base at Nyadzonia, Captain Rob
Warraker. He died when FRELIMO downed his aircraft just inside
Mozambican airspace.

Warraker was flying in a Canberra jet bomber piloted by Flight Lieutenant Ian 'Don' Donaldson; Air Sub Lieutenant Dave Hawkes was
navigator. They were part of a complicated operation in the south-
east involving a night attack on a large ZANLA camp at Madulo Pan,
75 kilometres inside Mozambique on the flood plains of the Limpopo
River, just north of Mapai.

The No. 5 Squadron leader, Randy du Rand, led a formation of
three Canberras in the inky pre-dawn blackness at only 300 feet above
the ground to bomb the Madulo target. The Canberras were carrying Peter Petter-Bowyer's newly developed Alpha 'bouncing bomblets'

– the first time these weapons had been used operationally in Mozambique and at night.

In a daring and brilliant effort, Schulie Schulenburg, who had left the SAS to join the Selous Scouts, sneaked right up to the ZANLA camp to lay a radio-activated flare on the camp perimeter and another further away to give the Canberras a line and target.

Ron Reid-Daly remembered that when Schulie, assisted by Steven Mpofu, had reconnoitred the camp in daylight, they had 'seen a tree at the edge of the camp. In pitch darkness they found the same tree where they laid the target flare.'

Ian Donaldson, flying the fourth Canberra at 30000 feet to ensure good communications with Schulie, fired the flares by radio signal at precisely the right time. This gave Du Rand the visual markers and line he needed to find the camp target in the pitch dark. The bomb run was bang on target.

When helicopters arrived at first light with troops, they were met by a fierce wall of anti-aircraft fire, which should have been neutralised by the Alpha bombs. The bombs had indeed wreaked havoc among ZANLA forces. The unexpected fire came from a FRELIMO battalion that just happened to be passing through the area when it was alerted by the Canberra strikes. The Mozambican Army soldiers, armed with anti-aircraft guns, moved in to assist ZANLA. Donaldson's Canberra, having conserved fuel at high altitude, was called in to neutralise the FRELIMO threat at Madulo.

Donaldson shed height in a wide descending turn above the thin layer of low cloud until he spotted a gap through which he could safely descend to his bomb-run height of 300 feet. However, he had the terrible misfortune of breaking cloud right over Malvernia, on the Mozambican–Rhodesian border.

Alerted by the Madulo attack, FRELIMO opened up on the giant bat-like Canberra with everything they had. Donaldson, Warraker and Hawkes had no chance to eject and the Canberra went straight in, killing all three.

Sergeant Kevin Milligan of the Air Force Parachute Training School recalls: 'I knew Rob Warraker pretty well. He was in the SAS before the Selous Scouts and came through PTS quite regularly for continuation training. He was the sort of guy you took to, a good officer and a good leader. His passing was a great shock to all of us.'

Operations in the south-east continued, to clear the area around

Mapai, a town on the banks of the Limpopo River, 90 kilometres inside Mozambique, and São Jorge de Limpopo, a small settlement on the Maputo–Malvernia railway line. Infrastructure was also destroyed.

There were further airborne assaults by the RLI on the ZANLA camp at Madulo Pan and another base called Rio on the Nuanetsi River. The Selous Scouts moved down the main railway line, flushed out the ZANLA guerrillas and destroyed the line. The operation went well, and there were large caches of war materials unearthed in villages around Mapai.

A Dakota from Buffalo Range flew in shuttles, bringing in supplies and carrying captured weaponry back to Rhodesia. As the vintage machine was about to leave with its third load just after dark, disaster struck.

Just as Flight Lieutenant Jerry Lynch hauled the Dakota's main wheels off the runway, the well-lit aircraft came under withering fire from small arms and rocket-propelled grenades. An RPG hit the starboard engine and small-arms fire came crashing through the cockpit, narrowly missing Lynch but hitting Bruce Collocott, the co-pilot.

Fighting the severe yaw caused by the failed engine, Lynch had a split second to react. He quickly cut the power on the good engine to reduce the now violent yaw and put the stricken machine back down on the runway, struggling to keep the swerving aircraft straight with differential braking. The laden and now burning Dakota slewed around and lurched to a halt just before the trees at the end of the runway.

Lynch unstrapped and tried to help Collocott out of his seat, but quickly realised his co-pilot was beyond help. Lynch and his technician, Flight Sergeant Russell Wantenaar, just managed to escape the inferno before the fuel tanks blew up.

The loss of Bruce Collocott was felt deeply by his colleagues in No. 3 Squadron and by the jump instructors at the Parachute Training School. Kevin Milligan again summed up the sad feeling:

> Bruce Collocott had such a quick wit and he was good fun, we really took to him. The pilots would come to PTS for a briefing and tea before a lift of paratroopers. The repartee between Bruce and the parachute jump instructors was always a humorous event to look forward to. Bruce could not understand why sane men would jump out of a perfectly serviceable aircraft. He would always ask witty questions, like 'How many meatbombs will we be dropping

on the enemy today?' It was hard to believe that Bruce was gone. His death in Dakota 3702 just added to the feeling of loss. This was one of our favourite aircraft, which, in earlier times, had been Air Force One, the personal aircraft of former South African prime minister Jan Smuts.

Smuts had donated the Dakota, built in 1944, to Rhodesia in 1947. With international sanctions and tight foreign currency, these aircraft were irreplaceable, further eroding this small air force. The loss of the Dakota also reflected the obvious: the war was really getting serious.

The government responded by announcing, in April 1977, that all men aged 38 to 50 were required to do military service, causing another rush of emigrants to take the road south to Beitbridge in what was known as the 'chicken run' or the 'owl run', depending on one's point of view.

20

ComOps is formed

The OCC was disbanded in early 1977 and a new overall military structure was set up, named Combined Operations (ComOps). The new post of supreme military commander went to someone who was a great supporter of offensive warfare and external operations, Lieutenant General Peter Walls. Air Marshal Mick McLaren, the recently retired head of the RhAF, was appointed deputy commander. Curiously, Walls remained at the rank of lieutenant general, which meant he did not outrank his colleagues. This was probably because the predecessor to ComOps, the OCC, had worked well on the basis of equal ranks among the army, police, air force and CIO.

Five years earlier, in 1972, Peter Walls had been appointed commander of the Rhodesian Army, replacing General Keith Coster. The serving term for chiefs of staff was four years, meaning Walls would retire at the end of 1976. Then tragedy intervened. Walls's natural successor, John Shaw, was killed in a helicopter accident. Prime Minister Ian Smith immediately asked Walls to stay on.

'I already had a job lined up in South Africa as a director with the Rennies Group,' said Walls. 'The CEO decided to keep the post open for me, filling the role himself for a year.'

But Walls and Rennies were in for a surprise. Four months into Walls's extended year, Ian Smith told him: 'No, you haven't been extended for one year; you're extended for as long as the war lasts and I want you to be commander of combined ops.'

Walls was taken aback. The prime minister had shown no inclination for a supreme commander, despite a well-argued case for one by Major General Andy Rawlins a year earlier. Nevertheless, Walls suddenly found himself in a position of strength: 'I told him that I didn't want to accept the job unless I got the authority to call the shots when necessary.'

He added another condition, arising from his distrust of the CIO and the police: 'I want intelligence to come to me, I don't want it to come second-hand from a whole group of people.'

Smith agreed, although it would take a while to actually happen – there were still deep rifts within the services.

As a young man, Peter's father, Reginald Walls, had given him a book, *Defense Will Not Win the War*, written by Lieutenant Colonel W.F. Kernan of the US Army and published in 1942. This book had a huge influence on Walls: 'I really believed in this philosophy of taking the war to the enemy.'

As commander of ComOps, Walls changed the philosophy to search and destroy, whether that was inside the country or beyond its borders. This ethos was outlined in a paper produced in April 1977, in which the call for external operations as a strategy was explicitly made to 'counter the terrorist's ability to escalate the war on all fronts'. Importantly, the paper was underpinned by an urgent recommendation to secure an early political settlement. The four signatories were Peter Walls, his deputy, Mick McLaren, Peter Sherren (police commissioner) and the CIO head, Ken Flower (who reproduced parts of the paper in his memoirs).

Peter Walls knew that Rhodesia's south-east posed the greatest strategic threat, despite frequent attacks on ZANLA bases and the infrastructure between the border town of Malvernia and Mapai. Josiah Tongogara kept pushing more insurgents into the area. These guerrillas frequently attacked Rhodesia's vital artery to South Africa, the Rutenga–Beitbridge railway line. The adjacent road link to South Africa was also attacked, forcing the deployment of armed convoys and sometimes aircraft top cover to protect motorists and commercial traffic.

In May 1977, reports were reaching Walls that ZANLA guerrillas were not simply passing through the Mapai area, but were also establishing a large presence in and around the town. The general was itching to deal ZANLA a decisive blow in the south-east. Ian Smith also understood just how serious was the threat, yet he had been warned not to antagonise Vorster any further. But this was in the wake of the Geneva debacle, and Smith was pretty angry, saying it was 'better to go down standing and fighting, than crawling on our knees'.

He backed his new ComOps leader and authorised the first large-scale, overt and sustained attack on Mozambican soil. The RLI, Selous Scouts and elements of the Territorial Army entered Mozambique.

The 'mini-invasion' was reported by the *Rhodesia Herald* on 1 June 1977, with the headline:

TROOPS SEIZE MOZAMBIQUE TOWN
Raid achieved object – Walls

Security Forces have seized Mapai, the first major main town inside Mozambique in the Gaza Province, and will stay in that country until terrorists have been eliminated from that area, the Commander of Combined Operations, Lieut.-General Peter Walls, said yesterday.

'Troops will be withdrawn from Mozambique as soon as they complete their task of eliminating ZANLA (the Zimbabwe African National Liberation Army loyal to Mr Robert Mugabe) terrorists from the area in question and destroying or removing ammunition, arms or equipment dumps or caches,' said General Walls.

The usual condemnation followed swiftly from the UN chief, Kurt Waldheim, and from America, Britain, the OAU and others. In some cases, it didn't just involve condemnation; pressure was also applied in no uncertain terms. Ken Flower revealed in his memoirs that cabinet secretary Jack Gaylard had warned a meeting of senior ministers and ComOps after the Mapai attack that '[t]he South Africans had told us that the United States would apply sanctions – and worse – to them if they did not immediately cut off oil and other supplies to Rhodesia if we were extending our war into neighbouring territories'.

21

Autumn in spring

Have you seen
The Msasa trees burn
Red to green?
A cooling flame
Between the sun's blaze
And our tired eyes.
— 'SPRING' BY R. KNOTTENBELT

August is the beginning of the warm season on the high plateau of Rhodesia known as the Highveld. Technically it is spring, but it looks more like autumn as the msasa trees come into leaf after the brief, cool, dry winter. In a reversal of the typical autumn process, the msasa leaves first burst out in a wonderful deep claret colour, then change to bright reds, brilliant oranges and then yellows before turning green. It is a wonderful sight.

Salisbury's spring colours in August 1977 seemed to go unnoticed by the politicians, however. Ian Smith faced a right-wing revolt when 12 of his Rhodesian Front MPs resigned in protest about him giving too much ground to the nationalists. The rebels, who became known as the Dirty Dozen, formed a new organisation, the Rhodesian Action Party. Smith called their bluff with a snap election on 31 August, winning all the contested seats. This election result was a huge boost for Smith, who now had the unequivocal backing of the white electorate to pursue a settlement while vigorously prosecuting the war.

On the very same day, an event just across the border in Mozambique would have a profound and long-lasting effect on Rhodesia. Robert Mugabe was elected supreme leader of both ZANU and ZANLA at a specially convened meeting at New Farm, the ZANLA HQ near Chimoio.

It was also that month that terror came to the streets of Salisbury when ZANLA terrorists bombed a Woolworths department store in the city, killing 11 and injuring 76 shoppers. Ironically, ZANLA had chosen a department store frequented mostly by black people. The bombers had recently been through training at ZANLA's massive HQ complex at Chimoio – a fact that was not lost on the military hierarchy.

On the international front, the British and American governments wasted no time. Another settlement plan was concocted, which brought two new personalities onto the stage, both rising stars in their administrations. Andrew Young was the new US ambassador to the UN and David Owen the new British foreign secretary. Owen, in particular, wanted Smith to hand over power to the guerrilla forces swiftly.

Inevitably, the South Africans called Smith to Pretoria for a meeting. On 12 September 1977, Vorster told Smith that he had received a letter from the Carter administration warning of 'dire consequences if the South Africans did not bring peace to the region'. Smith was shocked when Vorster told him that the South African government now expected Rhodesia to go beyond the Kissinger agreement by accepting a majority of black people in both Parliament and the cabinet. He dropped another bombshell, explaining to Smith that the growing pressure on South Africa was making it more and more difficult for his government to continue supporting Rhodesia. This was the final blow – South Africa was pulling the plug.

'Poor Rhodesia,' Smith wrote in his memoirs. 'We had enough problems with our enemies, without this kind of treatment from our few friends.'

The situation was indeed problematic. Special ammunition trains, codenamed 'barrage trains', would regularly pass through Beitbridge from South Africa and were then escorted with air cover to their destination, such was their importance. But the frequency of the barrage trains dropped, which seemed odd in an escalating war. The reason was simple: Rhodesia was running out of money. Peter Walls recalled the difficulties:

> I remember sitting in Milton Building listening to the sitreps being read. The Repulse area sitrep reported a skirmish at Malvernia where our guys, in retaliation, had lobbed a number of 80-mm mortars into Mozambique. I knew that we were down to our last 30 mortar shells in the main armoury in Salisbury. I said, 'How the hell do we tell these troops not to fire mortars because we only have 30 left?' Morale would have plummeted. So all I could do was to tell them to be restrained.

The situation was dire. We couldn't get the ammunition through. The South Africans would say, 'Sorry, we can't get that train through.' They were also threatening to cut our petrol; it was pretty tough going.

Ian Smith sent for Walls, telling him: 'You are now the only contact we have with the South African government. We need a $600 million loan. The Treasury can't talk to the South Africans, the minister can't talk to them and Vorster won't talk to me. You are the only person who can put over why we need this loan.'

Walls had a close relationship with his opposite number, the chief of the South African Defence Force, General Magnus Malan. The South African strongman acquiesced to Walls, Rhodesia got the desperately needed advance and the barrage trains started running again.

Later in September, a bolt came from the blue when Zambia's president, Kenneth Kaunda, invited Smith to Lusaka for secret talks. Tiny Rowland, chief executive of the Lonrho mining company, had facilitated the meeting and laid on his executive jet to fly Smith to Zambia. It was a pleasant gathering, but nothing really came of it because although Kaunda had influence over Nkomo, he had none over Mugabe.

When news broke of Ian Smith's visit to enemy territory, hardly anyone believed the story. Most shocked of all was Vorster, but he could hardly condemn Smith for talking to his old 'friend' Kaunda.

Smith knew that negotiating with Mugabe was futile because the guerrilla leader believed he was winning the war, as did quite a few prominent people in the international community. One way to remould this opinion was to eliminate Mugabe or land a very heavy blow on ZANLA in Mozambique ... or both. He asked Walls to come up with a plan.

The answer lay in an operation codenamed Dingo, the brainchild of Norman Walsh and Brian Robinson. General Walls asked for the plan to be presented again. He commented afterwards that 'Dingo was very risky, but well worth doing'.

Intelligence reports suggested that Robert Mugabe and his ZANLA war council, the Dare reChimurenga, would be meeting at their Chimoio HQ during the week starting 21 November 1977. The prospect of knocking out ZANLA's HQ and its top commanders was an opportunity too good to miss, even though it meant delaying the operation for a few days and risking adverse weather as the summer rains approached.

Another important factor was the moon phase. It is dangerous to fly an Alouette 3 helicopter on a dark, moonless night because the pilot needs a distinct horizon as his visual reference point, especially when flying slowly or hovering. With an operation of this scale, it was wise to assume that the Alouettes may well have to fly in the dark. The next full moon was due on 25 November 1977, falling between the Chimoio and Tembue attacks, which was ideal.

All Peter Walls now needed was the prime minister's approval to attack both Chimoio and Tembue. 'Although I had my difficulties sometimes with Mr Smith,' recalled Walls, 'I knew what he would agree to, or probably agree to. I had the greatest admiration for his probity; if I asked him or told him anything, it never went any further. I'm afraid the same can't be said about other people in the establishment. So I went to him direct.

'The PM referred to South African pressure. I responded by saying that far be it from me to say what he could and couldn't get away with, but my gut feel was that he would agree with this one. He pondered, then said: "Yes, all right, you can go ahead."'

Smith knew the timing was good. Vorster was facing a general election at the end of November, which made it unlikely that he would condemn the raid publicly because the white South African electorate was largely sympathetic towards Rhodesia. Also, the world press was now focused on the Middle East, where President Anwar Sadat of Egypt had just arrived in Israel on a state visit – the first Arab leader to visit Israel and address the Knesset.

Walls commented:

We agreed I would keep Smith updated on the strategic aspects of the operation. I chose to fly in a command Dakota near the battle, with a telex link direct to the PM's office, because, as ComOps commander, I felt that the place to be was where you got the feel of it – the battle – and you could make instant decisions, which I think helps at times because if you refer things back to committees or ComOps, you are not going to get an answer quickly. But I must emphasise that I was merely the strategic commander. The chaps from the air force and army did the job – they were the kingpins.

The door was now open for biggest clash of the war.

22

Walls between the SAS and RLI

Brian Robinson did not have sufficient SAS troops to envelop the targets during Operation Dingo; he would have to rely on other corps. He had no hesitation choosing his old unit, where he had received his first commission as a second lieutenant: the Rhodesian Light Infantry. The crack Fireforce commandos would supplement the SAS nicely.

The SAS and RLI had something in common: Peter Walls had commanded both units. He was the first man to command the Rhodesian SAS, although at the time it was a squadron of the British Special Air Services.

In the early 1950s, the SAS was resurrected from David Stirling's original SAS, which had been disbanded after World War II, to enter the Korean War. Two squadrons, A and B, were formed from volunteers under Brigadier Mike Calvert, who then went to Rhodesia to recruit more volunteers, which resulted in the formation of C Squadron. One of the Rhodesian volunteers was Peter Walls, a Sandhurst-trained officer, who had served with the Black Watch before returning to his native land.

As it turned out, the SAS was not required in Korea; instead, the Far East volunteers were sent to Malaya to fight communist insurgents during the Malayan Emergency, which also became known as the War of the Running Dogs. The SAS unit thus became known as the Malayan Scouts, and later 22 SAS.

The plan was to send the Rhodesians to South-East Asia under the temporary command of Lieutenant Peter Walls. 'They said to me: "You will be made a temporary captain, and wear three pips with no extra pay. When you get there, a British Army captain will be put in command."'

With great fanfare, the 100 men in jungle gear marched past Salisbury's Cecil Square to the railway station, where over 3 000 well-wishers had gathered to see them off. And they had another memorable send-off when their ship sailed from Durban for South-East Asia.

The men could feel the air getting hotter and muggier as the ship steamed eastwards across the Indian Ocean. By the time they reached the Andaman Sea, the humidity was so high that the sweat never seemed to evaporate, and it got worse as they passed down the Strait of Malacca towards their destination, the island of Singapore, protruding from the southern tip of the Malayan peninsula, just one degree north of the equator.

The final leg of the journey for the Rhodesians was a train ride from Singapore to Dusun Tua, near the Malayan capital, Kuala Lumpur. The train lurched across the causeway linking Singapore to the mainland, the very same causeway over which the Imperial Japanese Army had poured nine years earlier to inflict the worst military defeat Britain had sustained since the Battle of Isandlwana against the Zulus. The causeway was a sombre reminder to Walls and his men that the Commonwealth forces were not invincible. They would be facing a determined enemy – the Chinese communists, who were using terror as a brutal weapon to try to force Britain to relinquish control of Malaya.

At Dusun Tua, Walls learnt that the SAS had decided that these colonials from Rhodesia would not put up with a British commander, 'so they made me an acting major and I was only 23 at the time, a boy amongst all these decorated and formerly high-ranking officers,' said Walls.

It was a steep learning curve for the acting major. He learnt how to handle the jungle and manage his men in tough conditions. Discipline was a big issue, not helped by the fact his commanding officer, Brigadier Mike Calvert – a brilliant counter-insurgency officer – was investigated for misconduct. Calvert was dismissed from the British Army.

Walls managed to weed out and send home the bad apples in C Squadron. Slowly but surely, he and his men got to grips with the modus operandi of the Chinese insurgents, which wasn't easy in such thick tropical jungle.

In 1952, when his squadron was operating in the Cameron Highlands of Malaya, he lost his first man in action. 'We were advancing on a bandit camp when a sentry spotted us. Corporal Vic Visagie was walking just ahead of me carrying a British Army–issue map case. I think because of the case the sentry thought he was the officer and shot him between the eyes.' It was an awful shock to Walls, and made him wonder whether he had been too keen to attack the bandits, which may have led to some carelessness. Visagie's death taught Walls the importance of moving silently – a discipline that enabled his unit to chalk up enemy kills without further losses to C Squadron.

It was in Malaya that Walls noticed a corporal, a former post office signalman, who had potential. His name was Ron Reid-Daly. 'I promoted him to sergeant above a staff-corps man, who was pretty bitter. Reid-Daly became my right-hand man in many ways; he had a knack that others didn't have.' Reid-Daly would go on to command the Selous Scouts in the Rhodesian War.

One of the most uncomfortable experiences for Walls was when he discovered that a blood-sucking river leech had lodged itself inside his urethra. 'This leech had gone up my whatnot and I tried to get it out but couldn't. I started getting desperate, as it was going further up. One of the old Ibans [Dyaks] working with us stepped forward, took me off and got it out. I was so grateful to him.'

Walls was awarded the MBE in recognition of the contribution C Squadron SAS had made in Malaya.

Back in Rhodesia, his career continued on an upward path, and in 1964 he was appointed commanding officer of the RLI, a new regiment established in 1961. The RLI was formed during the Federation of Rhodesia and Nyasaland, and its initial instructors were drawn from the British Army. In 1965, under Walls's command, the RLI became a commando battalion divided into subunits, or commandos. The RLI, also known as 'The Saints', became very adept at counter-insurgency, making their mark as probably the best heli-borne troops in the world. They also established themselves as a crack parachute outfit when the Dakota was added to the Fireforce mix. The RLI almost certainly carried out more offensive parachute operations than any other unit in the world. The statistics speak for themselves: the RLI wiped out about 150 guerrillas for each man it lost in action, whereas the average for all Rhodesian forces was about ten guerrillas to one Rhodesian soldier.

'Commanding the RLI was probably the happiest time of my soldiering career,' said Walls.

The bad news for Mugabe's ZANLA was that these two crack units – the SAS and RLI – would be combining to assault its headquarters at New Farm, Chimoio, and the ZANLA Tembue base. The guerrilla movement was in for a torrid time.

23

Secret is secret

'If you reveal your secrets to the wind, you should not blame the wind for revealing them to the trees.' — KHALIL GIBRAN

Operation Dingo relied heavily on the element of surprise. Secrecy had to be paramount. 'Keeping the operational planning confidential,' said Norman Walsh, 'was one of the biggest challenges.'

Both he and Brian Robinson fretted that the plan would be leaked, especially as rumours suggested there was a mole in high places. Their concern turned to relief, however, on the day of the briefing; the secret was apparently still a secret. Norman Walsh recalled: 'Due to the uphill climb of getting to this point, we were pleased and relieved.'

The top-secret Dingo plan was restricted to a select few, and even then only revealed in parts on a need-to-know basis. Peter Petter-Bowyer (PB) was one of those select few. Norman Walsh had shown him aerial photographs of the Chimoio HQ complex as far back as January 1977 because Walsh needed PB's advice on the choice of weapons for an airborne attack.

Over the months leading up to Dingo, Walsh met regularly with PB, yet it was not until the last minute that PB learnt that the attack would include ground troops.

'Norman had not mentioned the use of ground forces until, at short notice, I learnt that I was to be the admin base commander for both operations, and that I was to attend a two-phase briefing at New Sarum on Tuesday 22 November,' PB admitted.

One problem with secrecy is that those who are kept in the dark become cheesed off. And some did. Norman Walsh remembered one of many cases: 'Randy du Rand was furious with me that I had not confided in him. He was officer commanding of flying at Sarum at the time and he felt that I should have trusted him. I did trust him, but secret was secret. No squadron commanders were briefed before the major briefing.'

Even in the field, secret was secret. The main helicopter staging base at Lake Alexander was in the middle of an operational area commanded by Major John Peirson, officer commanding of the 6th Independent Company, based in Umtali. Peirson recalled:

> One Wednesday afternoon in late November 1977, we had some spare time so my second in command, Captain Gavin Rawson, who was not only a very good fisherman, but a very lucky fisherman too, suggested we go up to Lake Alexander to catch some bass. As we came over the ridge by the lake, I was astonished to see a lot more than the eight helicopters I knew the Rhodesian Air Force possessed. Someone of senior rank came over asking what the hell we were doing in the area. As Gavin and I were in uniform and driving an army Land Rover, I retorted, 'I am in command of this area, what are *you* doing here?'

Peirson and Rawson were politely asked to leave, without even getting a chance to wet their lures. Said Peirson:

> As officer commanding the area, it peeved me that I had not been told of the op. Although I knew there were good reasons for this, I felt that the area should at least have been frozen to prevent my troops inadvertently walking in. My dissatisfaction was compounded by the fact that I had recently presided over two boards of inquiry into accidental deaths due to confusion over frozen areas.

Nevertheless, 'secret is secret' applied to everyone, even those having to perform vital functions before the op began. A good example was the helicopter recovery and repair facility at Lake Alexander, which needed to be established before the op started. Leading that effort was First Warrant Officer Charles Penney of the RhAF. 'My boss, Squadron Leader Derek Utton, told me to take helicopter spares, a full helicopter-recovery kit, tools and ammunition to FAF 8 [Grand Reef Airbase near Umtali], where I would be further briefed,' recalls Penney. 'I had no idea why we needed so many spares, which included a number of sets of main rotor blades, tail rotor blades, engines and general spares.'

Penney led the convoy of three trucks out of New Sarum Airbase on 22 November, the day before the operation (D-day minus 1). 'When we neared Rusape, I overtook a large air force convoy also heading east. We gave them a friendly wave and proceeded to Grand Reef.'

Two hours after Penney arrived, the large convoy pulled in, and Penney was instantly summoned to the ops room. 'I was crapped all over by Jack Lewis-Walker for passing the convoy. He said I was supposed to have been part of it – which was news to me. Anyway, we were still told nothing other than to leave at midnight for Lake Alexander to be on standby at first light.'

To make sure Penney didn't overtake any more convoys, his truck was placed at the front, right behind the escorting armoured car. 'We made camp near the lake in a clearing above and to the west of the public picnic area and then got a few hours of sleep. Just before 06:00, helicopters started landing in dribs and drabs from different directions. I eventually counted 32, yet still nobody would tell us what was going on.'

The answer was simple: Penney's group was there to recover downed helicopters. A casualty rate of at least 10 per cent was expected, so it was anticipated that his team would have to recover at least two downed Alouette helicopters.

To maintain the top-secret environment of the op for as long as possible, Robinson and Walsh decided that all the key participants would attend one mass briefing at New Sarum Airbase on Tuesday 22 November – the day before the operation. Pulling more than 200 soldiers from their operational areas at short notice and transporting them to Salisbury would most certainly attract attention and add grist to the rumour mill. The strongest rumour, probably planted, was that the raid was going to be on a ZIPRA base in Zambia.

Once the men were in the confines of New Sarum, they would be quarantined, with no access to telephones. The corporals' mess would be designated for all ranks, and stretchers with blankets would be laid out in the aircraft hangars.

Virtually all the available helicopters would be withdrawn from Fireforce ops and fly in to New Sarum at the same time to be serviced and made ready for Dingo. This meant that 22 Alouettes would arrive at New Sarum on the same afternoon. Another 10 Alouettes, discreetly loaned to Rhodesia by South Africa – probably without Vorster's knowledge – would supplement them. Then all the operational Vampires would fly in. Anyone just glancing across the runway from the main civilian airport would guess something big was about to happen.

Dave Jenkins, the helicopter technician who was chosen to fly with Norman Walsh and Brian Robinson in the command helicopter, recalled:

> I was deployed to Malapati [near the south-east border with Mozambique], flying with Mike Mulligan, Kevin Peinke and Nigel Lamb operating with the SAS. On 21 November, we were recalled to New Sarum and, on arrival, we suspected that something was brewing when we realised that all the choppers appeared to be returning to base, though nothing was let on to us. The first we knew about Op Dingo was when we all attended the briefing.

Mark McLean

The same code of secrecy applied to the few reservists called up for Dingo. Mark McLean, a highly experienced pilot, resigned from the air force in 1973 after 10 years of service to pursue his own interests. He did what most young people did in those days – he hopped on a plane and worked his way around Europe for a year. Then he returned to Rhodesia to begin a career in real estate. He worked for Fox & Carney and quickly became the agency's top residential property salesman.

Working as a civilian, however, did not exempt McLean from military service, and his first call-up was with Internal Affairs, where he spent his time recording all of the personal details of people in the rural villages. McLean was not only an experienced pilot, but a decorated one too. He had been awarded the Bronze Cross of Rhodesia in 1970 for some pretty hairy helicopter flying under extremely heavy enemy fire. Disgusted by the gross waste of his skills as a trained military pilot, he had a word in someone's ear and was transferred from Internal Affairs to the air force reserve. Call-ups became very regular; McLean recalls a particular one:

> I went to the office very early to clear up some last-minute things. Then I drove out to New Sarum to report for duty. I was hustled into a waiting chopper and sent post-haste to Mtoko. I arrived there just after the departure of the Fireforce, so I dumped my kit on the apron, pumped some gas and joined them. Three and a half hours after leaving the office, I was in a contact, shooting at people.

This lifestyle affected many Rhodesian reservists. McLean recalls:

> It was bizarre. You had to do a mental flick-flack, and it had its problems. For example, at FAF 4 in Mount Darwin, there was a Fireforce hooter that was blasted when we needed to scramble. One day, I was sitting in my office at Fox & Carney, having a meeting with two Greek businessmen, when a truck on the road outside sounded its horn. I was on my feet and heading for the door, before I realised I was nowhere near Mount Darwin. I got some funny looks from the Greeks as I sheepishly slunk back to my desk.

On 22 November 1977, McLean was ordered to report to New Sarum by 08:30 the next day for a routine call-up. When the long-haired, bearded reserve pilot drove his car into the airbase and saw scores of helicopters parked all over the place, he knew this was no ordinary call-up.

The venue

The 'secret is secret' rule also applied to the venue for the briefing – not an easy task because a hangar had to be cleared out, and seating and the massive models of the target moved in. Norman Walsh chose a shared hangar, one half occupied by the PTS, the other by the Radio Section. The hangar was divided across its breadth by offices. The briefing would take place in the Radio Section half.

The personnel in the PTS side of the hangar knew something was up: 'We noticed that the windows in our crew room, which looked through to the Radio Section, were suddenly taped up and we were told to keep the curtains closed,' recalls parachute jump instructor Sergeant Kevin Milligan.

On the other side of the taped windows, mapping expert Jacques du Bois and his team got on with laying out the Chimoio model on the floor; they then disassembled it and assembled Tembue in its place. At the main briefing, the switch from Chimoio to Tembue would have to be done during a 15-minute tea break.

The last bit of preparation entailed transporting the grandstands from the rugby field to the hangar to provide a small amphitheatre of seats. All was set for the largest military briefing in Rhodesian military history.

The consequence of concentrating all the country's firepower in Salisbury, ready to fly externally, meant that there was no Fireforce available to attack insurgents inside the country. 'We have 25 terrs visual, request Foxtrot Foxtrot' was a call that would usually have prompted a Fireforce scramble. 'Foxtrot Foxtrot is not available' was the disappointing reply. The armed section of the Police Reserve Air Wing (flying Cessna aircraft with a side-firing .303 machine gun), flown mostly by private pilots, became the stand-in Fireforce. The Police Reserve Air Wing crews, particularly the SALOPS Flight, which operated from Salisbury's small Charles Prince Airport, were inundated with call-outs and saw more action during the week of Operation Dingo than they had probably encountered during the entire war.

Number 11 Short Service Unit in 1958. Standing: Vic Wightman second from left, Ian Harvey fourth from left, Tol Janeke sixth from left. Sitting: Rich Brand sixth from left

Dermot 'Mac' MacLaughlin explaining formation position changes to student pilots Vic Wightman, Rich Brand and Bob Walsh

Norman and Merilyn Walsh on their wedding day in Salisbury

Peter Petter-Bowyer in RRAF uniform at the time of UDI

Rich Brand boarding his favourite Hawker Hunter

Mark McLean after receiving the Bronze Cross of Rhodesia

Lieutenant General Peter Walls

Keith Samler wearing a captured Soviet officer's hat (ushanka), at the time of his secondment to the Selous Scouts

Kevin Milligan kitting up for a fun jump at Delport Farm, near Salisbury

Flight Lieutenant Dick Paxton, No. 7 Squadron Alouette pilot

Rhodesians working with the Portuguese at Casa Katiza in Mozambique's Tete Province, 1970. Included in the group are Ian Harvey, Ron Reid-Daly, Chris Dixon, Bruce Collocott and Mark McLean

Mark McLean

Brian Robinson

Peter Walls and Ian Smith visit the bush. To the right of Smith are Junior Penton, Brian Robinson, John 'Fluff' Templar and Cocky Benecke

Keith Samler

Special Forces on a clandestine mission from Mtoko. From left: Winston Hart, Peter Stanton, Keith Samler, Scotty McCormack, Philip Conjuwayo and a FRELIMO soldier known as Lamek (kneeling)

Hawker Hunters, with RRAF markings, at Thornhill Airbase. Behind are de Havilland Vampires and propeller-driven Percival Provost aircraft

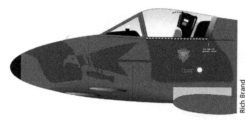

Rich Brand's favourite Hunter, showing an eagle-headed spear clutching a bomb

A display of the Hawker Hunter's armaments

Mark Jackson (wearing helmet) observing RLI troopies boarding his G-car Alouette helicopter during a Fireforce deployment

The G-car, with Mark Jackson firing the twin Browning machine guns

The K-car with the 20-mm Matra cannon. Note the army commander's seat in the left front bubble

RRAF Vampires in formation

Mark McLean

A Rhodesian Canberra jet in attack mode with bomb doors wide open

Dennis Croukamp

Greg Todd

RhAF Canberras moving into attack formation

Kevin Milligan

Kevin Milligan demonstrating a perfect static line exit position

Kevin Milligan

Mass parachute drop from Dakota aircraft

The bridge over the
Pungwe River destroyed
by the Selous Scouts
after the raid on
ZANLA's Nyadzonia base

Brian Robinson's lucky escape: the wreckage of the Lynx aircraft at Mtoko airbase

The remains of Jan
Smuts's former personal
Dakota, shot down
while taking off from
Mapai airfield in
Mozambique, claiming
the life of Flight
Lieutenant Bruce
Collocott

Photographs from cameras seized by Keith Samler and his SB colleagues during the Chimoio raid show ZANLA training at New Farm. *Above*: Women ZANLA guerrillas marching. *Right*: Josiah Tongogara, the ZANLA commander, making a point with his AK-47

Above: Women ZANLA guerrillas sharpening their skills with the AK-47 at the rifle range
Below: ZANLA recruits undergoing fitness training

The Vampire boys: Ken Law, Steve Kesby and Justin 'Varkie' Varkevisser (Phil Haigh is absent)

Steve Kesby

Keith Samler

Alouette helicopters arriving at lake Alexander before the attack on Chimoio

SB men Ken Milne and Mike Edden in a G-car en-route to Chimoio

Keith Samler

Keith Samler

The ZANLA HQ at New Farm

*Unexplored Alpha bomb dropped by a
Canberra near the HQ building*

Keith Samler

Keith Samler

Large quantities of ZANLA documents are drawn into the fire near the HQ building

A ZANLA anti-aircraft gunner lies dead near his destroyed gunpit

An RLI troopie raises the Rhodesian flag near the ZANLA HQ building at New Farm

Bob MacKenzie (wearing helmet) frantically calls off an airstrike on his commandeered Peugeot vehicle at Chimoio

Captain Bob MacKenzie, SAS

Lieutenant Neill Jackson, RLI Support Commando

Neill Jackson

Mark McLean

Mark McLean with swelling above his right eye, and, 33 years later, tracing the line the AK bullet took through his helmet

Ian Pringle

John Norman

John Norman's blood-stained casevac card showing his injuries and morphine doses

www.thezimbabwean.co.uk

Josiah Tongogara, the ZANLA commander

Helicopters arriving and being directed by a marshall at Chiswiti

A ZANLA guerrilla perished in the trench he was digging at Tembue

A guerrilla shows Keith Samler an underground bunker at Tembue

A destroyed DShK 12.7-mm anti-aircraft gun in a fortified gunpit at Tembue

Keith Samler

Keith Samler

A gunner's view from a G-car crossing Cahora Bassa dam after leaving Tembue

Peter Petter-Bowyer

A 'flechette' dart embedded in a tree

Vic Wightman's Martin Baker Club 'ejection' certificate

Vic Wightman

MARTIN-BAKER TIE CLUB

PRESIDENT: SIR JAMES MARTIN,
C.B.E.,C.Eng.,M.I.Mech.E.,F.R.Ae.S.,

Mr. C. L. Wightman

The Holder..........................
is registered as a Life Member
of the Martin-Baker Tie Club,
and is authorised to purchase
for his own personal use the
Club's distinctive tie.

....
Signature of Life Member.

1847
Life Membership No.

....
Secretary.

Rich Brand's logbook, recording the Dingo sorties. The underlined entries indicate that weapons were delivered

Rich Brand

Norman Walsh receives the Officer of the Legion of Merit medal for Operation Dingo from President John Wrathall, while Brian Robinson waits in the rain to receive his medal

Brian Robinson

The ZANLA war shrine in the distance framed by trees adjacent to the old ZANLA HQ at New Farm

Bob Manser

Remains of the ZANLA HQ and weapons now enclosed in a museum building at New Farm

Bob Manser

Bob Manser

Neglected mass graves at the site of Chitepo College, New Farm

Wall of Remembrance to the ZANLA men and women who died at New Farm

Bob Manser

24

There's a kind of hush

The anniversary of UDI was celebrated each year with a glittering ball attended by politicians, captains of industry and civic leaders. The star guest was always Prime Minister Ian Smith. The format was that of a New Year's party, with dinner and dancing before the prime minister made a short speech, and then, at midnight precisely, he would strike the Independence Bell. Modelled on the American Liberty Bell and donated by Friends of Rhodesia, this large bell hung from a stand made of solid Rhodesian mukwa hardwood, on which there was an inscription: 'I toll for Liberty, Civilisation and Christianity.'

Some 600 people dressed to the nines gathered at the Harry Margolis Hall in Salisbury on the evening of 10 November 1977 to celebrate the 12th anniversary of UDI. The ball took place as yet another peace deal was emerging. This time, David Owen and Andrew Young were the brokers.

The backdrop to this Independence Ball was an intensifying war. Ian Smith's speech, broadcast live by the Rhodesian Broadcasting Corporation, was fittingly sombre. He talked of the multiple settlement efforts and the risk of failure: 'Let me hasten to add as far as we in Rhodesia are concerned, we are ready to show great reason, and if there is a response from the other side I think the world would be agreeably surprised with the amount of reason that would be forthcoming from Rhodesians. But a fatal mistake would be to misinterpret our reason as weakness because that will mean failure.'

What Smith and only a few others at the ball knew was that in just 12 days' time, Rhodesian forces would deal Robert Mugabe's ZANLA forces in Mozambique a heavy blow in the largest air and ground attack of the war. Smith ended with a message of caution and hope:

I wish you well in the year ahead; I hope that, as before, Rhodesians will go forward and enter this 13th year of ours in good spirit and with strong resolution. We have got problems; don't let's pretend otherwise, but no doubt you have often in the past heard the well-known saying that no matter how dark the night, there will always be a dawn.

I believe this is very apt as far as Rhodesians in present circumstances are concerned. And, as you all know, the dawn with its fresh, cool, clear air is always the best time of the day and I believe that the dawn is coming to Rhodesia.

To humour the audience, Smith reminded them that the bell was not struck once for each year of independence, but always 12 times: 'You can imagine what the position would be when one of my successors, in due time, has to ring the bell 100 times,' Smith quipped to laughter and huge applause.

The party continued with the traditional first song of the new Independence Year, a rendition of the Herman's Hermits hit 'A Kind of Hush (All Over the World Tonight)'.

25

The Dingo commanders

Norman Walsh

From childhood, Norman Walsh had wanted to be an air force pilot. He was brought up in Queenstown, in South Africa's Eastern Cape, and attended Queen's College, a prestigious boys' school established in 1858 at the foot of the rugged Stormberg mountains. Being youngest in his class didn't faze Norman, except that it meant he was too young to leave school when he matriculated, so he spent another year doing a post-matric course at Grey High School in Port Elizabeth.

English-speaking Norman didn't fancy his chances of getting into the South African Air Force (SAAF), so he hit the Great North Road to Rhodesia, hoping to join the Royal Rhodesian Air Force (RRAF).

Why Rhodesia? 'Many people seemed to be going there, as the prospects seemed better,' recalled Walsh. But he found once again that he was too young; he also had to live in Rhodesia for at least six months to qualify as a resident before the air force would consider his application.

Norman found a job as a farmhand on Montezuma Farm, a tobacco outfit owned by Aubrey Leeuwen. Montezuma was 15 kilometres south-west of Karoi, a small agricultural town sometimes called the Town of the Little Witch, after its Shona name, *ka* (diminutive) and *royi* (witch). Tobacco farming was not easy work for young Norman, especially as the tobacco-curing barns had to be monitored for correct temperature and humidity at all hours of the day and night.

Soon Norman was old enough to bid farewell to the Town of the Little Witch and join the RRAF selection process in Salisbury. Norman whizzed through selection, and joined the air force in 1953 as a member of the No. 5 Course, Short Service Unit.

In no time, he was learning to fly the iconic de Havilland Tiger Moth, a wonderful biplane made of a Sitka spruce frame covered with fabric and ply; wire anchored the wings together. Built as a trainer, it had two open cockpits with tiny windshields to give the pilots a little relief.

The student sits at the back, so Walsh quickly got used to reading the body language of his instructor, Flight Lieutenant Colin Graves:

'He would whack the side of the aircraft if one made a major balls-up.'

But as Walsh gained experience, the whacking diminished. Then one day, Graves hopped out of his front seat, saying, 'Walsh, I want you to do one circuit and land – on your own.' Graves walked off to dispersal while Walsh bumped along, zigzagging the Tiger Moth so that he could see where he was going beyond the high nose. On a signal from the control tower, Walsh lined up the biplane on the runway centre line, applied full power, keeping the machine straight, with generous bootfuls of rudder lifting the tail up a bit, and soon the Tiger Moth was in the air.

It felt eerie seeing no head sticking out of the front cockpit – Walsh was on his own, but loving every minute of it. In what seemed like no time at all, it was time to land. A good three-point landing completed his first solo and his first major milestone in aviation. His next important landmark came the following year, when he was awarded his wings in August 1954 and later won the trophy for the best student on the course. Walsh was now set up for a brilliant air force career, which would see him go all the way to the top.

Yet beneath this cloak of professional excellence lurked a naughty, funny and rebellious spirit. Norman had the proverbial hollow legs and was renowned to be the last to leave the party – still standing. He also had a compassionate side for those who could not remain on their feet. On one occasion, a young pilot officer by the name of Hugh Slatter had turned 21. After flying duties were over for the day, he and others went to the officers' mess at Thornhill Airbase to celebrate. Slatter recalled: 'I don't remember the details, except that my "friends" mixed some suitable concoctions and in a few hours I was feeling a bit worse for wear. The pub was filling up as other officers came in for a drink after flying or sports, and I desperately needed some fresh air.'

He staggered outside to the car park and collapsed in a heap as the world spun around him. 'I knew I was flat on my back on the tarmac. I don't remember how long I stayed like that, but the next thing I remember was the officer commanding of No. 1 Squadron, Norman Walsh, standing next to me with his arm outstretched to pull me to my feet.

'Although I could stand, I was very unsteady, and Norman helped me to get into his car, whereupon he drove me to the single quarters and told me to get some rest, and drove off back to the pub. I was mortified ... here was the officer commanding of the Hunter Squadron, almost a god in pilots' eyes, helping a lowly pilot officer who clearly could not handle his drink, to recover.'

After the Tiger Moth, Walsh graduated to his first heavy-metal monoplane aircraft, the North American Harvard. Later, Walsh moved on to Vampire jets and then on to the impressive Hawker Hunter FGA9 fighter/ground-attack jet. If the wings are free of external fuel tanks, the Hunter can achieve supersonic speed in a shallow dive.

Walsh notoriously broke the sound barrier in his Hawker Hunter over thousands of people at an air show in Lusaka in 1963, at a time when the Federation of Rhodesia and Nyasaland was coming to an end. The supersonic boom, in reality an extremely loud double crack, was a show winner, but it angered many local residents as their shivering dogs scampered for cover, their hens stopped laying and the odd bit of glass was shattered – at least that's what the offended parties told their insurers.

Norman Walsh was soon forgiven, and the very next year he was promoted to squadron leader, taking command of No. 1 (Hunter) Squadron.

But despite the responsibility of his rank, the rebel was still in those bones. Hugh Slatter recalled another mess incident involving Norman Walsh:

Friday nights were pub nights, and one was expected to attend and socialise with one's fellow squadrons and support staff. On this occasion, in the mid-60s, there was a good attendance and everyone was having a good time, with plenty of beer and laughter, and the odd game of bok-bok [a rough type of collective wrestling] thrown in for added fun. Norman, if I remember correctly, was commanding 1 Squadron at the time and was present and enjoying himself like everyone else.

The commanding officer of the station was also present. Something caused the CO to call for quiet at the bar, and he went on to say that although it was good for everyone to let off some steam, damage to the pub was unacceptable and, in particular, the use of fire hoses in the mess for purposes other than fire was forbidden.

Then everyone returned to their drinks, including the CO – except for Norman, who immediately left the bar, fetched the fire hose from the lobby, turned it on full blast and aimed it at those of us drinking at the bar. The blast of water was powerful, and caught the commanding officer squarely on his chest. He managed to hang onto his glass until the blast was shut off and Norman put the hose back in place.

As Norman came back into the pub, the CO slowly put his glass down, and in the sodden silence invited Norman to see him in his office on Monday morning, and then left the mess. I don't know what happened in the CO's office on Monday morning, but he was a good man, and Norman still had two arms and two legs next time we saw him, and the incident did nothing to stop him becoming commander of the air force later in his career.

After Hunters, Walsh switched to the other speed extreme, and learnt to fly the slow, but extremely versatile, Alouette helicopter. There was only one problem: the new squadron boss of No. 7 (Alouette) Squadron had never flown a helicopter before. It was an inverted pyramid, with the top man having the least helicopter experience. The pressure was on; Walsh had to learn quickly.

Flying a helicopter poses challenges for fixed-wing pilots, especially when learning to hover accurately. The problem is that any control movement in a helicopter causes a dynamic reaction, necessitating a correction somewhere else. New helicopter pilots tend to tense up and over-control, making the helicopter look like a drunken dragonfly as it bucks and rolls around with increasing severity while the student inadvertently aggravates the situation.

Norman remembered the pressure: 'On chopper conversion I had pins and needles in my thumb from being so tense – it was so different.'

His instructor, Peter Petter-Bowyer, also remembered: 'None was more frustrated by the learning process than steely-eye jet pilot Norman Walsh. He simply could not understand why he could not control the Alouette in the hover.'

Walsh quickly got the hang of it, however, and no longer needed an area the size of a rugby field to practise hovering – half a tennis court would do. After only seven days, Walsh flew the Alouette solo for the first time and his full conversion training was done in a record period of six weeks. The new squadron boss was at last a qualified helicopter pilot.

As squadron leader, Walsh often had to fly VIPs around. His passenger on one of these assignments was the rather eccentric minister of defence, P.K. van der Byl, who always sported large, expensive sunglasses. They were returning to base from a tour of the operational area, when the minister was, as usual, trying to spot enemy forces in the bush. He leant out of the doorless Alouette a bit too far and his pricey sunglasses flew off into the thick bush below. 'Turn back, turn back – I know exactly where they are,' Van der Byl ordered. Walsh knew that finding the sunglasses would be impossible, so he continued flying back to base. The angry minister never forgave him for disobeying a direct order.

Not long afterwards, it seemed the minister had called on nature for retribution. Walsh was flying back to New Sarum, when an eagle smashed through the Perspex windscreen of the Alouette, hitting his technician in the chest. 'Benecke started thrashing about and went into convulsions. I had to restrain him while flying the helicopter.' Walsh managed to get the unconscious technician back to safety and to hospital. There was a massive hole in the left side of the bubble resembling the eagle's shape. 'When I visited Benecke later in hospital, I saw that the eagle had left an imprint on his chest too.'

Gone was the myth that bird strikes are not hazardous to slower-flying helicopters.

Norman Walsh had fond memories of his helicopter days: 'Choppers were probably the most rewarding aircraft to fly, because of the close association with the army and police. Having myself gone through a few courses with the army and police, counter-insurgency in particular, it was very good to get to know people on the ground and that they understood where we were coming from. It was a learning curve for everyone.'

Walsh's affinity with the 'people on the ground', and having previously flown attack aircraft, equipped him to quickly become adept at calling in and accurately directing air strikes onto targets from his helicopter. In one particular operation in 1968, against a group of 30 ZIPRA guerrillas in the Chewore area of the Zambezi Valley, Walsh and his gunner, Sergeant Tinker Smithdorff, came under withering ground fire as they deployed troops to contain the enemy.

As the battle raged, an RLI soldier was injured. Walsh flew right into the firefight to evacuate the man, but his helicopter took a hit from enemy fire. Fortunately, the damage wasn't terminal, and Walsh was able to drop the wounded soldier off for medical treatment before flying his damaged Alouette straight back into the battle, where he coolly and professionally directed frantan strikes right into the midst of the enemy. 'It made me realise that our training was good,' said Walsh after the battle.

Peter Walls remembered the event: 'I had tremendous respect for this bugger who flew into a valley to support and evacuate troops – in a helicopter!'

Both Walsh and Smithdorff were awarded medals for this action. The inscription on Norman Walsh's medal, the Bronze Cross of Rhodesia, has the following simple conclusion: 'There is no doubt that Squadron Leader Walsh's skill as a pilot, coupled with his complete disregard for his personal safety, contributed in no small way to the success of the action.'

This and many future actions confirmed Walsh as precisely the right person to plan and command the air attack in the massive Operation Dingo, nine years later.

Brian Robinson

Like Norman Walsh, Brian Robinson was born in South Africa and he too had a boyhood dream to become an air force pilot. Brian's father, David 'Robbie' Robinson, was passionate about aviation, and piloted the Douglas Boston light bomber with the rank of major in No. 12 Squadron, SAAF during World War II. After the war, Robinson senior continued to fly as a pastime, and served for many years as president of the Durban Wings Club. This private flying club is based at Virginia Airport, an idyllic airfield almost on the beach on the wild Indian Ocean, just north of Durban. Young Brian grew up in an environment that revolved around aviation, often flying with his father in his Aero Commander and Mooney.

As soon as he finished school, Brian headed for Pretoria to undergo the pilot selection process at the SAAF Gymnasium in the suburb of Valhalla. When he wasn't marching around the parade ground, called the Sahara, he was excelling at sport. This proved useful for Robinson, as pilot selection was biased against English-speakers in those days, but being good at sport counted in his favour. Robinson won the Transvaal three-metre board-diving championship and was selected to play rugby for Transvaal Under-19s as a centre alongside Syd Nomis, a promising player who would go on to play for the Springboks in 55 Tests.

Brian was soaring. He was superbly fit and ready for the pilot aptitude tests, decompression tests and a very extensive medical examination. It should be a shoe-in for the rugby player. Soon the young man would be following in his father's footsteps. At least, that's what it seemed like, until he had his eyes tested.

To Brian's shock and dismay, the medical team found that he had a very slight red–green colour deficiency, which meant a failed medical. The young man's dream was well and truly shattered. 'I was devastated. The only jobs open to me in the SAAF were cook, clerk or musician, so I borrowed 10 quid from my dad and bought myself out.'

Robinson slowly picked himself up and found a job with a timber merchant. The company needed someone to travel to neighbouring Rhodesia to relieve the depot manager in Salisbury on a temporary basis.

Two things about Rhodesia immediately impressed Robinson: they had television and played rugby on Sundays. In South Africa at the time, the ruling Calvinistic National Party prohibited television, which it regarded as an evil black box. Sport and most other unholy activities were banned on Sundays.

'One day, walking down First Street in Salisbury, I came across an army recruitment office,' recalls Robinson. 'The poster showed some bod jumping out of an aircraft. They suggested I go on an officer's selection course as a civvy. If I failed, I could walk away without any obligations. If I passed, I could either go to Sandhurst or Gwelo.'

Robinson passed easily – the slight colour blindness was not an issue this time – and went to the school of infantry in Gwelo. Although not in the air, he was back in his element. He sailed through officer selection and was commissioned into the RLI as a second lieutenant. The 'bod jumping out of an aircraft' poster still played on Brian Robinson's mind, however. He needed to be near aircraft even if he couldn't pilot them legally.

After a year with the RLI, Robinson saw an opportunity to join the SAS when C Squadron, 22 SAS Regiment, under Major Dudley Coventry, was moved from Ndola in Zambia to Salisbury at the end of the federation. Robinson grabbed the chance, and joined the SAS as a second lieutenant.

It wasn't long before Robinson was sent to England on attachment to the mother unit, 22 SAS Regiment, Hereford. Attachments were normal in colonial times. Robinson's arrival in England coincided with the period when the new Federation of Malaya was squaring up to Indonesia over the control of Borneo. President Sukarno of Indonesia objected to the northern part of Borneo, the three regions known as Sabah, Brunei and Sarawak, joining the Federation of Malaya. Indonesia already controlled the biggest chunk of Borneo, the southern part, called Kalimantan. Sukarno wanted the whole island.

In December 1962, armed Indonesian insurgents tried to take power in Brunei. This was followed by incursions of armed bands of insurgents that engaged in propaganda and sabotage missions, which led to what was known as Konfrontasi – a confrontation that would last until 1966.

Looking after its former colonial interests in Malaysia, Britain responded by sending in 22 SAS's A Squadron. With only 100 men to defend 1 500 kilometres of border between northern and southern Borneo, the SAS deployed four-man teams to work very large areas, with the help of friendly locals, or 'border scouts', to disrupt Indonesian forces and supply lines behind enemy lines.

The men would deploy into Kalimantan for three-week spells, each man carrying his own supplies – dehydrated food, water and ammunition. Because of their small numbers, the SAS focused on clandestine warfare, gathering intelligence, disrupting enemy supply lines and occasionally hitting Indonesian troops and then vanishing into the jungle – a technique known as 'shoot and scoot'.

This type of warfare was very effective and made life tough for the insurgents; it also avoided dragging Britain into overt war with Indonesia.

Brian Robinson studied in detail the SAS tactical deployment methods for Borneo while he was in Hereford. Then it was time for him to try it out first-hand in Borneo. But it was November 1965, and history intervened. 'I was actually on the flight manifest to go to Borneo with one of the squadrons of 22 SAS, when Prime Minister Ian Smith declared UDI.'

Rhodesia had rebelled against the Crown, and this meant Robinson and his fellow Rhodesians were no longer welcome in Britain. Robinson found himself on a long-haul flight, but heading south instead of east. He was on his way back to Salisbury and life in the Rhodesian SAS. Life would change dramatically in the wake of UDI as sanctions bit and the black nationalists chose war in a conflict that would last 14 years.

Robinson would go on to become the longest-serving officer commanding of the Rhodesian SAS, from 1972 to 1978. His natural flair when it came to outsmarting the enemy coupled with his knowledge of the SAS's counter-insurgency techniques used in Borneo would play a significant part in that war.

Death comes close

Eight months before Operation Dingo, Brian Robinson's passion, flying, very nearly cost him his life. An SAS callsign in Mozambique was under fire from the enemy and desperately trying to break contact and slip away. In the process, they lost long-range radio contact with SAS HQ. Robinson knew there was only one way he could make contact – by using line-of-sight VHF radio. The only way to do this was by air. The RhAF provided a plane for him from FAF 5, the forward airfield at Mtoko.

It was the Ides of March – a particularly dark night falling right between the last quarter and the new phase of the moon. Robinson and his pilot, Air Sub Lieutenant John Kidson, clambered aboard their Lynx aircraft. The Lynx was a French-built Cessna 337 (the model number reflecting the wing area in square feet).

Kidson started the Lynx's two engines, one at the front and one aft, which gave the Lynx its other name, 'push and pull', sometimes derogatorily translated to 'huff and puff' or 'suck and blow'. Kidson chose Runway 09, facing east. It was a logical choice, as the threshold was much closer to dispersal than the other end, and he would already be pointing towards Mozambique.

There was plenty of hard-surfaced runway ahead of them – 1100 metres of it, with a very gentle downhill slope towards the other end. After the end of the runway, however, the ground rises gradually to 11 metres above runway level, but by this point an aircraft should be well established in a climb much steeper than the angle of the sloping ground.

On a dark night with no visual reference after the runway lights disappear, it is imperative to establish a positive and sustained rate of climb, using nothing but the aircraft instruments. The pilot immediately and systematically scans all the critical instruments. One of these shows the aircraft rate of climb, the vertical speed indicator, or VSI, a sensitive pressure device showing climb or descent in feet per minute. If the aircraft is climbing, the needle points up from the neutral nine o'clock position, and vice versa.

Kidson lined up on the runway facing east, completed his preflight checks, applied full power and released the brakes.

'We probably got airborne halfway down the runway,' recalled Robinson. 'We were airborne for at least 20 seconds. I was about to ask Kidson what the hell was going on with the VSI sitting at the six o'clock position, when we flew into the ground on the other side of the road.'

It seems the Lynx had taken off normally, climbed a bit and then started descending until it ploughed into the rising ground just on the other side of the Mtoko–Mrewa main road. The Lynx quickly ground to a halt.

Kidson shouted, 'Get out, get out!' but his door was jammed. Robinson reacted immediately: 'Amazing how fire helps with the unlocking sequence of the door. The plane actually exploded as we made a hot exit.'

Both men were very lucky to get out alive. Kidson had bruised ribs and Robinson needed 15 stitches to close a head wound, and treatment for burns to his face. The aircraft was destroyed by fire.

Always ready to make light of a serious situation, Robinson commented later: 'I believe I raised the morale of the squadron for at least 10 minutes, until they found out I had survived!'

26

The Dingo briefing

'Are you fucking mad?'
— ANONYMOUS SOLDIER

Bringing over 200 people together, quarantining them from the outside world and then telling them nothing breeds frustration, anxiety and speculation. 'Are we going to colonise Zambia?' 'Are we going to occupy Maputo?' These were just some of the theories flying about. People wanted to know.

The anxiety kept building and when the side door to the Radio Section hangar was opened at 13:00 on Wednesday 22 November 1977, the tension was electric.

Peter Petter-Bowyer remembers walking in: 'We came in and there were tiered seats on the left and at the rear and there was this huge target laid out on the floor. It was in proper relief, so where there was a dip in the ground, the model replicated the same thing.'

'Everyone including his dog seemed to be there,' thought Kevin Milligan when he walked into the hangar. 'Everyone who was anybody, that is. I then saw the huge model on the hangar floor. Then I knew why our Parachute Training School windows had been sealed. This just confirmed my suspicions that this was big – far bigger than anything we had seen before.'

Keith Samler of the Special Branch had different thoughts; he was worried to see so many people at the briefing. His detective instincts warned him that the law of averages meant there was a very strong possibility of a leak.

People occupied their seats or clambered up the rugby grandstands, set out like a theatre. The SAS were surprised to see RLI soldiers, and vice versa. Combined ops between these two units were rare. All eyes were on the large target model on the floor.

What particularly impressed PB about the model was that by being on the floor, it gave the same perspective one would have from the air. There were marked tapes across the target, indicating a simple alphanumeric scale – letters from left to right and numbers from bottom to top. This turned out to be vital, especially before calling in air strikes. The aircrew and ground commanders were given their own photographs of the target with the grid lines clearly marked.

'Norman Walsh would not give his pilots map references. Instead, he would give them a grid reference from the photograph. Then he could turn away and focus on the next task, confident that the target was about to be zapped,' PB added.

Walsh had also asked the modellers to superimpose clear, easy-to-follow 'circuit patterns', a series of red curved arrows, for the pilots to follow to reduce the chances of mid-air collision.

The buzz from the audience turned to silence as SAS Intelligence Officer Captain Scotty McCormack stepped forward. 'He stood right in the middle of the target, with no microphone,' remembers PB, 'and then walked around inside the target, on the many stretches of open ground, as he explained what the various areas were and what they were called.'

McCormack explained that the massive complex laid out on the floor was a model of New Farm, the military headquarters of ZANLA in Mozambique, the very nerve centre of the organisation. He pointed out that Robert Mugabe, Josiah Tongogara, Rex Nhongo and most of the ZANLA hierarchy spent much time at Chimoio. He pointed to Mugabe's sleeping quarters on the model for effect. The attack was planned on a day that the ZANLA war council, the Dare reChimurenga, was known to be meeting, presenting an opportunity to decapitate the organisation.

McCormack reminded the audience that although the HQ was a prime objective, the real issue was to attack the vast numbers of trained and semi-trained guerrillas before they could enter Rhodesia.

Flight Lieutenant Mark McLean, who flew a K-car on the op, remembered:

They listed all the friendly forces, the RLI, SAS and aircraft that would be involved, and you could see it was going to be a very big operation. The friendly forces added up to about 200 people. Having done that, they turned to enemy forces, saying that they estimated about 5 000 Charlie Tangos [communist terrorists].

It was the first time in my life that I had heard a tremendous collective gasp, a huge intake of breath by 200 people ... everyone was stunned.

Then some wise guy at the back, using the punchline from a well-known Japanese kamikaze flying joke, shouted in an appropriate accent: 'Are you fucking mad?', whereupon everybody burst out laughing loudly, which broke the tension.

After the tension-releasing laughter had died down, McCormack spoke about a constant stream of new arrivals coming in from Tanzania, Ethiopia and China, so there might be a lot more than 5 000, he warned the audience. Up to 8 000 had been estimated from an earlier aerial photograph, which brought another collective gasp from the audience. McCormack described each major target in turn, its function and the numbers of personnel expected to be there. All in all, there were 17 targets, each given an alphabetic letter.

If that weren't bad enough, McCormack mentioned that in Chimoio Town, there were expected to be large numbers of FRELIMO troops, supplemented by elements of the Tanzanian Army and up to 100 Russian and Cuban advisers. What made the airmen shudder was the mention of Strela heat-seeking missiles, backed up by 12.7-mm and 14.5-mm anti-aircraft weapons. The mention of tanks and armoured cars at Chimoio Town worried the infantrymen.

Second Lieutenant Neill Jackson of the RLI recalls:

We were given an exceptionally professional and clear briefing at New Sarum by SAS Intelligence Officer Captain Scotty McCormack. I remember being stunned by the vast scope of the operation, but drawing much confidence from the coolness and professionalism of the SAS soldiers that I had befriended on a diving course, as we all listened to the briefing and made the relevant notes.

Ever since Mugabe and Tongogara had cracked down on the poor discipline at their HQ, the ZANLA routine was to assemble on the parade square each day at 07:00 for drill and to listen to speeches by commanders and political commissars. This process would usually keep them on the parade square for an hour. The timing of the initial air strike would be built around this ZANLA routine.

After McCormack's spellbinding presentation, Group Captain Norman Walsh took the floor. Using military terms for the day of the operation (D-day) and the time it would commence (H-hour), he announced: 'D-day is November 23; H-hour is 07:45 Bravo.'

As it sunk in that the attack would start at 07:45 the next morning, a buzz of adrenalin-fuelled murmurs swept through the hangar – these guys are serious and in a hurry, was the thought running through many heads.

Walsh explained the air-strike sequence. First, a DC-8 cargo jet would fly over the target as a decoy, making as much noise as possible. When the assembled terrs heard the DC-8, they were likely to scatter and dive into the trenches or man the anti-aircraft guns. When they realised it was a false alarm, they would start reassembling on the parade square, by which time Red Section would be about to launch the initial strike. The DC-8 would also mask the sound of the approaching Dakotas and helicopters.

It was unprecedented to use a civilian jetliner at the leading edge of a major air attack. The aircraft in question belonged to Air Trans Africa, a Rhodesian sanction-busting airline operated by a former World War II Spitfire pilot, Jack Malloch. Jack was sitting in the audience. He would not be flying the DC-8 himself; instead, he would fly a propeller-driven DC-7, the aircraft every helicopter pilot would rely on for fuel.

Walsh continued:

> At precisely H-hour, Red 1 will strike the HQ building complex here, with Golf [percussion] bombs, while Red 2 will plant Golf bombs here, on target Mike [Chitepo College], and Red 3 will drop frantan here, on Lima [Pasidina 2, a guerrilla convalescence centre]. The weather forecast is good, but if there is cloud, frantan will replace Golf bombs. Red Section's strikes will be the markers for Green Section, which will strike with Alpha bombs at H plus 30 seconds.

Walsh explained that the Vampire squadron would strike the recruits' camp nearly seven kilometres to the north-east with rockets and 20-mm cannon, also at H-hour.

As the Canberras of Green Section were releasing their bombs, Walsh wanted the next wave of Hunters, White and Blue Sections, to be already in their dive profiles to attack the four main anti-aircraft-gun emplacements. 'Gentlemen, timing is crucial,' warned Walsh, 'because by now, the six Dakotas of Silver Section will be approaching to drop the troops here and here,' indicating with his pointer stick the two sides of the 'box', or target. 'The G-cars of Pink Section will drop the helitroops on the lee side of this ridgeline, making up a third side of the box. At H plus five, the 10 K-cars will attack these targets ...' Walsh pointed out six target zones, four of which would be attacked by pairs of K-cars to ensure a constant presence when one ran out of ammo or fuel. He amplified the orbit patterns and warned his pilots of the risks of mid-air collision.

'Pink Section, once you have dropped the troops at the target, fly directly to the admin base,' said Walsh, pointing to a mark on a large map, 'which is 13 nautical miles north on a heading of zero-zero-three degrees magnetic. It should take you nine minutes to get there. Land and refuel; wait for further instructions. However, don't get in the way of the K-cars – they have refuelling priority.

'Yellow Section, your task is to fly men and equipment between Lake Alexander and the admin base, as listed on the schedule and as directed by me or the command Dak.'

Walsh emphasised again just how crucial timing was. It had to be down to the precise second. If just one element in the chain erred, the entire operation could be compromised.

'Gentlemen, there is no room for error. Any questions?'

Major Brian Robinson then strode up, commanding absolute attention as he outlined the plan for the attack troops. By definition, this had to be very detailed, even down to how many water bottles and rations each man should carry. He also reminded the men to write their blood group on their shirt, a necessary instruction, but one that always got the adrenalin going.

Dingo was essentially a Fireforce operation, only 11 times bigger. And besides scale, there was another difference. A typical Fireforce operation worked on a ratio of two enemies to one Rhodesian troopie. With Dingo, the most favourable ratio would be seven enemies to one Rhodesian, but that ratio could rise to 40:1. The odds seemed overwhelming.

Dave Jenkins, the technician tasked to fly with Norman Walsh in the command helicopter, remembered the concern about Rhodesian casualty estimates: 'If I recall correctly, we were told that losses could be as high as 10 per cent. I might be wrong about the exact percentage, but I remember it was quite high. It was definitely a topic of discussion after the briefing.'

Lieutenant Mark Adams, officer commanding the RLI's 12 Troop, 3 Commando, remembers a projected casualty figure of 30 per cent. 'I also found out later that two entire floors had been quietly cleared out in the Andrew Fleming Hospital [Salisbury's main hospital] to handle a big influx of casualties.'

Robinson told the men that six Dakotas would drop 144 paratroopers on two sides of the target box, and another 40 RLI troops would be choppered in to the third side. The thought going through many soldiers' minds was: 'It will be no problem getting 184 troopies in there, but if things go badly, how the hell are we all going to get out?'

Robinson made it clear that the G-cars would fly in to extract the troops only when the battle was over, adding that the parachutes and helmets would be lifted out first; the troops would leave last.

'On landing,' he said, 'get out of your harness, link up with anyone in your immediate area, take good cover, wait and shoot.'

Having outlined the sweep plan that he would control from the command helicopter, he then gave details of radio-communication frequencies, callsigns, withdrawal, emergencies, and so on.

After questions and clarifications, a tea break was ordered. Everyone filed out into the other half of the hangar, the PTS side, where tables with tea and biscuits were waiting.

Meanwhile, back in the briefing hangar next door, the model makers were scurrying about removing the Chimoio model and replacing it with the one of Tembue.

During the tea break, the leader of No. 1 (Hunter) Squadron, Squadron Leader Rich Brand, approached Norman Walsh. 'Sir, if taking out the ZANLA leaders in the HQ is key, then may I suggest I use guns rather than bombs?'

Brand was the air force's top marksman; he was deadly accurate with the 30-mm cannons. Walsh saw the wisdom of the suggestion. 'Okay, but then both your wingmen must carry Golf bombs.'

When they walked back into the hangar, the new target caused another buzz of excitement. A very different-looking target now occupied the floor. This was the second phase of Dingo, codenamed Zulu 2. This target was simpler than Chimoio, with only three camps along the banks of a river running north–south, making for easy orientation. Much of the operational detail had already been discussed, therefore the briefing for Zulu 2 was much shorter. Afterwards, Walsh called everyone's attention to a master clock with a large face and a second hand. Everyone was to synchronise their watches to that clock – to the second.

The command structure was then explained. Group Captain Norman Walsh was the airborne commander, with Squadron Leader Harold Griffiths, the helicopter squadron boss, as his deputy. Major Brian Robinson was the ground-force commander, with Major Mike Graham nominated as his deputy, but also serving as commander on the ground.

If the command helicopter became disabled or needed to leave the battle area, Griffiths would extract Graham from the battlefield and the two of them would then assume the role of the command helicopter. In such an event, the ground-force command would pass from Major Graham to Major Jeremy Strong of the RLI.

After a final question-and-answer session, Lieutenant General Peter Walls, the supreme commander, addressed the hushed gathering and emphasised the importance of Operation Dingo to the bigger picture, then wished the men well. People filed out of the hangar, all deep in thought, arranging their minds around what needed to be done over the next 18 hours.

'During the briefing,' recalled Dave Jenkins, 'the need for absolute secrecy was impressed upon us, to the extent that we were not allowed to leave camp.' Indeed, to ensure secrecy, most of the men were quarantined in New Sarum.

After the briefing, people broke up into their own groups for further briefings and discussions. That is when Jenkins found out he would be flying with 'Boss' Walsh in the command helicopter. 'It was after the briefing that Geoff Dartnall told us who we were flying with. Why I was tasked to fly in the command chopper I'm not sure. However, I remember Geoff saying to me that I was to make sure the aircraft stayed in the air at all costs. I was a bit miffed, and probably replied along the lines of "how the fuck do you do that when you get shot out of the air!"'

It was a busy afternoon for Derek de Kock and his parachute jump instructors: 'All the PJIs were involved. We took our individual sticks and went through the aircraft drill and general para refresher training.'

The 40 RLI troops who would go in by helicopter to close the northern side of the box boarded trucks together with a paratroop reserve for the four-hour drive in convoy to Grand Reef, the Fireforce base near Umtali. In the early morning, the heli-borne troops would leave Grand Reef for Lake Alexander, a picturesque drive through the mountains – although not best viewed from the back of a covered truck just before going into battle against enormous odds.

To reduce congestion at New Sarum and for better mission secrecy, the 10 reserve, or 'Polo', helicopters of Yellow Section would fly to Grand Reef for a night stop, and leave for Lake Alexander in the morning.

Thornhill

Squadron Leader Rich Brand flew back to his Midlands base at Thornhill, deep in thought. In the morning, the responsibility fell on him to fire the first shots and start the battle at exactly 07:45, not a few seconds early or late, but on the button and on target.

It was an enormous responsibility. Not only that, but everyone was expecting him to shoot Mugabe and his generals while they reviewed the parade from the porch of the HQ building. But Brand felt calm. He knew he could fire accurately; he also knew that the more planning he did, the easier it would be on the day for him and his men.

By the time Brand was back in his office at Thornhill Air Force Base, he had already worked out the bones of his plan. Now, with maps, a pencil, protractor, ruler and calculator, he quickly worked out the finer detail. He would brief his Hunter section at 17:00 in the pilots' briefing room, where the ground-crew chief and the meteorology man joined them. Each pilot had his own gridded photos of the target. Brand reminded them of the objective:

> Gents, our mission is to attack targets, neutralise anti-aircraft sites and provide top cover. We will open the battle with Red Section hitting three prime targets at 07:45:00 local time, here, here and here. At 07:45:30, as the Cans come through, White and Blue Sections will hit these four anti-aircraft pits. Thereafter, we will form a cab rank and attack targets, as directed by Delta Zero, 'Boss' Walsh's callsign in the command helicopter. I will lead Red Section, Vic Wightman will lead White and John Blythe-Wood will lead Blue.

Brand outlined the route, timings, contingencies and other details. 'Gents, the mess will be open for breakfast from 05:45; we will have a recap briefing here at 06:30. Any questions?'

Back at New Sarum, Dave Jenkins and his fellow technicians had checked and serviced their aircraft; now it was time for a few beers. 'The corporals' mess was designated an all-ranks mess for that night. I think most of us had a few chibulies [beers], but without getting too pissed, after which we made our way back to the hangar, where we dossed down on our stretchers,' Jenkins recounted.

A silence settled over the base. It was a balmy late-November night in Salisbury. After seven months of the dry season, the atmosphere hung heavy with the expectation of rain. Soon, the Indian Ocean monsoon would blow moist air across Mozambique. As the air collided with the solid wall of the Rhodesian Highlands, it would be forced upward, cooling rapidly and forming mountains of white cumulus cloud.

As the moist air spread across Rhodesia, massive late-afternoon thunderstorms were caused by heat rising from the ground. You could almost set your watch by the regular afternoon thunderstorms in Salisbury. At about half past four, just as people were preparing to knock off from work, the ferocity of a storm would be unleashed with surprising regularity.

There is something very special about the first storm after the dry season. First, huge white cumulus clouds grow and grow, towering as high as 40 000 feet. Then it gets darker as the heavily pregnant cloud struggles to hold its water. At this stage, just before the wind starts blowing furiously, the unique metallic smell of fresh rain hits the nose, an indescribably wonderful aroma. Then it's time to run for cover to avoid getting drenched and, more importantly, to avoid the lightning, Africa's biggest natural killer on the Highveld. It all ends quickly, then the sun comes back to cast wonderful rainbows and orange glows across the sky. High above, the cloud changes from the shape of a mushroom to that of a blacksmith's anvil, the death shape of the storm.

Norman Walsh fell asleep at home, hoping Mother Nature would hold off for another four days. It wouldn't.

Part 2
Zulu 1: Chimoio

27

Short Handle

When each major milestone during Operation Dingo was reached, a code word would be reported back to the command structure. Nine milestones were set, each with a code word derived from cricket, starting with 'Short Handle' and ending with 'Off Spin', the point at which all troops were safely back on Rhodesian soil.

'Short Handle' would let the commanders know that the first major task had been completed, namely setting up the helicopter assembly area at Lake Alexander. This would be the main helicopter transit point, where RLI troops and other support personnel would board the Alouettes. A medical resuscitation unit and a helicopter spares, supply and repair point would also be established at Lake Alexander.

The lake – actually a dam on the Odzani River – nestles in the Stapleford Forest, making it an attractive venue for rowing, fishing, camping and picnicking. The planners chose the largest open camping area for the helicopter landing zone. A gently curving dirt road framed the longest edge of the LZ, providing ideal access for transporting troops and fuel.

Lake Alexander was an ideal compromise, being less than four kilometres from the Mozambican border, yet far enough away from the prying eyes of populated areas, particularly the lovely city of Umtali, 25 kilometres to the south. There was only one problem. At 5 725 feet above sea level, the thin air at Lake Alexander would rob the Alouette helicopters of weight-bearing capability, especially the G-cars, with four fully kitted infantrymen and a crew of two. This meant the helicopters would have to carry less fuel.

Men from the air force began to arrive and stake out 22 places along the edge of the dirt road. A further 10 spots were staked out in a second row behind. Fuel drums would be dropped off at each stake to demarcate where each helicopter should land. The spaces had to be far enough apart to allow the helicopters to land safely next to each other. The rotor diameter of the Alouette is 11 metres, and there was a buffer zone of five metres between helicopters. The distance from the first to the last stake would be just over 300 metres.

Later that afternoon, the growling of a convoy of trucks carrying 160 drums of helicopter fuel interrupted the tranquillity of Lake Alexander. Initially, two drums were dropped off at each stake. Most of the 22 target-bound helicopters (K-cars and troop-carrying G-cars) would land along the edge of the road.

Fortunately, the Rhodesians had managed to borrow 10 Alouette helicopters from the South African Air Force. Known as Polo helicopters, these machines were not permitted to fly near the target; they would act in a support role, ferrying men and equipment between Lake Alexander and the admin base across the border.

Typically, the Alouette G-car would fill up with one 200-litre drum of fuel, enough for about 40 minutes' flying time, with a small reserve. The helicopters would fill up with fuel to their capacity in Salisbury to minimise refuelling time at Lake Alexander. Therefore, most would only need to top up at the lake to have 230 litres in the tank, which would bring the machine close to its maximum weight limit. This fuel load would be just enough to reach the target, drop the troops and fly to the admin base, leaving a contingency reserve of no more than 10 minutes' flying time. The lighter K-cars would load more fuel, giving them an endurance of at least an hour and a quarter.

Given its proximity to the Mozambican border, Lake Alexander was certainly not a secure area in 1977. It was vulnerable to attack by ZANLA, so 20 RLI troopers with 81-mm mortars were needed at Lake Alexander to provide protection for the helicopters, personnel and equipment until the operation was over.

By early evening, all the work had been done in preparation for the arrival of 32 helicopters, truckloads of RLI troops and lots of support staff. After a final inspection just after dawn, the RLI protection troop officer at Lake Alexander transmitted the first key radio message of the operation: 'Short Handle complete. I say again, Short Handle complete.' The message was received by the SAS radio facility at the Grand Reef Airbase near Umtali and quickly relayed to Salisbury. Robinson and Walsh ticked off the first critical milestone. The next critical stage would be Cover Point.

Cover Point

The admin base over the border in Mozambique would serve a similar purpose to Lake Alexander – a refuelling and staging post for the helicopters, with facilities for repairs, medical resuscitation and initial prisoner screening. There was, however, one big difference: 'Cover Point', its code name, needed to be close to the target and, therefore, well inside hostile, foreign territory.

This was a challenge for the planners. The base needed to be within 10 minutes' helicopter flying time from the target, but away from roads and populated areas. It also had to be large enough to accommodate up to 32 helicopters.

Areas to the west and south were out of the question; these were heavily populated and well defended. The only feasible option was to the north. The planners scanned aerial photographs of the area between the Pungwe River and New Farm, looking for a flattish, open area. Ideally, it would also be near some high ground to allow an army mortar team to take position to protect the vulnerable helicopters from attack.

Some ground near the foothills of a modest elevation called Monte Utumece, 25 kilometres north of the target, looked ideal, at least from the pictures. It afforded a high area to the east; it was 17 kilometres from Highway 102, linking Chimoio and Tete, and seven kilometres south of the lightly populated banks of the Pungwe River. What the two-dimensional pictures didn't show was that the grass was tall, and so were the clumps of dense bush – not ideal terrain for helicopter landings. Validating the area before the raid, however, was not an option, so if there were obstacles, Peter Petter-Bowyer, the admin-base commander, would have to make a plan.

Ideally, PB would land at the admin base before H-hour, giving him time to quickly familiarise himself with the lay of the land and then supervise the all-important fuel drop from the DC-7. The key tactical advantage for the Rhodesians, however, was total surprise. Therefore, it was too risky for even a single helicopter to fly across Mozambique ahead of the main attacking force. To reduce the risk of compromising the element of surprise, Norman Walsh modified the original plan and allowed PB's admin helicopter, flown by Flight Lieutenant Bill Sykes, to tag along with the main helicopter assault force and separate en route to arrive at the admin base a few minutes before the DC-7. This would give PB the opportunity, albeit brief, to assess the terrain and figure out where best to drop the fuel. PB would talk the DC-7 onto the drop zone by means of a portable VHF radio.

28

D-day

'Dingo was just another op, so I had no problem sleeping,' Norman Walsh remembered. 'But I did have to sneak out with my flying gear, as my wife, Merilyn, had no idea I would be flying on an op.'

The bedside alarm clock jangled loudly at 03:15, and Walsh silenced it quickly as he slipped out of bed. He pulled on his flying suit, and slid his feet into the comfortable *veldskoens* that were standard uniform issue. Walsh grabbed his flying helmet, briefcase and an overnight bag, and sneaked out of the house. He drove off in the dark to New Sarum. The pre-dawn air was fresh and cool; there had been light rainfall during the night – not something the weathermen had forecast.

The New Sarum base slowly came to life. The first people out and about at just after 03:30 were the helicopter technicians, who removed the covers and prepared the 22 helicopters scattered around the base and on the sports fields. Torchlights flashed like fireflies as the techs in poorly lit areas busied themselves in the inky darkness just before dawn.

In the shadows of the west apron stood seven Dakotas and a DC-7; Alouette helicopters randomly occupied empty spaces. On the northern apron stood four giant bat-like Canberra bombers, with their canopy and engine covers in place. Seven Vampire jets were lined up neatly nearby, also still covered.

Norman Walsh arrived at 03:45. After a weather briefing and a quick cup of coffee, he and Brian Robinson set off to find their command helicopter. Dave Jenkins, Walsh's flight technician, greeted the two commanders as they strode up to the Alouette. In the gloom, Walsh barely noticed that there were strange covers over the machine-gun barrels. Jenkins explains: 'Henry Jarvie found two cylindrical cardboard containers the evening before, which he promptly stuck over the two barrels of my twin Brownings, saying that the gooks might think it some sort of secret weapon, which would stop them shooting at our command aircraft. Needless to say, the cylinders blew off as we got airborne.'

Henry Jarvie was probably the best-liked No. 7 Squadron technician and one of the funniest. His idea of the secret-weapon joke backfired because, as it turned out, the gooks did shoot at the command aircraft – accurately too.

Walsh and Robinson were strapped in and ready at 04:25. Jenkins remained outside, resting against the Alouette's fuselage while he waited to check the helicopter during the wind-up process. Walsh flicked on the battery master switch, bathing the cockpit in a soft glow from the instrument lights. He turned on the radio, set it to the check-in frequency and waited.

The brooding silence was broken when the man leading the helicopter armada, Squadron Leader Harold 'Griff' Griffiths, called 'check-in', which prompted a response from the rest of the first section of helicopters to lift off that morning. The calmness of the morning was shattered as one Turbomeca gas turbine engine after another screamed into life. The noise of the helicopters seemed to act as an alarm, spurring on the base. The Canberra armourers seemed to work faster; the Dakota technicians put more urgency into preparing their ancient machines; and everyone started walking around more briskly. In the rising din, Air Marshal Frank Mussell, the air force commander, strode out of the main building to wave the machines off.

Griff tuned his radio to 118.1 MHz, to talk to the civilian control tower on the other side of the runway: 'Alpha 7, request lift-off', to which there was a quick reply: 'Seven, circuit clear, lift-off at your discretion.'

Anyone monitoring the public frequency, as they often did, would assume this was a routine departure of a helicopter from New Sarum at first light. Little would they know this was the largest helicopter armada to fly into battle since the Vietnam War.

Griffiths lifted the collective lever and started taxiing the heavily fuelled Alouette forward; he then lifted it free of the ground into nose-down forward flight. The horizon was quite distinct by now as the steely dawn lit the eastern sky.

Norman Walsh lifted off with the first section of helicopters. 'As we left Sarum, I felt an immense relief. Relief that after all the planning and briefings, we were now on our way.'

Operation Dingo had started.

As the last helicopters were lifting off from Salisbury, the man to initiate the attack, ace marksman and leader of No. 1 Squadron, Rich Brand, was just waking up in his home at the RhAF Thornhill Airbase in Gwelo, 210 kilometres away.

29

Brand – the marksman

'What is your name?'

'Officer Cadet Brand, sir.'

'You big dick!'

'Yes, sir.'

'Why don't you play rugby?'

'Because I don't particularly like the game, sir.'

'Do you feel this pace stick on your head?'

Brand squeaked out a painful 'yes, sir'.

'If you don't play rugby, I will stick this pace stick up your arse and give you a double backbone. Understand me?'

The scene was a group of student pilots at Thornhill Airbase in the Rhodesian Midlands undergoing basic drill instruction, the first stage in the process of learning to fly. The victim was Rich Brand, one of the cadets.

'My first experience was not flying, but drill,' recalls Brand. 'Our drill instructor was Sergeant Major Ron Reid-Daly. It was a cold morning. Ron Reid-Daly asked us who played rugby. Most of the guys put up their hands, except me. I had played rugby at school, but it was on dirt, and the game didn't really appeal to me. Needless to say, after that morning I played rugger enthusiastically.'

Rich Brand wanted to be an astronaut. His ambition was well grounded. His father's brother, Sir Quintin Brand, had been the first pilot to fly an aircraft from England to Cape Town. Many years after his Silver Queen adventure, Air Vice-Marshal Quintin Brand commanded the South-Western Sector in England during the Battle of Britain in 1940.

Rich was also influenced by his brother Basil, a flying instructor on Harvards at the South African Air Force flying training school at Dunnottar. Rich Brand seemed destined to simply push open the door and enter his chosen career. Instead, the young man would have to deal with deep disappointment and rejection.

Rich Brand descends from Dutch sea captains whose original name was Burgaardt-Brand, who made early contact with South Africa, arriving in the Cape of Good Hope in 1619 as they plied the trade route to the Dutch East Indies. Brand has some famous ancestors. Sir Christoffel Brand, an advocate and passionate democrat, was the first speaker in the Cape Legislative Assembly. Sir Christoffel's son, Johannes Hendrikus Brand, became the fourth president of the Orange Free State, a position he held for 24 years until his death in 1888. Jan Brand, as he was popularly known, coined the phrase *alles zal recht komen als elkeen zijn plicht doet* (all will be well if everyone does his duty). This became shortened over time to form the popular modern Afrikaans saying *alles sal regkom*.

President Brand was asked to become president of a proposed Boer Union, which would unite the Transvaal and Orange Free State. He declined because he strongly believed in a policy of strict neutrality with Britain, knowing the powerful empire opposed the concept of a Boer Union. The Brands' history of neutrality with Britain and the fact that Quintin, and Christoffel before him, was a Knight of the Realm and chose to speak English may well have had unintended consequences for young Rich.

After matriculating at a school with the unlikely name of the College of the Little Flower, a Catholic institution run by Belgian monks in Pietersburg, Brand joined the SAAF for a compulsory stint of national service, which was the right place to be to start the application for pilot training. About 200 other aspiring pilots gathered at the SAAF Gymnasium at Voortrekkerhoogte to compete for the few places on offer.

Brand sailed through the medical and aptitude tests, and was confident when he entered the final phase, the interview. A week later, a list of successful candidates was pinned to the Gymnasium noticeboard. Rich Brand anxiously searched for his name, but couldn't find it. There must have been a mistake, so he searched again. It soon became clear that Brand had been rejected.

Rich's brother Basil, a serving SAAF pilot, asked a contact in the aptitude section to find out where his brother had come unstuck. To his astonishment, Basil discovered that Rich had achieved the top mark in the pilot aptitude tests. Somebody did not want Rich Brand in the SAAF.

Brand is not an English name, but the fact that Rich was an English-speaker was impossible to hide in the interview. This was the late 1950s, when the predominantly Afrikaner National Party was consolidating the power it had won a decade earlier, and moving inexorably towards breaking with the Commonwealth to become a republic.

He was devastated, his dream of becoming an astronaut well and truly shattered. After finishing his national service, he started picking up the pieces. He had to look elsewhere and the obvious place was the Royal Rhodesian Air Force. So he trekked up to Rhodesia and went straight to Quo Vadis, a farm near Umtali in the beautiful Eastern Highlands owned by his famous uncle, Sir Quintin Brand.

Like Norman Walsh before him, Brand had to live in Rhodesia for six months before he could apply to the RRAF. Sir Quintin provided the opportunity, teaching his nephew the fundamentals of farming, driving tractors and rifle shooting, first at targets, then live quail. The young man excelled at shooting, a skill that would serve him well in the air force.

The six months flew by, and soon Brand had to go through the same process of medical and aptitude tests he had undergone a year earlier in South Africa. This time, the door opened and Brand joined 11 lucky young men in the 11th pilot intake of the RRAF in 1958. Some of them would also become legends, such as Ian Harvey, Tol Janeke and Vic Wightman.

Reid-Daly drilled the men relentlessly and no cadet was immune from his attention. Brand recalled an event: 'On the tarmac early one morning, we were lined up facing the control tower when a squawking bird flew past. Reid-Daly looked at Tol Janeke and said, "Janeke, answer that bird." Of course, Janeke said absolutely nothing.

'Reid-Daly glared at the hapless officer cadet: "Janeke, you are going to regret that you did not answer that bird, because one day you will be flying along in your aeroplane and you will have to bail out, and your parachute won't open. And you would have had the opportunity to stick your little finger up that bird's arse and drift gently down to the ground."'

Such was the quaint humour of this larger-than-life personality who would go on to establish and command the Selous Scouts, a man who was known affectionately as Uncle Ron.

Then it was time to learn to fly. On 10 March 1958, Brand met his instructor, the irrepressible Mick McLaren, also a South African. Brand has good memories of McLaren, a man who had a big influence on his flying career:

He taught me very early the value of a properly trimmed aircraft, a prerequisite for accurate flying. One day, I had not trimmed the aircraft properly, and Mick picked up a crowbar he kept in the Percival Provost cockpit, banged me on the helmet with it and said, 'Brand, trim the fucking aircraft!' He went on to lecture me about TAFIO, a common mnemonic pilots used to remember this drill – T, trim the aircraft; A, asseblief, trim the aircraft; F, for fuck's sake, trim the aircraft; I, I must trim the aircraft; O, Oh shit, trim the aircraft.

On April Fool's Day in 1958, McLaren climbed out of the Provost, telling Brand, who had 15 hours' total flying time in his logbook, to fly a circuit on his own. Thinking it was an April Fool's Day joke, Brand did nothing – at least not until he saw McLaren reaching back inside the aircraft for the crowbar.

'I guess I landed okay because I continued flying.'

After 124 hours of prop flying, Brand joined the jet age, and started flying Vampires.

'After Vamps, I was posted to No. 3 Squadron, flying Dakotas, which I hated with a passion.'

Brand did not hide his feelings, and told his superior officers at every opportunity that his heart was in flying jets. To make up for the tedium of flying big, slow machines, Brand applied himself to building and flying model aircraft, at which he excelled – he won the Rhodesian Aeromodelling Championship title 11 times and the South African title seven times, earning his Springbok colours.

After 300 hours on Daks, Brand's persistence paid off. He was posted back to No. 1 Squadron and Vampires, this time to learn weapon firing and bombing, under the expert instruction of Norman Walsh. He showed a high aptitude for delivering weapons accurately, and averaged only 14 yards in the high dive-bombing profile, a fantastic achievement in anyone's book. His gunnery results showed a 35 per cent hit rate, also impressive for a student. And, recalls Brand, 'I always remembered to trim the aircraft well; Mick McLaren's TAFIO was well and truly ingrained in my flying.'

The Hunters come

After another mandatory stint at HQ as operations intelligence officer, Brand returned to No. 1 Squadron as weapons instructor, a job he was good at. Then came some exciting news – the squadron was to take delivery of a dozen Hawker Hunter FGA9 jets. This was a fighter and ground-attack jet capable of supersonic speed, a bigger, faster and much more exciting machine to fly than the Vampire.

Late in 1962, Brand was told he was going to the UK to learn to fly the Hunter and ferry one of the 12 back to Rhodesia. His first experience with the Hunter was in a simulator at RAF Chivenor in Devon, which did not feel good: 'I thought the Hunter was a most dangerous aircraft, as everything that could go wrong in the simulator did.'

His fears proved unfounded after three dual flights in the Hunter T7 two-seat trainer. Then Brand was told to fly solo in a single-seat F6, essentially the same machine as the FGA9. The single-seat layout was broadly similar to the T7 he had just flown, but there was one big difference – the F6 punched out a lot more thrust than the trainer.

It was late afternoon on a wintry January day in 1963. Brand strapped in, fired up and lined up on the runway as the sun was slowly reddening in the west. As he brought the thrust lever up to 4 500 rpm, Brand could feel the difference.

He applied full power, hearing a howl as the hungry engine sucked in air. The aircraft accelerated, reaching the unstick speed of 145 knots pretty quickly, and Brand was airborne, above the cloud in the cold twilight sky. He was enjoying the experience so much that he hardly noticed it was rapidly getting dark, and he had to snap out of his reverie and land quickly before he lost the airfield in darkness.

Soon it was time to fly the FGA9s to Rhodesia. The route would involve four refuelling stops between Lyneham in England and Thornhill in Rhodesia – Malta, Libya, Khartoum and Nairobi.

'As we left RAF Lyneham, our boss, Squadron Leader Mike Saunders, lost his radio, so flying as No. 2, I had to take the lead. There was total cloud cover below; I never saw the Channel or much of France. Two hours and 45 minutes later, with our low-fuel "bingo" lights glowing, we landed in Malta. The rest of the ferry flight was uneventful,' Brand recalled.

His passion for perfection and need for constant improvement when building his world-class model aircraft were key ingredients in Rich Brand's constitution throughout his air force life, enabling him to add important modifications to Rhodesian warplanes. When he was with

No. 5 Squadron, flying the Canberra jet bomber, Brand soon noticed that the bombsights were not harmonised across the fleet, meaning that each Canberra was slightly different for the navigator. Working with a team, Brand devised a system to harmonise the sights, thus enabling a navigator to jump from one Canberra to the next, confident that the sights would be the same. The Hunter also needed harmonising for air-to-air gunnery, something Brand carried out with the help of Rick Culpan.

In February 1976, Brand's dream came true: he was appointed leader of No. 1 Hunter Squadron at Thornhill.

That jungle dustbin

Shooting accurately became the hallmark of No. 1 Hunter Squadron; its pilots were often referred to as the Steely Eyes. Word got out about this, and a newspaper published an article claiming that RhAF Hunter pilots could hit a dustbin in a jungle clearing with their 30-mm cannons. This article drew the attention and mirth of rival squadron members, who, as a challenge, presented Brand and his squadron with a rusty old dustbin in a 'formal' ceremony in the officers' mess at Thornhill.

Brand took up the gauntlet. The next day, he asked 'Kutanga Mac', the range officer at the RhAF firing range near Thornhill, to place the rusty dustbin on the range. Brand took off in a Hawker Hunter, fired a quarter-second burst (five rounds) and drilled the dustbin.

The seriously holed and dented exhibit, now the air force world's most famous dustbin, was chrome-plated and returned to the officers' mess, where it stood proudly. The inscription on the dustbin lid, still bearing the old Royal Government Issue OHMS stamp, read: 'That jungle dustbin – Alpha.1.1280 – five rounds fired, one hit.' (The squadron boss always took Alpha, followed by the squadron number, hence Alpha 1. The Hunter serial number was 1280.)

'The Hunter is very stable when firing those guns. The 30-mm cannons are deadly, deadly accurate,' recalls Brand. 'In fact, the cannons were too accurate for the type of war we were fighting. If ground forces called in a Hunter strike, say on a group of terrorists under the third tree from the left, and the troops couldn't see from the ground that it was actually the fourth tree, the third tree would be destroyed, but the terrs would go unscathed.'

Help was at hand. The inventive Peter Petter-Bowyer was developing yet another new weapon, the Golf bomb, which would give the Hunter a lot more clout. PB had been studying fuel-air explosives, which the Americans were using to clear large areas of landmines. The massive blast pressure of the fuel-air bomb detonated unwanted mines over a wide radius. The American version used ethylene oxide, an expensive and unstable explosive.

PB, always driven to make something effective but more cheaply, decided to test an alternative: ammonium nitrate and fuel oil, known as ANFO. After many tests and modifications, PB and his team perfected an extremely good high-pressure weapon, which exploded and then imploded, causing lethal damage to any living thing in an area 95×135 metres. Anyone surviving the blast and the shrapnel would have ruptured eardrums and be badly stunned and disorientated.

Rich Brand was involved in the development of the Golf bomb, in particular in the aircraft bombing profile. The typical dive profile was to release the bombs at 4 500 feet, but Brand wanted to improve accuracy, which meant dropping them at a lower height. The solution he developed was known as the glide profile. This was a technique of approaching the target in the Hunter at 10 000 feet. Then, at 10 nautical miles from the target, the pilot throttled back to idle, in effect turning the jet into a silent glider. The descending Hunter would then pinpoint the target, turn in and commence a 60-degree dive, releasing the bombs at 3 000 feet above ground level, followed by a six-G-force pull-out, which gave just enough margin for the aircraft to avoid flying into its own bomb blast.

'The advantage of the glide attack was that the aircraft would not be seen or heard until the pull-up, by which time it was too late to escape,' said Brand.

Dive-bombing accuracy without modern technology is largely proportional to the steepness of the dive and how close the aircraft can get to the target. In other words, the steeper the dive and the lower the pull-out, the better. However, this has obvious dangers because while the pilot is concentrating on keeping the target in his bombsights, it is very easy to inadvertently pay less attention to the altimeter. The most serious case of this scenario is known as target fixation, when the pilot flies straight into the ground.

Fortunately, this problem is usually spotted and resolved early during training. Nevertheless, the risk of pulling out late at only 3 000 feet in a 60-degree dive is high: a few seconds too late, and the pilot will almost certainly overstress the aircraft during the 'oh shit' pull-out.

Brand had a brilliant solution. He asked the instrument technicians to install a small additional altimeter next to the sights. Coupled to this altimeter was a light that would start flashing at the optimum altitude. This enabled the pilot to focus more closely on accuracy without having to constantly scan the altimeter. This invention – an early type of head-up display now common in military aircraft – greatly increased dive-bombing accuracy.

The last Rhodesian Parliament

No. 1 Squadron often performed fly-pasts, a wonderful spectacle. The sight of a squadron of Hunters approaching rapidly, silently and in tight formation would impress even the most aerophobic observer. The first sound to reach the audience on the ground is the howl of multiple 'blue notes', the term used for the sound emanating from the 30-mm cannon ports, like a greatly amplified version of blowing over the mouth of an empty Coca-Cola bottle. Following the blue note comes the sound of the jet tearing through the air and then, finally, the deafening roar of the Rolls-Royce Avon 207 engines as the formation passes by – a truly memorable show.

On 27 June 1977, at the height of the war, No. 1 Squadron was asked to do a fly-past for the opening of Parliament. Very few realised at the time that this would be the last opening of the Rhodesian Parliament. Coincidentally, the fly-past also commemorated Squadron Leader Rich Brand's 1 000th hour of flying Hunters. The proud squadron leader briefed his team, Mark Aitcheson, Cocky Benecke, Dave Bourhill, Martin Lowrie, John Annan, Chris Abraham, Jock McGregor and Mark Vernon: 'Gentlemen, the mission is to fly a diamond nine at the opening of Parliament in Salisbury at 11:00 local time. To polish up, we will route to Bulawayo in tight formation, do a fly-past over the city, then proceed to Salisbury.'

In a wartime economy hampered by economic sanctions, this was an expensive way to celebrate, but it did have two spin-offs. Firstly, it showed the world that Rhodesia was still capable of putting up a formation of nine Hawker Hunters, a feat deemed impossible by some

RAF 'experts' in Britain. Secondly, it gave Brand and his pilots a chance to practise precise timing over 'target' and brush up on their formation skills.

The people of Bulawayo rushed out to see the perfect diamond nine formation go by. The Hunters then flew north-east for 28 minutes to Norton, a farming town south-west of Salisbury named after the family brutally massacred there in the First Chimurenga. As the formation passed over the Umfuli River, Brand called: 'Red Section, tighten up, three minutes to IP.' Norton was Brand's initial point (IP), the final turning point to bring the formation onto a magnetic heading of 085 degrees and straight over Cecil Square, the park in front of Parliament, with its gardens designed in the form of the Union Jack. This was the spot where Rhodes's pioneers first hoisted the Union flag and named the place Salisbury 81 years earlier.

'Lead turning right … now,' Brand called as the formation approached Norton, and he eased slowly into a right turn. Leading a formation looks like the easy job, as everyone else has to work hard to stay in position, but it's not. The leader must fly very smoothly with accurate speeds, positions and altitudes. Any sudden corrections are amplified, causing the formation to become ragged and untidy.

'Target one minute ahead, nice and tight please' was Brand's final command. At precisely 11:00, the Hunters, in a perfect diamond nine, flew directly over Cecil Square to the delight of the large crowd gathered to witness the formal opening of Parliament on that clear winter's day in 1977.

Just three months later, the same aircraft, armed to the teeth, would open the attack on Robert Mugabe's ZANLA headquarters in Mozambique.

30

Lake Alexander

As the crow flies, the distance from New Sarum to the helicopter assembly point at Lake Alexander is 198 kilometres to the south-east. The Alouettes were fully fuelled to save time at the rendezvous, which meant the helicopters were heavy and slow, initially managing to fly at only 130 kilometres per hour. But as fuel burnt off, the machines became lighter and faster. Allowing for dog-legs to provide deception, the total flying time to the lake would be about one hour and 20 minutes.

For Dave Jenkins, peering over the barrels of the twin Browning machine guns in the command helicopter, the flight to Lake Alexander was 'like any other call-out'. For Norman Walsh, piloting his first operational flight in many a year, the feeling was similar: 'It felt as if I had never been out of it.'

The sun was quickly changing from a red ball to a brilliant spotlight in the sky, shining into the Perspex bubbles of the Alouettes and causing some discomfort to the pilots as they headed south-east. Twenty minutes after lifting off, the first gaggle of helicopters passed over Longlands Dam, just north of the thriving town of Marandellas. After a similar interval, the helicopters crossed the main Salisbury–Umtali road a few kilometres north of Rusape. Soon, the topography started changing from hilly, rolling farmland to larger, bald granite features. The mountains of the Eastern Highlands were looming in the distance. This was territory both Robinson and Walsh knew well.

As the formation skirted the highest terrain near Osbourne Dam, Walsh could see the deep green of the Stapleford Forest area; he knew they were close to their refuelling point. He also noticed something he did not want to see: low cloud hugging the mountains in the distance towards Mozambique.

Keith Samler, accompanied by his SB colleague Ken Milne and the head of SB, Mike Edden, drove to Lake Alexander in Samler's car. The Triumph 2000 pulled into the lakeside picnic area just after 06:00, as the last section of helicopters was landing. Samler took out his Super 8 movie camera and filmed the landing helicopters in the early-morning mountain air. Samler would film parts of both phases of Operation Dingo, the only moving record of the raids.

The last trucks bringing in the RLI 2 Commando heli-borne troops arrived. The clatter of rotors, whine of turbines, revving truck engines and people milling about in the dust gave the impression of absolute chaos, but there was order in the din. The RLI troops were positioned in front of their specific helicopter landing spot, in the same order they would be dropped off at the target. The SB men and other support staff were told which helicopters they would be flying in. Things quietened a lot once the last gaggle of helicopters had landed at 06:15 and wound down their engines.

The long section of gently curving dirt road at Lake Alexander that the planners had chosen as the assembly point worked well, except for one thing – the helicopters were spread a long way apart. The first helicopter was nearly half a kilometre from the last. This in itself was not a problem, but while the techs were refuelling the Alouettes, the pilots needed to gather around their squadron leader's machine for a final briefing. This meant some serious jogging to get to and from Griff's helicopter.

Mark McLean, flying a K-car, was one of the unfortunates who had to make up a lot of ground to catch up with the lead helicopter: 'All the helicopters went to Lake Alexander and filled the LZ. I was parked well back, and had to cover quite a distance. We then got together for a chat, smoke and nervous pee. It was one of those situations where everyone was pretending to be casual, but they were quite tense.'

Harold Griffiths delivered his final briefing, essentially a high-level recap, and he once again emphasised the need for precise timing. He warned them that the low cloud would get worse as they crossed the higher ground between Lake Alexander and Mozambique. 'Right, gentlemen, let's go.'

It was 06:45, plenty of time for the pilots to reach their machines, strap in and be ready for the call to start at 07:00. Griffiths had allowed enough time for the wind-up and sequential take-off, with a little extra added for insurance, taking into account the old adage that losing time in the air is easy, making it up can be impossible.

The enormous number of brooding Alouette helicopters in the tranquil picnic ground was quite a sight. It was just before 07:00, and the tension was electric – this was the real thing. The 40 RLI attack troops and officers sat in the 10 trooping Alouette G-cars; the 10 K-cars and command heli were also ready.

In the command helicopter, Brian Robinson waited quietly; Norman Walsh chewed frantically on his pencil as he cast a worried eye at the low cloud hugging the mountains to the east. These 21 helicopters were the attack force, which would fly straight to the target area. The 22nd helicopter tagging along carried the admin base controller, Peter Petter-Bowyer. The remaining 10 Polo helicopters, the borrowed machines from South Africa, were on standby to fly men and equipment to and from the admin base; they were not permitted to enter the target area.

For the second time that morning, the lead helicopter's banshee whine shattered the silence as it started, catalysing the others into action. Soon there was a cacophony reverberating off the trees and cliff faces. One by one, the rotors started turning as all 22 helicopters wound up. They were all ready when Griff lifted the collective lever, bringing the lead K-car into a hover. After a few vital checks, he eased the cyclic stick forward, countering the increased torque with his pedals.

The morning coolness gave the thin air a bit more viscosity. The helicopter started moving forward, flying low over the ground, initially above a dirt road and then skimming over the treetops of the deep-green forest – not a good place for an engine failure. One by one, in strict order and at precise intervals to allow for safe separation, the rest of the armada lifted off and followed the squadron leader.

Seeing such a vast number of helicopters flying off was a magnificent sight, something etched forever into the minds of those on the ground. Watching the departure somewhat nostalgically was Wing Commander Rex Taylor, who, a few days later, would be manning a major refuelling point deep inside Mozambique on the second phase of Operation Dingo.

Taylor was told to drive to Lake Alexander with his flying kit to be on standby as a reserve helicopter pilot. 'Before dawn on Wednesday 23 November, I drove to Lake Alexander and floated around waiting for Wing Commander Ted Stevenson to send me off in a chopper.'

With the mixed emotions of badly wanting to fly, yet not wanting to have to replace an injured pilot, Taylor watched the last of the helicopters depart, and waited ... and waited.

An hour passed, and then the sound of Dakota engines invaded Taylor's thoughts: 'I was overwhelmed when I counted every Dakota that we'd sent out earlier, now flying low over Lake Alexander on their way home. My emotions were high; I even shed a tear. Knowing the anti-aircraft weaponry at Chimoio and the low altitude at which the Dakotas flew, I had believed that the chances of survival of the whole squadron were slim.'

Taylor's mood changed quickly: 'I was suddenly fired up and buoyant – if the Daks could get away with it, the rest of the aircraft would too! By midday, it was apparent that my services in an Alouette would not be required and I set off in my service Renault 10 to Mount Darwin.'

What Taylor could not have known was that the departing helicopters were having trouble crossing the border. Squadron Leader Griffiths knew that the cloud would be covering the high ground, so he needed to find a valley deep enough to reach below the cloud base. Griff had already marked out a valley on his map, one that was deep and required only a minor deviation from track.

Skirting the highest ground, the line of helicopters, resembling a gigantic snake, followed the leader into the valley. Griff noticed with mounting concern that the low cloud was getting worse. As he flew down the valley, the cloud closed up, shutting the doorway into Mozambique. Griff had no alternative but to turn back. He banked through almost 180 degrees, and, like a snake's body following the head, the Alouettes followed his path.

PB, flying in the admin base helicopter 10 places back from the leader, describes the U-turn: 'Helicopters flying the loop caused by this diversion presented an impressive sight.'

Norman Walsh was getting very worried: 'I had emphasised again and again the need for precise timing. Now we were blowing the timing because of the unexpected weather.'

If the helicopters were late, ZANLA would have plenty of time to escape through the two uncovered sides of Brian Robinson's carefully planned box. Walsh knew that if they did not find a way through soon, the consequences might be disastrous. Not only would the helitroops be late, but the G-cars would have insufficient fuel to drop the troops and make it back to the admin base. They would either have to get back to Lake Alexander or route via the admin base to refuel. Furthermore, there would be no airborne commanders to direct the troops and air strikes. Operation Dingo had hit a serious and unplanned hurdle.

While the helicopters were struggling to find a way into Mozambique, the Canberras had just taken off, the DC-8 jetliner was taxiing, and down in the Midlands, Rich Brand was signalling the start for his Hunter Squadron. All was going to plan, except for the main helicopter force.

General Peter Walls, sitting at his desk in the command Dak, was blissfully unaware that the helicopters had encountered problems entering Mozambique. Harold Griffiths was due to break radio silence only when the helicopter formation crossed the border. This message was due at 07:18, failing which the alarm bells would start ringing loudly in the command Dak.

It was looking desperate for the helicopters; there was no way out of Rhodesia. PB describes what happened next: 'Griff shouted that he had a break. He turned hard left ahead of us and we all followed through this gap. We got through, but only just. It closed so fast that I think the last few helicopters in the line actually went through some mist.'

Brian Robinson was anxiously mulling over in his mind the consequences of the helicopters being late. Nevertheless, he still had time to admire the skills of the formation leader: 'The armada of helicopters was going up a re-entrant which was 8/8 clampers [complete cloud cover]. Squadron Leader Griff Griffiths had to do a 180-degree turn and map read his way to the target – all on a 1:50000 scale map, with no door on the heli, no time to get out rulers and protractors, and no GPS.'

Walsh and Robinson were intensely relieved to see the brighter daylight of Mozambique ahead, but they knew the slack that Griff had built into the timing had gone. At 07:20, just two minutes after due time, Griff made the short call 'Alpha Seven crossing', which let those who needed to know that the helicopter assault force had crossed the border and all was well.

Once over the low ground of Mozambique, the shape of the helicopter formation changed as the 10 G-cars moved into line abreast forming the front of the formation.

31

New Sarum

After the last gaggle of helicopters had left New Sarum for Lake Alexander just after 05:00, the apron at New Sarum was abuzz. Next to get airborne, at 06:00, would be the six Paradaks of Silver Section, followed by the command Dakota carrying General Peter Walls and his command team.

Preparation for the 06:00 departure of the Daks had begun well before first light. The men of the Parachute Training School woke up from a fitful sleep on coir mattresses on the hangar floor at 04:00 to start sorting 144 parachutes. The men were soon milling about in the cold hangar, arranging the chutes into six areas, 24 chutes per group. The parachute jump instructors recorded the unique number of each parachute on a manifest so that the chute's history and the name of the packer were traceable. The parachute jump instructors, assisted by two army dispatchers, laid out the chutes in two rows of 12 for the paratroopers sitting on the starboard and port sides of the Dak. The commanding officer of the PTS, Derek de Kock, mucked in too – he would be flying in the lead Dak.

At 05:15, 144 SAS and RLI troops filed into the PTS hangar. It looked chaotic, but each commander knew exactly which group of parachutes was his. The men lined up in reverse order of jumping, first in last out, and donned their chutes. The dispatchers checked each man front and back, numbered them off and marched them to the waiting Dakotas. As they marched across the apron, one of the paratroopers, Colour Sergeant John Norman of the RLI, proudly looked down at his brand-new para boots, which his father had recently sent to him from Australia. It was last time he would wear those boots.

The parachute jump instructors had already left to do preflight checks of the equipment in the Dakota cabins. Sergeant Kevin Milligan made his way to his Dakota, where he met his pilot, Flight Lieutenant Vic Culpan. Milligan hopped inside to check the seats and belts, the static line cables, and the like, while Culpan and his co-pilot did an external check of the old machine.

The pilots climbed up the small steps and entered the rear of the

Dakota just as the paratroops arrived. The Dakota is a taildragger (there is no nose wheel), which means that when not flying, the cabin floor tilts aft at quite a steep angle. The pilots hauled themselves up the steep incline to the flight deck, passing two rows of rudimentary folding canvas seats, one on each side of the fuselage, for the paratroops. There was no first, business or even economy class – the paratroops would sit in two long rows facing each other. There was no superfluous padding, just bare ribs and skin and a hard metal floor. At the flight deck, the pilots settled down and prepared for the flight.

At 05:40, the Dak leader, Bob d'Hotman, pressed his transmit button and called, 'Silver Section, check in.' The response was quick – 'two, three, four, five, six'. Soon, the gurgling and wheezing of the starter motors interrupted by loud coughs and pops added to the din as the ancient Pratt & Whitney radial engines burst into life in a cloud of white smoke. The command Dak also fired up.

At 05:45, D'Hotman led the Dakotas out across the main runway onto the taxiway for the slow trip to the take-off point on Runway 06. It was a sight not seen since World War II, a line of Dakotas laden with paratroops going to war.

Moving well forward on the runway to allow space for the rest of the Dakotas to line up behind him, D'Hotman advanced the throttles to full power while his co-pilot ensured that the throttle, propeller pitch and mixture levers were all fully forward – balls to the wall. The engines roared, shaking the whole machine.

'As we took off, the paras were quiet. Conversation is difficult for any length of time because of the noise. Most closed their eyes and rested, or tried to,' recalled Milligan.

D'Hotman pedalled on the rudder bar to keep the long machine straight; then, as the speed increased, he eased the control column forward, bringing the tail wheel off the ground. Not too much, or the propellers would strike the runway; not too little, or the aircraft would lift off too early.

At the right speed, the grand old bird eased off the runway. Once the aircraft was climbing, it was time to raise the undercarriage and reduce power. The vibration and noise eased as D'Hotman coarsened the pitch to reduce the propeller speed. This had a calming effect on the paratroops, albeit a temporary one. D'Hotman started a slow bank to the right so that the rest of the Daks could take the inside lane to catch him.

He glanced through the right window at a house on Delport Farm, its white walls glistening through the msasa trees. This was Bob's house, conveniently situated away from suburbia, but close to work. His wife, Trish, would have no idea that this was anything other than hubby and his colleagues doing a routine early-morning parachute drop or a bit of circuit training ... until five more Dakotas flew over the farmhouse in rapid succession.

The next aircraft to leave New Sarum was one of the most important to the operation, the DC-7. Every single helicopter was relying on its cargo – 16 000 litres of helicopter fuel contained in 80 drums, which would be dispatched along with ammunition for the K-cars by parachute into the admin base. The DC-7 also carried another important cargo, of the human kind – 16 RLI paratroops whose responsibility was to protect the base from hostile forces.

The Douglas DC-7 was the last and largest piston-powered airliner to be built. The four-engine machine was capable of maintaining a cruise speed of 550 km/h. It was the first airliner to fly non-stop from New York to London. This particular DC-7 was cobbled together from parts of two former KLM Dutch Airlines DC-7s to haul freight for Air Trans Africa. The aircraft was transferred to the RhAF in 1976. Jack Malloch, an active air force reserve pilot, was at the controls, assisted by Squadron Leader George Alexander.

Twenty-five minutes after the last Dakota had blended into the morning sun, the DC-7 roared down the runway. As the aircraft eased into the sky and past the hangars on the civilian side of the runway, another Douglas aircraft was preparing for flight. This was a DC-8, the jet-powered successor to the DC-7, also hauling freight for Air Trans Africa. The DC-8's mission was to create deception. It would fly reasonably high over the target at H minus 4 (exactly four minutes before the Hunters would open the attack on New Farm), making a lot of noise. After the DC-7 had departed, New Sarum fell silent, but not for long. At 06:45, Squadron Leader Chris Dixon led his Canberra Green Section from the crew room to their aircraft – four pilots and four navigators. Dixon eased his way into the awkward hatch on the side of the aircraft's belly, and pulled himself up into the cockpit of his English Electric Canberra light bomber.

A few minutes later, the leader of No. 2 Squadron, Steve Kesby, led the last group of pilots out onto the apron. This was the de Havilland Vampire section, callsign Venom, which would attack the recruits' camp seven kilometres north of the ZANLA HQ, also at H-hour, then take over from the Hunters as they ran out of ammo. There were seven Vampire jets parked on the apron; these 1940s vintage birds would fill a firepower gap nicely in the operation.

'To carry out the required tasks for Op Dingo,' recalled Kesby, 'HQ needed six aircraft, four FB9s for the initial attack, supported by two T11s [two-seat trainers]. We would operate in three sections as top cover after the attack.'

The extra Vampire was a spare in case there was a problem with any of the other machines. The two trainers, the T11s, were easily distinguished by their much larger nose and canopy sections. They raised a few eyebrows. Why, some thought, were trainer aircraft on the mission? The answer lay in necessity and the privileges of rank. Group Captain Tol Janeke, the commanding officer of Thornhill Airbase, and Group Captain Hugh Slatter, officer commanding flying at Thornhill, had 'jammed' their way onto the mission.

'Whenever we could,' recalled Slatter, 'we would "scrounge" any "leftover" aircraft and join the operation. Who says rank doesn't have its privileges? But I found the T11 very uncomfortable for me because of the ejection seat and my relatively short back and long legs, and I sort of hung forward in the seat, which made for some discomfort, especially when pulling "G".'

The two senior officers would fly in support of Venom Section, and also relieve the Hunters from top-cover duties. They had their own callsign – Voodoo.

The four Canberras were ready to start. Before sanctions, these jet bombers were usually started by means of a cartridge, an expensive explosive device resembling the cartridge of a gigantic starter pistol. The explosion, a rapid expansion of gases, would spin a starting turbine, which, in turn, rotated the main engine fast enough to get it started. But at about £100 per bang, these cartridges were expensive. In typical Rhodesian fashion, some innovative person decided that the same thing could be achieved with air, which was free but for the small cost of the electricity used to compress it. The result was a compressed air starter. But because the four Canberras had to start simultaneously on that day, the old cartridge system was used.

As Chris Dixon signalled the start with a twirl of his left index finger, he pressed the No. 1 engine start button with his right index finger. The cartridge fired with a loud hiss and a cloud of black smoke as the explosive charge sent highly compressed gas into the jet's starting turbine, spooling the main engine to 1 100 rpm, sufficient to start the Rolls-Royce Avon engine. More ear-piercing hisses of the cartridges reverberated as the other Canberras followed suit.

As the eight engines of the Canberras stabilised into their loud jet turbine sound, an altogether different sound engulfed the apron as the de Havilland Goblin engines of the ancient Vampires screamed into life.

The Canberras would fly to the target at low level, passing about 15 kilometres north of Lake Alexander. The Vampires, on the other hand, would climb to 20 000 feet – a fuel-conserving measure that enabled them to take over from the Hunters when their fuel ran low. The last aircraft to leave New Sarum just behind the Canberras and Vampires was the big DC-8 cargo liner.

The air armada, virtually the entire Rhodesian Air Force (only the slow and noisy Trojans were left out), was on its way to deal Mugabe's nerve centre a massive blow.

A gentle easterly breeze stirred the silence that now enveloped New Sarum. The aprons were empty; the ground crews were inside having a well-deserved cup of tea.

The silence did not last long, however. Soon the Canberra and Vampire ground crews were out again, busily preparing to rearm and refuel the aircraft when they returned from Chimoio.

32

The magnificent seven

H-hour, the time the attack on Chimoio New Farm would commence, was 07:45 on Wednesday 23 November 1977. Opening the attack would be the RhAF's top marksman, the commander of No. 1 (Hunter) Squadron, Rich Brand.

In air force parlance, the word 'walk' describes both a time and an action. The leader sets the walk time, which signals precisely when the crews should leave the crew room and make their way to their jets. The walk is the first physical step on the way to the target. Brand set the walk time for Operation Dingo by working back from H-hour, 07:45. He knew the straight-line distance from Thornhill to Chimoio was 388 kilometres, which, at the Hunter's low-level cruise speed of 420 knots (778 km/h), was 30 minutes' flying time.

Although Brand was very good at low-level navigation, he left nothing to chance. He studied the route meticulously and memorised it in his mind's eye. He chose not to fly on a direct course, but along a series of zigzag tacks as a ruse to make it difficult for anyone who saw the formation to guess its destination.

The Hunter's navigation equipment was pretty elementary, consisting of a radio-beam automatic direction finder and a distance-measuring device that measures distance to a VHF transmitter, usually at an airport. Both of these instruments, however, were useless on a low-level precision raid. Brand would rely on the traditional instruments – a compass, stopwatch, map, and the best instrument of all, the mark one eyeball. At each turning point, Brand would fine-tune the timing by slowing down or speeding up as necessary, to ensure he would arrive at Chimoio precisely at H-hour.

Brand also factored in time to allow for the take-off roll, formation positioning and acceleration to 420 knots. Losing time is easy, but making it up can be impossible, so Brand also built in a few minutes of slack as an insurance policy. He calculated the wheels off the runway time at 07:25; engine start at 07:15; strapping in at 07:05; walk at 06:55. The final refresher briefing would be 06:30, which would take 15 minutes, allowing time for the mandatory toilet visit before walking.

Breakfast was ready in the mess from 05:45, but most pilots didn't have much of an appetite that early. The pilots also knew better than to have more than one cup of coffee – being strapped to an ejection seat for at least two hours with a full bladder is not a good idea. Brand knew what this discomfort felt like from experience. Shortly after the Hunters had first been commissioned in Rhodesia, he was tasked to fly in formation on a maximum-range exercise. The flight was from Thornhill across the border to South Africa, past Johannesburg and on to Bloemfontein, where they would turn and retrace the same route back – a planned flight of three hours, 20 minutes. 'The moment I got airborne, I wanted to pee,' recalls Brand. 'By the time we were abeam Johannesburg, I was desperate. I needed to pee … now! I started thinking up an excuse to declare an emergency and land at Jan Smuts Airport.'

In the end, the pressure of finishing the sortie exceeded Brand's bladder pressure – but only just. He bit his lip and continued on the most agonising flight of his life to Bloemfontein and back. When at last he saw Thornhill through a painful haze, Brand landed immediately, taxied back to dispersal at almost take-off speed, screeched to a halt, slammed the high-pressure cock closed and flew out of the Hunter to the hangar, where he had the longest pee of his life against the hangar door. 'I vowed then and there that if it ever happened to me again, I would take off one of my flying boots and pee in it.'

The pilots and crew chiefs were already assembled in the briefing room when Rich Brand walked in just before 06:30 on D-day. The Thornhill meteorology man, Harvey Quail, had some disturbing news at the briefing. 'We have reports of low cloud in the Eastern Highlands and into Mozambique,' said Quail.

Norman Walsh had covered this eventuality at the main briefing. Low cloud would rule out the steep dive profile needed for the Golf bombs. The alternative weapon would be frantan, requiring a much flatter dive to disperse the flaming gel. Brand quickly ordered the crew chief to change the Golf bombs on Red 2 and 3 to frantan. With typical RhAF efficiency, the rearmament was completed in a matter of minutes.

Just before 06:55, the pilots left the crew room for the engineers' office to sign the flight authorisation sheets, the process of accepting their aircraft from the engineers. At 06:55 on the dot, the seven Hunter pilots strode out into a clear summer's morning – Rich Brand, Dave Bourhill, John Annan, Vic Wightman, Spook Geraty, John Blythe-Wood and Martin Lowrie. Waiting for them, looking menacing on the apron, were the fully armed Hunters, with a spare machine as a back-up. The ground crew were standing by to help strap the pilots in and launch the aircraft. The pilots each checked their aircraft and armaments before climbing up the ladder to strap into the compact Hunter cockpit, first checking that the two ejection-seat handle pins were still in.

Rich Brand hopped into his favourite machine, the 'eagle' Hunter, emblazoned with an eagle's head morphed with a spear and clutching a bomb in its talons. He slid into the ejection seat and secured first the parachute harness, then the straps that would secure him to the ejection seat and the leg restraints that would automatically draw his legs into the seat if he ejected. The last item he donned was his yellow helmet customised with red stars. He then said to his crew chief, 'Ready for pins', as he removed the pin from the lower ejection handle, or seat pan, while the crewman extracted the upper, or face-screen, pin. The seat was now live.

All the pilots were ready with time to spare ahead of the start. The tension was building as they waited. At 07:00 precisely, Brand pointed to the sky, rotating his index finger, the signal to start. The silence was shattered as the seven Hawker Hunters, almost in unison, let out a whistle-like sound from the purging motors followed by a massive hissing noise as the Avpin starting fluid exploded in the starting chambers to spin the turbines, bringing the Rolls-Royce Avon engines to life. The cost of the highly volatile starting fluid was the same as a bottle of the finest cognac.

A few minutes later, all the jets were ready. Brand hit his radio transmit button: 'Red Section, check in.' The crisp responses followed quickly, 'two' then 'three', as Dave Bourhill and John Annan confirmed to their leader that they were on frequency. Brand repeated the check-in procedure for White Section, led by Vic Wightman, and Blue Section, led by John Blythe-Wood. The Hunters were ready.

'Tower, Red Section ready taxi.' The control tower replied immediately: 'Red Section, clear taxi for Runway 13.' Brand eased the power up to 3 800 rpm, testing the brakes as the Hunter eagerly started moving forward. Thornhill is laid out in a triangle, the runway forming the base and dispersal the apex, joined by long taxiways to each end of the runway.

Brand moved onto the left taxiway, taking him to the north-west end of the runway. He had plenty of time to complete the vital preflight checks. He entered the runway and moved well forward, allowing room for his number two and three to line up behind him. Over his right shoulder, he could see that Vic Wightman was halfway down the taxiway, with the rest of White and Blue Section neatly spaced behind him.

Brand looked again at the map and the photograph of the target that was mounted inside the Hunter's crowded cockpit. He had gone over the route in his mind many times and knew exactly what to expect. He reviewed the turning points and had a long look at the most important one – Monte Hombe, a tall, shark-fin-shaped koppie in Mozambique, rising 230 metres above the surrounding ground. This was the IP, the initial point, where he would turn his formation directly towards the target. Brand had plotted his course so that the IP was 22.4 nautical miles, or three minutes and 12 seconds, north of the target. Take-off time was approaching; Brand checked the instruments and settings one last time.

At precisely 07:09, Brand signalled to his wingmen and eased the throttle forward, holding the Hunter still with the brakes while the Avon engine howled as air was greedily sucked through the twin air intakes into the jet engine. The brakes now barely held the straining machine as the engine reached 7000 rpm. The Hunter lurched forward as Brand released the brakes and applied full power, sending over 10000 pounds of thrust through the jet pipe.

'Check 8100 rpm, check jet-pipe temperature, check fire warning out,' Brand said to himself as the Hunter began accelerating smoothly – to 80 knots, 100 knots – then, at 120 knots, he tugged the stick back to bring the nose wheel just off the runway, a position he maintained until the main wheels followed suit, gently leaving the tarmac at 150 knots. As soon as a good climb rate was established, he squeezed the brake lever behind the stick to stop the wheels spinning, stabbed the gear-up button, moved his hand instinctively to the pressurisation switch and flicked it to 'on', and then raised the flap retract switch. With the drag out of the way, the Hunter accelerated eagerly.

Brand banked the jet to the right onto a southerly course. Over his right shoulder, he could see Red 2 and Red 3 taking the inside lane to catch up and formate loosely on him. He knew that White and Blue Sections would be going through the same routine, staggered according to their strike times. The Hunters passed over Prime Minister Ian

Smith's farm, Gwenoro, meaning 'the place of the kudu', then past the nearby town of Selukwe. Brand then banked left for quite a long time until he was on a north-easterly route towards Gutu.

The Hunters were flying at about 100 metres above the ground, low enough to go unnoticed by radar. Those on the ground close to their flight path, however, would hear a deafening roar as the jets tore through the morning air, underscored by the blue note, the characteristic howling sound coming from the four cannon ports.

Brand started making speed adjustments as he passed his early landmarks to ensure Red Section was dead on time. The earth was whizzing by at 13 kilometres a minute, yet time seemed to stand still. It felt like forever, but it took barely 25 minutes for the Hunters to cross the high mountains of the Eastern Highlands and into the People's Republic of Mozambique. Brand noticed a lot of low cloud on the escarpment, but the way to Monte Hombe looked clear enough at low level. He followed the ground as it dropped away into the Mozambican lowlands.

Soon the big shark-fin shape of the IP was visible in the distance, right on the nose. The Hunters were dead on track, and now within four seconds of the required timing. Brand quickly checked that all four guns were selected and then unlocked the trigger with his thumb. The trigger flew out like a flick knife, turning the graceful jet into a deadly weapon.

It was unusual to use all four guns at once, because each one fires 20 rounds per second, which means it takes only seven seconds to empty the magazine of 540 rounds. However, given that Robert Mugabe, Josiah Tongogara and Rex Nhongo were expected to be in the building, or standing on the patio outside, it made sense to put down as much fire as possible.

Red Section was now just over four minutes from the target, and the adrenalin was coursing through Brand's veins, making everything seem to slow down. As he crossed the Pungwe River, three kilometres before Monte Hombe, he initiated a steep right turn and checked his stopwatch. The timepiece confirmed what he instinctively knew: he was within one second of the planned IP time.

Now he had exactly three minutes and 12 seconds to run to target. Brand pressed the radio transmit button on the throttle lever and made the announcement Norman Walsh and the rest of the air armada were tensely waiting to hear: 'Red Section at IP.' General Peter Walls heard the transmission from the command Dakota, but Walsh and many in the low-flying aircraft did not.

Brand now focused on two things: bringing the Hunter quickly onto a precise magnetic heading of 172 degrees and scanning the stopwatch. The IP was also the signal for Bourhill and Annan to drop back slightly into a looser battle formation, allowing sufficient space for safety. With precisely 17 seconds to run, Brand would pull up to the perch, a position 3 000 feet above ground, from where he would confirm the target and begin the dive attack.

Time dragged by ever more slowly for Peter Walls in the command Dakota. Norman Walsh and Brian Robinson, flying at low level in their command helicopter, were tense, waiting to hear from Red 1. They were anxious to know if total surprise had been achieved or whether they were flying into an organised ambush.

'Twenty seconds to go, 19, 18, 17, pull.' Brand felt the G-force tugging at his whole body as the Hunter rose majestically into the Mozambican morning sky, the upper surface of the wings now totally covered by white vapour. The rapid climb changed the vista dramatically; he could now see for miles, and there it was, exactly where he expected it to be – Mugabe's headquarters complex.

Brand's voice crackled with tension as he hit the transmit button, announcing 'Red 1 target visual'. This time, everyone heard the call. The Battle of Chimoio was about to commence.

Just before reaching his perch altitude, keeping the target as his constant reference point, Brand rolled the climbing Hunter to his left, almost inverted, arresting the climb, and brought the plane gracefully and neatly through a 90-degree left turn and into a perfect 30-degree dive, while maintaining positive G throughout.

As the HQ building started filling the gun sight, Brand released the back pressure on the stick and rolled the aircraft the right way up. As he fine-tuned his aim, he noticed tracer from anti-aircraft fire rising up from his eleven o'clock position. 'Someone's awake,' he thought as he squeezed the trigger and let loose with all four Aden 30-mm cannons, pumping out 80 rounds per second.

The Hunter shuddered violently from the recoil caused by sending nearly 200 shells towards the HQ and adjacent buildings, which slowed the machine down markedly. Just as he was about to pull up, Brand saw the first strikes glinting and kicking up dust in front of the main building. 'Perfect,' he said to himself. In his peripheral vision, he saw people scattering in all directions.

At the optimum moment, Brand released the trigger and pulled the Hunter's nose up until the G-meter registered 5, the minimum G-force necessary to avoid crashing into the ground. This rapidly arrested the dive and put the juddering Hunter into a rapid climb to safety – and out of the way of his wingmen, just as they planted frantan canisters on their designated targets.

In the climb, with one eye on the high cloud base, Brand rolled the Hunter gently to his left to see Mugabe's HQ complex clouded in dust and smoke, and, for the first time, he saw the massive armada of aircraft converging on the target: Hunters, Canberras, Dakotas, Alouettes and Lynxes.

He saw black frantan smoke rising from Chitepo College and the guerrilla convalescence centre (Pasidina 2), Bourhill's and Annan's targets, respectively. 'Excellent markers for the Canberras,' thought Brand. In the distance, he could also see Steve Kesby's Vampires attacking the recruits' camp seven kilometres away.

A frantic call interrupted Brand's grandstand view: 'Red 1, this is Delta Zero. Did you hit the target?' It was Norman Walsh approaching in the command Alouette with Brian Robinson.

'We had naturally maintained radio silence,' recalled Robinson. 'But at H + 10 seconds, Norman Walsh could no longer contain himself. "What a question," drawled Rich Brand sarcastically. I cannot describe the relief felt by the group captain and me.'

Green Section

The perspective was quite different for Chris Dixon, flying his lead Canberra bomber at just 90 metres above the ground. He would not have the luxury of pulling up to a perch to fine-tune his aim. But he did have the benefit of another sharp pair of eyes – those of his navigator, now lying on his stomach peering out of the bomb aimer's bubble.

Being so low and still five kilometres away when Brand opened fire, the Canberra crews had to rely on precise compass headings, stopwatches and map reading, at least until they saw the smoke rising from the initial Hunter strikes, particularly the black smoke from the frantan attacks, which were the precise markers for Green 2 and 4. Green Lead would drop on the HQ and Green 3 on the Nehanda and Chaminuka complexes lying east of Chitepo College.

The target smoke should have been coming from the right of a hill to the north-west of the target, which had now just come into view. There was no room for error; any rapid course corrections were dangerous in formation and so close to the ground, and any violent manoeuvring could overstress the Canberra's wings.

As the Canberra formation reached its IP, command subtly shifted to the navigators. Although the pilot was still the commander, from now on he would be told exactly what to do. When the navigator wanted a compass heading of 110 degrees, the pilot was expected to fly 110 degrees, not 109 or 111.

Flying with such accuracy was pretty demanding in an aircraft bumping along in low-level air turbulence. The pilot would also be expected to achieve the precise airspeed called for, and quickly. Chris Dixon's first major command from his navigator would have been: 'Acceleration point coming up, stand by ... accelerate.' At this point, the Canberras would accelerate from their cruise speed to their bomb-run speed. Dixon pressed the transmit button: 'Green Lead accelerating', giving the rest of the formation notice, so that they would not be caught unawares and be left behind.

All four Canberra pilots moved their thrust levers forward to a position they knew from experience would give them a steady 330 knots with the bomb doors open. The vigorous Rolls-Royce Avon engines nudged the machines forward to the faster airspeed. Norman Walsh heard the acceleration call from his helicopter and knew, with satisfaction, that the Canberras of No. 5 Squadron were also going to be bang on time.

As the speed of the Canberras stabilised, 'switch and doors' was the call and response between navigator and pilot. Dixon pressed the bomb-door switch and the doors started parting, extending into the slipstream to reveal the bomb bay, glistening with 300 Alpha Mark II fragmentation bombs in the hoppers. The opening doors distorted the smooth, aerodynamic shape of the aircraft's belly, causing the Canberra to start shaking and shuddering. The tension was electric.

'Come right a bit, steady, the heading is one-zero-eight, steady. I can see the smoke. Two degrees right, steady, I've got the target, back onto one-zero-eight, quickly. Right, right, steady, steady ... bombs gone. Spot on target, fucking grrreat.'

Like a heavy-metal shower, the Alpha bombs from Dixon's Canberra bounced and exploded around the old Antonio farmhouse, ZANLA's

HQ building, ripping branches from trees and cutting down the ZANLA personnel who hadn't yet legged it after Brand's attack. Green 2 and 3 simultaneously carpeted the huge area housing Chitepo College, Chaminuka and Nehanda camps, and Mugabe's residence, while Green 4 hit the complex housing convalescing combatants.

As quickly as they came, the threatening, bat-like Canberras were gone, leaving behind a massive cloud of dust, smoke and death.

With split-second timing, even as the Canberras were dropping their bombs, Vic Wightman and his wingman, Spook Geraty, were diving their Hunters towards the menacing anti-aircraft emplacements. The anti-aircraft gunners were now switching their aim away from the disappearing Canberras to the Hunters and the big, lumbering Dakotas approaching for the mass paradrop.

Wightman and Geraty opened up on the anti-aircraft emplacements with 68-mm rockets, and then attacked with 30-mm cannons. Wightman's Hunter took a hit in the port air intake from ground fire on his second attack. John Blythe-Wood's Blue Section Hunters attacked the other main anti-aircraft pits, following up with attacks on infrastructure targets. These attacks by the Hunters were absolutely crucial. Had they not attacked and reattacked when they did, it is virtually certain that serious damage would have been caused to the Dakotas.

All quiet at New Farm

Before the haunting howl of the blue note from Red 1 had interrupted things, the ZANLA HQ was going about its normal business. Some guerrillas were on parade and many more were receiving instruction under the thick tree cover that was characteristic of New Farm. The area around Chitepo College was a hive of activity as instructors lectured guerrillas in various aspects of military theory. Down the road to the east, the vehicle mechanics tinkered away on ZANLA vehicles in the garage.

The dirt thoroughfares around the HQ building, lined with neatly spaced palm trees planted by the farmer who had owned the land, were neatly swept in the African tradition. The atmosphere was calm, the inhabitants oblivious to the impending storm. The passage of the DC-8 flying high overhead did not cause panic, although some anti-aircraft crews manned their weapons. Generally, the inhabitants felt very secure.

Brian Robinson's key tactic, the element of surprise, had been well achieved.

Oppah Muchinguri, a secretary to the ZANLA high command, was near the HQ building when the attack started. She told the ZBC 33 years later:

> We saw planes, about 10 initially, flying towards the camp. We did not suspect anything, as we thought they were Mozambican. We had been attacked before at Nyadzonia. The planes started dropping bombs and parachutes. Rhodesian ground forces had already been dropped and had us surrounded, so the planes were targeting their bombs at our camp. As the bombs fell, those who tried to escape faced helicopters, which were targeting the outskirts of the camp. The camp had about 5000 people. As secretary, I was responsible for the safekeeping of all party and war documents so I dug a hole and buried them in the ground.

Muchinguri may have taken care of the war documents, but the Rhodesians still managed to retrieve masses of ZANLA classified material.

33

The mass paradrop

The oldest aircraft deployed on the raid, the Dakotas, rumbled along at 130 knots (240 km/h) in a loose formation. As the 'old birds' crossed into Mozambique, or 'Indian territory', as it was called, the dispatchers and parachute jump instructors hooked each paratrooper's static line to the overhead cable. This was a precaution in case the aircraft was seriously crippled by anti-aircraft fire – at least then those on board could jump out. This routine also served to ratchet up the tension; it was now getting serious.

The Daks were still 17 minutes from dropping – too long for some of the paratroopers, who were feeling a bit nauseous as they descended suddenly from the high ground to the Mozambican lowlands.

Kevin Milligan was standing near the open door of his Dakota. For the first time, he saw the helicopter armada as the faster Dakotas passed the Alouettes. Over his headset, he could hear the Hunter, Vampire and Canberra pilots talking in clipped, tense tones as the aerial attack continued.

Vic Culpan's voice over the intercom interrupted his thoughts. 'Prepare for action,' the No. 2 dispatcher bellowed. 'Stand up, check equipment.' The checks were done quickly: static line hooked up, safety pin fitted, helmet secure, Capewells secure, reserve-chute ripcord secure, body band secure, quick-release box secure. The paras then turned to face the open door at the rear of the aircraft, each man checking the parachute of the man in front. Then the dispatcher shouted: 'Tell off for equipment check.' Immediately, the furthest para from the door called out, '12 okay', '11 okay', and so on, down to the first man in each stick, who respectively called out, 'One okay, starboard stick okay'; 'One okay, port stick okay.'

Bob d'Hotman levelled his lead Dak off at 500 feet and slowed the machine to 95 knots. Vic Culpan followed suit, staying in line-astern formation. The timing and separation had to be perfect to avoid mid-air collision both of the aircraft and the paras. Each trailing Dak positioned itself slightly to starboard and about 50 feet above the one in front.

The 144 paras on board the six Daks would form two sides of

the box. Stops 1, 2 and 3 covered the western side, 3.2 kilometres long; Stops 4, 5 and 6 would cover the southern side, 3.6 kilometres in length.

As the Daks started positioning for the run-in, two minutes out, the dispatchers took up their positions near the door of the swaying aircraft. This brought on a new surge of adrenalin in the paratroopers. 'Will my chute open? Will I land on a rock? Will the gooks be waiting for us?' were some of the thoughts rushing through their minds.

Then Culpan called 'action stations' over the intercom, which Milligan repeated immediately to the No. 2 dispatcher, who, in turn, yelled 'action stations' to the ready and poised paras. The stick of 12 men on the port side shuffled to their position, one pace from the door. Culpan flicked the red-light switch, illuminating the bright red light above the open door. 'Red light on; stand in the door,' shouted the No. 2 dispatcher. The lead para took up his position in the door while the rest of the stick shuffled up to ensure they were tightly packed for the exit.

In the lead Dak, Derek de Kock counted off the paratroops as they jumped; this was transmitted by Bob d'Hotman over the air. As the second-last man jumped, Vic Culpan flicked the green-light switch in his Dak. Milligan shouted, 'Green light on, *go!* [slap on the shoulder], *two* and *three* and *four ...*'

Unlike in the case of Fireforce deployments, the dispatcher had to pause for a brief moment between jumps to ensure the men would land far enough apart to cover a side of the box. Travelling at 95 knots, the Daks covered the ground at a rate of 48 metres per second, meaning all 72 paras in the leg would be spread over a distance of 3.4 kilometres, exactly what was needed. The paras' adrenalin was flowing, and Milligan remembers that it was 'hard to slow them for a slower stick. They were used to exiting in one fast, flowing movement.'

In fact, it was impossible to slow them down. Lieutenant Mark Adams, commanding the southern half of Stop 1, explains:

> The RLI were used to jumping from the Dak in Fireforce operations. The key for us was to get a stick [four men] together as soon as we could after landing. The concept of an individual troopie staying where he lands and then fighting on his own some distance from the remainder of his stick was foreign to us. Also, when bullets are cracking around, the infantryman does not like to be in a confined

space, be that an aircraft or a vehicle, where he is unable to use his weapon to defend himself.

The powerful slipstream violently snatched each man as he stepped out of the door, the static line now his only attachment to the aircraft. It was a very brief attachment, as the static line quickly reached the end of its length and hauled the chute from the pack before breaking free. None of this was visible to the paratrooper. He waited for the reassuring tug of the parachute opening, and then shouted, 'Look up, check canopy.' The ground was less than 500 feet away.

The green chutes mushroomed from the Daks, a sight resembling large mammals giving birth to multiple young in flight. Soon the sky was filled with parachutes, but not for long – as the last paratroops were hurling themselves into the Mozambican sky, the first were already landing.

Derek de Kock was pleased to see that his drops had gone to plan. He was also happy there was good tree cover. This would snag many parachutes and slow the landing speed, reducing the risk of injury – provided the men remembered the golden rule: keep your feet tightly together. This wasn't simply a gender-saving precaution, but also a good branch-breaking technique, and, of course, the correct position for landing on terra firma.

Bob MacKenzie

SAS Captain Bob MacKenzie, an American veteran of the Vietnam War, wrote up his experiences of Operation Dingo, later published in the magazine *Soldier of Fortune*. MacKenzie was commanding Stop 4:

> I stood in the door of my Dakota while red and green tracer rounds zipped by, signalling the beginning of the battle for Chimoio 500 feet below. Inside the crowded fuselage of the Dak, my men were already standing and hooked up, and were finishing their pre-jump checks. A last look from the door revealed a landscape billowing with smoke and dust, and I saw the other half of my 'A' troop start jumping from a Dak ahead and slightly below the one in which I stood.
>
> With rounds popping like popcorn outside, I gave the thumbs-up to my long-time comrade and troop colour sergeant, Koos Loots, and to my men – silent, sweating, and grim-faced after an hour of

flying. The buzzer and green light went on and they started shuffling to the door and out, the 60 to 70 pounds of equipment hanging under their reserve chutes, making graceful exits impossible. 'Fuck me, get me out of this flying target,' I thought.

Hanging in my harness, drifting down from 500 feet, I could see terrorists running beneath me through the bush, firing wildly over their shoulders into the air. I gave a brief moment of thanks for the wretched marksmanship and lack of fire discipline exhibited by most African terrorists, and was pleased to see the long line of green canopies descending through the heat haze into the bedlam. My boots crashed through the branches of a Mopani tree and on down, coming to a halt six inches off the ground.

Pounding my quick-release box, I dropped out of my harness and took cover behind a tree. My first day at Chimoio had begun.

As the Daks finished the drop, they dived to low level to get away from the target zone and avoid the heavy anti-aircraft fire. This increased their speed significantly, 'which made it a real bugger to get the static lines and bags in,' recalled Derek de Kock.

As the parachutes were descending, the 10 trooper helicopters, now flying abreast in a staggered line, began dropping the men from the RLI on a ridge at the northern part of the box. Norman Walsh steered his command helicopter right to the edge of the battle zone, from where he and Brian Robinson could now assess the situation and establish command.

'As we came overhead and pulled up, there was still a lot of dust and smoke, and among all that there were hundreds of people running in every direction,' recalls Dave Jenkins, flying in the command helicopter. 'There was constant radio chatter, non-stop. Callsigns on the ground were reporting gooks everywhere.'

It was not easy for the commanders. Massive clouds of dust from the Canberra bombs hung in the morning air, obscuring visibility. The Hunter strikes had set scores of huts ablaze, and the problem with burning thatch is that before bursting into flame, it emits vast quantities of extremely thick white smoke. To add to the gloomy mix, the hot air rising from the fires into the moist air above cooled and condensed into little, puffy, man-made cumulus clouds, further obscuring visibility for the jet pilots.

The K-cars, now only four miles away, had a grandstand view from their bubble cockpits. Mark McLean recalled:

> Running in is something I remember very clearly because it was one of the most exciting times of my life. My initial thoughts then were on a television series called *Twelve O'Clock High*, about the US Air Force Flying Fortresses attacking Germany, with scenes of cigar-chewing Yank pilots bouncing around in their seats as the flak burst around them. It seemed to fit the scene as we ran in to target. Hunters barrelling in, explosions, bombs streaming out of the Cans – it was a totally impressive sight. Then the parachutes blossoming. Our own little Arnhem, I guess.

From his prime viewing position, McLean knew that this was a very big punch-up: 'It was definitely a "yahoo" moment – really, really exciting.'

Major Simon Haarhoff, the commander of the RLI's 2 Commando troops being carried in the 10 G-cars of Pink Section, described the scene as something like 'a swarm of angry bees – the air force's entire strike capability throwing any and every ordnance they could carry into the camp area'.

Norman Walsh, witnessing the same spectacle from his helicopter nearby, quickly spotted the major threat: many anti-aircraft weapons were still firing. These had to be silenced, and quickly too. After the initial attack, the Hunters orbited above the target area, forming a 'cab rank'. The next one in line would respond to Walsh's command, 'Blue 2 from Delta Zero, hit gun pit four with guns, then ZZ193061 [the grid reference on the photo map] with rockets.'

Martin Lowrie, next in line in the Hunter cab rank, looked at the gridded photograph of the target area in his cockpit, and knew instantly that Walsh wanted him to attack gun pit no. 4 with 30-mm cannon, then the mill and stores complex beyond the gun pit with 68-mm Matra rockets. 'Blue 2, roger' was Lowrie's crisp reply as he rolled his Hunter into an attacking dive, neutralising the weapon with a hail of cannon shells and returning to pump 24 rockets into the mill and stores beyond, setting scores of buildings alight.

However, the anti-aircraft guns seemed to pop up like mushrooms – as soon as you stood on one, another popped up elsewhere. The pre-raid photographs clearly showed the main fixed anti-aircraft gun pits.

These emplacements were ringed by thick walls of logs, making them easy to spot. Less noticeable, however, were the anti-aircraft guns placed on what were thought to be lookout towers. But the most dangerous weapons were those almost impossible to see – mobile anti-aircraft guns that were well camouflaged among the heavy tree cover.

The extent of the anti-aircraft defence came as a surprise, and it would take three more hours to silence all the heavy-calibre guns. It was not surprising that virtually every aircraft that engaged targets was hit.

Once the set-piece air strikes and early restrikes were over, it was the turn of the K-car gunships to move in and engage their allocated targets. Most of the K-cars sealed with their cannon fire the fourth side of the box, attacking east of the HQ complex. The remaining K-cars were to attack two targets outside the box, the convalescence centre, to the west of the HQ, and the recruits' camp, seven kilometres to the north-east.

Mandi Chimene, a ZANLA medical orderly, told the ZBC: 'Before anyone realised what was happening, we were under attack. In confusion, I left the barracks and went outside. A helicopter was hovering above me, spraying petrol down onto our building. I ducked inside as the soldier inside the helicopter started firing at me.'

The K-car fire might easily have been mistaken for petrol, as the 20-mm cannon shells exploded and set thatching alight.

The K-cars sent to Pasidina 2, the combatants' convalescence centre built around the old De Sousa farmstead, near where Chimene had her helicopter encounter, were in for a surprise. As they approached to engage, a withering wall of small-arms fire rose to meet them. Clearly, the convalescents were well armed and pretty sprightly. One of the K-cars was damaged almost immediately and had to retire. The convalescents continued to make a stand. The awkward thing was that Pasidina 2 was outside the box and about a kilometre behind Colour Sergeant John Norman's Stop Group 1, which, at the time, was engaging enemy to their front. Turning the RLI paratroops around or splitting them to attack the convalescents was not an option. Robinson had no choice but to ask Walsh to pacify the so-called convalescents with Hunter strikes.

Further to the east, at the fourth side of the box, Mark McLean arrived at his target zone:

I pulled up into my attack orbit and started shooting. There was quite a lot of long thatching grass and reasonably dense tree cover, which presented a problem, in that you could see a dozen or so enemy rushing in one direction, but as soon as we engaged them, they would throw themselves to the ground and disappear in the tall grass. So you would have needed to be directly above to spot them.

I was surprised that the high-explosive shells from our cannon did not set the grass alight; it must have been wet or quite green.

McLean was right – the grass was still damp from the rain the night before, which allowed quite a few guerrillas to slip through this part of the box.

The SAS stop groups were in the thick of it from the time they left the Dakotas. Hordes of ZANLA guerrillas were fleeing south, running away from the air strikes and straight into the SAS men just across the dry Massua River. The urge to escape the air assault seemed to make many of the guerrillas totally oblivious of the devastating ground fire they were running into.

There was also plenty of action for Simon Haarhoff's helicopter troops as they sealed the north side of the box. Guerrillas fleeing from the air attacks on the Takawira and Pasidina 1 camp areas covered ground so quickly that the men of 2 Commando hardly had time to deplane from the Alouettes before they were confronted by the van-guard of the sprinting guerrillas. Haarhoff explained:

Within minutes, firing started all along the line of sticks as terrs began breaking cover in front of the ridge and were picked off. It was like a badly organised turkey shoot, with the air force as the beaters and 2 Commando as the shooters.

Lieutenant Graeme Murdoch, whose stick was in the first G-car to land on the western extremity of the RLI stop line, was separated from the rest of 2 Commando. He recalls: 'It took me nearly 40 minutes to literally fight our way to join up with the rest of the commando after being dropped off, as the bad guys were desperately trying to flee out of box.'

Haarhoff's 2 Commando would account for more than 150 ZANLA in those early encounters.

The recruits' camp

The six Vampires had a target all to themselves: the recruits' camp, named Tango, which was seven kilometres north-east of the main target. Tango was also struck at H-hour.

At the time of Dingo, there were only three Vampire pilots in service in the RhAF, and all three also happened to be pilot attack instructors. These were Squadron Leader Steve Kesby and Flight Lieutenants Justin 'Varky' Varkevisser and Ken Law. All three were also rated on Hunters. Any non-current pilot volunteering to fly the Vampire would first need a flying and weapons-familiarisation check with one of these officers. The 'jammers', Janeke and Slatter, were first to volunteer. Flight Lieutenant Phil Haigh, who had just recently been posted to No. 1 (Hunter) Squadron, found out that because of his inexperience with Hunters, there was no Operation Dingo role for him. Anxious not to lose out, he volunteered to fly a Vampire. It was a fateful decision.

The Vampires taxied out, careful not to stop anywhere for too long, as the downward-angled jet efflux had a reputation for melting asphalt surfaces. The Vampires took off from Runway 06, and Kesby led his section east, climbing to 20 000 feet. Kesby and Varky would attack the anti-aircraft positions, so in addition to a full load of 20-mm cannon, they carried four three-inch, 60-pound rockets.

The Vampires worked on achieving a ground speed of five nautical miles per minute, which meant a flying time of 30 minutes to the recruits' camp. Kesby recalled:

> As we approached the eastern border, we were in contact with Grand Reef Airfield and learnt about the extent of the cloud cover from feedback from the helicopters already in Mozambique. I could see that we would have a problem descending through the cloud without compromising our attack. I then elected to descend to low level and thread our way through the mountains to our IP.

This was easier said than done. Descending from high altitude when one has visible landmarks is not a problem, but with cloud below and having to fly through holes in the white stuff, precision navigation can be difficult. The last thing Kesby needed was to inadvertently fly over the main target area. 'We always built in a "fudge factor" for timing,' he said, 'so that we would be able to lose or gain time in order to leave the IP as required to make our strike time.' Kesby quickly picked up his landmarks and made the IP on time, ensuring the gun sight and armaments were set correctly for the attack. There was an anxious moment for Kesby, however:

> On pulling up, I searched for the target, but only managed to fully identify all aspects of it three-quarters of the way up. I then positioned for the rocket attack and turned in. The rocket profile requires at least four seconds of steady tracking with the gun sight uncaged, during which time no evasive manoeuvring is possible. At this stage, I saw many of the camp inhabitants start to bombshell away from the parade square.
>
> The camp appeared as the photo intelligence indicated. A large open parade square with many persons on parade at the time. There were four large barrack blocks and a number of smaller huts. I was able to identify both the anti-air positions. There was evidence of ground fire, but there was also evidence of many bodies fleeing the scene in all directions.

As Kesby pulled up from his rocket attack, he heard his pilots all call 'off target' as he set his sights to guns only. 'Lead in' was his call as he attacked the barrack blocks with 20-mm cannon.

The Vampires had caught the inhabitants of Tango by complete surprise. The ZANLA trainees were lined up on the parade square as the jets pounced. For many, however, this was their lucky day. Had a Canberra or two come this way, the casualty rate would have been much higher.

34

Cover Point chaos

While the battle was blazing at Chimoio, another vital milestone had to be achieved: setting up the admin base near the target. Every attack helicopter needed to land there – inside Mozambique – to refuel and rearm. The code word for this milestone was Cover Point, which would be relayed to the command helicopter.

The admin base commander, Peter Petter-Bowyer, and his pilot, Flight Lieutenant Bill Sykes, left Lake Alexander with the main helicopter attacking force of 21 Alouettes. Sykes positioned his helicopter between the trooper G-cars in front and the K-cars behind. Exactly 12 minutes from the target, Sykes left the formation and broke left onto a north-easterly route towards Monte Utumece, the prominent feature alongside the area chosen for the admin base.

En route, PB saw the much faster DC-7 fly past, turn back and overtake them again. The plane was obviously early. As their Alouette approached the site, PB was in for another surprise: 'I was startled to find that this was not the open area of ground that I had expected ... it was covered with fairly high grass interspersed with clumps of dense scrub.'

PB had barely climbed out of the helicopter when he saw the lumbering DC-7 already positioning for its first run. The time was 07:58; the big airliner was a full two minutes early. The original plan had been modified to allow PB to land just ahead of the DC-7 so that he could talk it in, ensuring the fuel, ammo and troops would be dropped in the most suitable place. But there had obviously been a misunderstanding. The DC-7 started disgorging the protection troops some distance from where PB wanted them, despite his frantic calls on the radio. The DC-7 did a circuit and started another run, this time to drop the first load of fuel drums, almost in the same spot as the troops, risking flattening the soldiers beneath the heavy pallets. In an attempt to rescue the situation, Bill Sykes took off in the admin base helicopter to try to get the attention of the DC-7 crew.

For a while after Sykes's departure, PB stood completely alone in the middle of the Mozambican bush, armed only with a radio. Sykes did manage to attract the attention of the DC-7 crew. However, the co-pilot, George Alexander, cursed him for getting in the way of the drops. The curses reached Dave Jenkins, flying in the command helicopter over the target: 'I recall George Alexander losing his rag over the air ... he was always quite temperamental.'

By now, the trooper helicopters, having offloaded their troops at New Farm, had started arriving from the south, and landed near where PB stood, and then some of the K-cars that were either damaged or out of ammo started arriving too. To make things more difficult, some of the Polo helicopters started arriving early from Lake Alexander, one carrying the Special Branch team. Unsurprisingly, the post-Dingo debriefing made the point that the Polo admin helicopters should not have landed at the same time as the attack helicopters. It looked chaotic – drum and ammunition pallets raining from the sky while helicopters started converging on the base.

The 10 G-car trooper helicopters had done their work for now; refuelling them was not a priority. But it was critical to turn the K-cars around fast so they could return to battle and secure the eastern side of the box.

'I had abandoned any hope of getting fuel and ammunition down to where I needed them,' recalls PB. 'I had no choice but to move the admin base to where the drums were. In these circumstances, you must forget errors and blame, and just sort things out as they are.'

The 16 RLI protection troops were supposed to get onto the high ground quickly to observe and react to any hostile enemy movement. Says PB: 'The RLI officer sent only two men with a mortar onto the high ground. The rest of the troops remained behind to give us a helping hand. The G-car pilots and technicians also pitched in. You didn't have to ask for help – everyone mucked in. They were fantastic.'

PB's main concern was that there might be an accident. The K-car pilots, keen to get straight back into the heavy battle raging at New Farm, had little option but to land close to the fuel drum pallets. This exposed them to the risk of the collapsed parachutes billowing in the rotor wash and snagging the rotors. But the pilots were wise to this and there were no accidents.

Mark McLean, now out of ammo and needing to refuel, takes up the story: 'When we landed, we just tucked in and helped ourselves to fuel. I landed near a fuel pallet, hopped out and helped my technician roll drums to the chopper. We also collected our own 20-mm ammo – there was no problem.'

PB decided the immediate priority was to clear areas near the drums and remove the parachutes from the pallets. At the same time, men shifted the heavy 20-mm ammo boxes to the clearings. PB remembered the moment: 'I was running around like a blue-arsed fly trying to get things sorted.' It was not until 08:15 that the words 'Cover Point' were transmitted to the command helicopter.

Just as PB thought he was getting on top of things, Sod's Law struck again. Suddenly, Norman Walsh's command helicopter arrived – way ahead of schedule.

35

Long Stop

The next major phase of the battle would be tightening the noose. The paratroops would start sweeping towards the central area. As this began, Robinson would radio the code words 'Long Stop' to General Peter Walls in the command Dak. 'Short Leg' would be the code words used later to indicate that the sweep was complete.

Brian Robinson was anxiously watching as a large group of ZANLA south of Chitepo College tried to break out towards Stops 4, 5 and 6. Because of the dense tree cover around the central target area, most guerrillas had probably not seen the parachutes coming down and had no idea they were running straight into a trap.

The stop groups stuck to their orders from Robinson: 'On landing, get out of your harness, take good cover, wait and shoot.' One SAS paratrooper in four was carrying an RPD light machine gun chucking out 650 rounds a minute, so the firepower was devastating. Waves of panicking guerrillas were cut down. The same was happening on the western flank, where the RLI engaged enemy as they broke cover from a riverbed between them and the HQ area.

There was little that Robinson could do until the battle stabilised. Finally, at 08:10, 25 minutes after H-hour, he was able to call his commanders to establish whether their sticks were all right. It was quite a challenge controlling 184 men. Each stop group had its own radio frequency, and the seven commanders also monitored the main battle frequency of 132.20 MHz. With the paratroops scattered over nearly seven kilometres and behind cover, it was not obvious where the lines were, and the haze didn't help. Robinson had planned for this, however, telling the men at the main briefing: 'The man on the extremity of each stick is to carry a white-phosphorous grenade, ready to throw on my command.'

But now was not the time, as the battle was raging all over the place, from the convalescence centre in the west to the recruits' camp in the north-east. So heavy was the fighting that soon many of the K-cars ran out of ammunition, and retired to the admin base for rearming. Norman Walsh filled the K-car gap with additional jet strikes. Walsh's voice was virtually continuous on the battle frequency as he prioritised targets for the jet pilots and coordinated the effort with Brian Robinson, and all this while piloting the command helicopter. The workload was intense.

Then disaster struck. A loud bang startled the occupants of the command helicopter, and the Alouette started vibrating badly. ZANLA men firing a 12.7-mm heavy machine gun had found their target. One round went harmlessly through the tail boom, but another hit the main rotor system, causing the severe vibration. Although a bit rusty on helicopters, Walsh acted quickly, and lowered the collective for a rapid descent to tree level, both to avoid further fire and to assess whether he needed to put the helicopter down immediately. 'Controlling the helicopter became a problem because the hydraulics were affected by the vibration and the controls went sloppy,' recalled Walsh. 'Had the vibration got worse, I would have landed immediately; but it remained constant so I flew back to the admin base.' Dave Jenkins praised his pilot:

> Boss Walsh had been off operational flying for a while prior to the op. He did a quick refamiliarisation course on choppers, and I suspect that on this occasion it was the first time he had come under fire from a 12.7-mm. When the gun opened up on us, I think he said something to the effect of 'What's that funny noise?' [First you heard the rounds go past, then the sound of the weapon firing.] As soon as the first round hit us, as quick as a flash, he dumped the collective and put us on the trees.

There was a contingency plan. If the command chopper became incapacitated, Squadron Leader Harold Griffiths would take over from Norman Walsh, picking up Major Mike Graham to stand in for Brian Robinson. Unfortunately, Alpha 7 (Griffiths's callsign) was heading back to the admin base to get ammo and refuel. And Graham was on the ground in a heavily wooded area, unable to be picked up.

Brian Robinson had no option but to call his commanders; he told them to 'hold current positions until I am back'. Walsh too had to think quickly as he tried to control the stricken helicopter: 'Alpha Four from Delta Zero, take command of the air effort until I am back.' With that order, Walsh instructed the lead Lynx pilot to assume airborne control. Walsh had barely transferred control when the Lynx also took a hit from ground fire. This was the worst possible time to lose airborne command.

Bob MacKenzie, commanding Stop Group 4, heard the exchanges on the battle frequency:

> The command net crackled and I heard that the C & C [command and control] helicopter had taken a hit and had to retire. Robinson said he would be back soon and ordered all units to hold their present positions until then. Attempts were made to get a chopper in to pick up the alternate commander, but he was engaged in a firefight far from an LZ and was too busy being a rifleman to take command.
>
> The ground war tapered off to sporadic bursts as Mugabe's finest tried to escape through the closing Rhodesian lines. For more than an hour, officers and men waited in the heat, fuming at the delay, knowing the enemy must be slipping away through the inevitable gaps in their lines and through the side of the box that was supposed to be closed by K-cars. The gunships were much diminished in their number now, due to refuelling and rearming.

The admin base commander, PB, was just bringing order to the rather chaotic situation caused by the DC-7 dropping the fuel in awkward locations, when suddenly he saw the command heli stagger in. 'Norman Walsh arrived, way ahead of time. His command helicopter was shot up and he needed to borrow another in a hurry. Both he and Brian were deeply frustrated by their unplanned absence from the action at the most critical time in the battle, but there was no aircraft immediately available.'

There was another problem. The command helicopter had a special multi-radio stack to allow Brian Robinson to simultaneously monitor and talk to a number of callsigns on different frequencies. It would be incredibly difficult using a single helicopter VHF radio, so it was essential to repair the command ship quickly. PB explained how he got things going:

> There was no hope of switching the complex radio system on the command aircraft, so I asked the No. 7 Squadron technicians present if they thought it possible to substitute the command helicopter's

damaged main rotor head with the good one from the aircraft requiring a tail-cone change. 'What a question, sir! We will have it done sooner than you think.' With no rigging equipment whatsoever and no special tools, half a dozen technicians and two pilots descended on both aircraft with standard tools and plenty of energy.

Norman Walsh picked up the story: 'Brian Robinson went off in an interim helicopter, until I had my aircraft repaired. The techs were fantastic, as usual. They did a high-speed blade change, then Brian was called back and we went off in the command helicopter again.'

A rotor blade is a heavy piece of kit, so removing one and carrying it to another machine is hard work. Even harder is lifting the blade up to the rotor head for attachment. The technicians and pilots climbed onto fuel drums and guided the blade onto the mast. Once attached, the blade needed adjustment to be in harmony with the other two blades. Special tools are needed for this, but the technicians only had a few spanners. Nevertheless, they completed the task in 45 minutes, probably a world record for a rotor-blade change in the field, and a tribute to the skill and can-do attitude of the No. 7 Squadron technicians. Walsh and Robinson lifted off again at 09:25, just under an hour after the aircraft had been hit.

While the command ship was being repaired, many aircraft over the target area were also taking hits, including most of the K-cars. At 08:40, a chilling call came over the airwaves: 'Venom Two is hit.' It was a distress call from Air Lieutenant Phil Haigh in his Vampire FB9. His squadron boss, Steve Kesby, recalled:

On positioning for the third attack, I heard No. 2 call: 'I've been hit.' I immediately turned to where I knew he would be and told him to continue straight ahead. I then told Varky and the rest of the squadron to make their own way back. I caught up with Phil and moved into tight formation as we climbed through the cloud cover. Once above the cloud, we changed radio channels and I carried out a thorough close inspection of his aircraft. I couldn't see any obvious damage. He reported that all indications were normal, except for the JPT [jet pipe temperature], which was indicating off the clock. A further inspection of this area revealed nothing.

Phil was rightly worried, and I suggested he could land at

Marandellas Airfield, which had a tar strip, if he felt that there was a major problem. He replied that the aircraft was handling okay – but the JPT was a threat. We levelled off at about 15 000 feet and throttled back as far as we could and headed for base. I positioned myself about 100 yards line abreast, with his aircraft on my right.

Kesby switched radio frequency to Grand Reef and explained the situation. After this radio exchange, he reset the domestic channel and called Phil: 'No reply. I looked for where he should have been, but was unable to see him. I realised then that there must have been a development with Phil and his aircraft. He never replied to my desperate calls.' What Kesby did not know was that a bullet had entered the Goblin engine, rupturing a burner tube.

Haigh nursed the stricken Vampire towards Rhodesia, but soon the engine failed completely. The Vampire was now a glider, with only precious height keeping it flying. He had two options: bail out or find a suitable field for a forced landing. Unfortunately for Haigh, the FB9 variant of the Vampire was not equipped with an ejection seat, so he would have to escape manually. This involved jettisoning the canopy, climbing out, jumping clear and pulling the ripcord – easier said than done. All Vampire pilots knew that they risked colliding with the twin-tail boom assembly when jumping from an FB9. This is probably why Haigh chose the forced-landing option. By the time the Vampire had crossed the Eastern Highlands of the Rhodesian border, Haigh was running out of sky and would not make it to an airfield – he had to land.

He chose an open field, near Inyanga, but, sadly, there was a concealed ditch traversing the field, and a pilot gets only one shot at a forced landing. Haigh touched down in the right place, but the thin Eastern Highlands air meant the Vampire needed a greater-than-normal landing distance, which extended beyond the ditch. The aircraft collided with the edge of the ditch and flipped over. The engine broke free and crumpled the cockpit, killing the pilot instantly.

Steve Kesby had already radioed Grand Reef for helicopter assistance. Then he headed for the most likely field, diving down to about 1 500 feet above ground. 'I saw a large plume of black smoke in the middle of the field. I flew overhead and saw that I would not be able to help in any way – the aircraft was very badly damaged.'

Kesby returned to New Sarum critically short of fuel. 'The mood was very sombre, but with all that was happening, we had little time for reflection.'

Air Lieutenant Philip Wilfred Haigh, a direct-entry pilot from the RAF, became the first Rhodesian casualty of Operation Dingo.

Often forgotten after an air crash are the people who have to deal with the wreckage and remains of the pilot, and those who have to inform the loved ones. First Warrant Officer Charles Penney was sent from Lake Alexander to recover the wreckage. 'It looked like a perfect forced lob, but the Vampire hit this big donga and flipped over. The first thing I found was the pilot's watch.'

The task of informing Phil Haigh's wife, Dot, fell to a fellow pilot, at the time the officer commanding Administration Wing at Thornhill, Squadron Leader Prop Geldenhuys. 'Advising next of kin of a fatality is a job I would not wish on my worst enemy,' wrote Geldenhuys in his book *Rhodesian Air Force Operations*.

He found Dot Haigh at the airbase canteen shop and broke the awful news to her in her car, then drove her home, where medical staff were waiting to take over.

Second Lieutenant Neill Jackson of the RLI, who was part of Operation Dingo, paid tribute to Haigh: 'I was particularly saddened to hear of the death of Vampire pilot Phil Haigh, who had extricated me from a very difficult situation earlier that year with some very skilful flying and excellent close-quarter weapons delivery.'

Steve Kesby described Phil Haigh as 'an Englishman who readily fitted into our air force and society. He was quiet, with a good sense of humour, and flew well.'

36

Rubbernecking and the sweep

Back at Chimoio, while the command helicopter was out of action, there had been no overall command. It was a tribute to Norman Walsh's detailed briefing and the professionalism of the pilots that the jets and K-cars continued attacking key targets, harassing the enemy and neutralising many anti-aircraft sites. The commanders on the ground were using their wits and initiative by calling in jet air strikes to neutralise enemy positions. This wasn't without its problems. K-car pilot Mark McLean was engaging targets in his zone:

> With all the shit that was going down, a lot of smoke and haze had built up over the target area, and, to make matters worse, we weren't on the same frequency as the guys on the ground calling in the air strikes. I was in my attack orbit when I saw a Vampire suddenly pass in front of my gun barrel, underneath me and very close. In reaction, I pulled up and then looked back and there, sure enough, was his number two coming for me. So thereafter I was not looking at my target, but rubbernecking [looking for other aircraft], searching the grey haze for aircraft coming down the slope, and sure enough, there they would be.

McLean knew the modus operandi of the jet pilots from his earlier days of flying Vampires and Hunters: 'It was quite exciting for us because the guys would have been concentrating on the gun sights and probably not thinking too much about a camouflaged helicopter drifting out of the haze into their flight path.'

Fierce firepower was pouring out of the triangular area bounded by the HQ, Chitepo College and Nehanda Camp. The Canberras, now refuelled and rearmed, were again approaching Mozambique. As Walsh and Robinson rejoined the battle at 09:35, the first thing Walsh did was to direct one of the Canberras to strike the troublesome triangle.

This meant Brian Robinson would again have to hold off with the sweep until the Canberra strikes were over. Green 3 dropped a load of Alpha bomblets between Chitepo College and Chaminuka Camp, taking two hits from ground fire in the process – the element of surprise had now long worn off. Walsh requested another Canberra strike, while Robinson asked Stops 1 to 3 to throw smoke, initially to give a marker to Hunter pilot Vic Wightman to attack the enemy in front of them, and to give Robinson an accurate fix of where the stop groups were as he prepared to start the sweep.

At last, more than two hours after H-hour, Robinson was able to give the order that the ground troops were anxiously waiting for: 'Stops 1, 2 and 3, prepare to start sweep. Stops Alpha to Juliet and Stops 4 to 6, to watch out. Sweep from present loc towards target area.' Robinson was moving the western side of the box in towards the HQ area, with the northern and southern groups holding ground, ready to pick off any ZANLA flushed out by the sweep. But as he did so, an enormous volume of fire erupted from the central area, forcing the advance to take defensive cover.

The sweep was put on hold while another Canberra was brought in to soften the target. A Hunter of Blue Section marked the spot for the Canberra, but the haze was so bad that the Canberra crew never saw the marker, and planted its load 200 metres beyond the target. More Canberra strikes were brought in, with better effect. However, most of the guerrillas had taken cover in the elaborate zigzag trench system that surrounded the main target area, which protected them from the Alpha bombs. Like most battles, the ground forces would have to finish the job.

Robinson, now very concerned about the time, ordered the sweep to resume, letting General Walls know that 'Long Stop' was under way. Robinson asked the general how long the attack troops could stay. Peter Walls, sitting at his table in the command Dak, poring over his maps and scribbling on his notepad, replied: 'Nine, this is Zero. You can continue the sweep, but do not get bogged down.'

The commander-in-chief, knowing that FRELIMO had not yet made any attempt to intervene, was allowing Robinson to push the time out, but only if there were no more hold-ups. Captain Bob MacKenzie was worried:

With the all-important element of surprise having been used up, there was a growing apprehension that some of the enemy commanders could be organising their forces for a concerted attempt at breaking out of the box, or worse, a counter-attack. Even a concentrated group of 30 or so guerrillas would have little trouble in smashing through the one-man-thick Rhodesian line. Clearly, the enemy had scant idea of how few troops were attacking them, and the constant presence of the air force was both deadly and demoralising...

MacKenzie had summed up the situation well. After Rich Brand's opening attack, ZANLA were preoccupied predominantly with their escape and survival. It was only when the braver ones realised there was a wall of enemy between them and escape that they decided to defend or fight their way out.

Stops 1, 2 and 3 eventually started sweeping in earnest towards the HQ and Chitepo College area. RLI Colour Sergeant John Norman, part of Stop 1, marshalled his 11 Troop sweep line across some clear ground and then into thick tree cover. Norman was standing in as troop commander for Lieutenant Rod Smith, who was away on a Selous Scouts selection course.

Suddenly, all hell broke loose. 'There was the sound of heavy firing from above,' recalled Norman. 'I thought the gooks were firing at us from up in the trees and I told my men to move forward to engage them. When I tried to stand up, I couldn't.' Norman had not yet realised that he had been seriously wounded in five places by pieces of flying shrapnel from a 20-mm cannon. Also injured were three of his men: Troopers Furstenburg, Hooley and Grobler.

In the haze and confusion, a K-car had mistaken 11 Troop for ZANLA forces and opened fire. 'Stop, stop, stop!' was screamed over the radio and the K-car backed off. Paul Furstenburg, the designated stick medic, attended to Norman, not yet realising he had been injured.

'Paul, is my eye still there?' asked the troop commander frantically; blood and swelling had closed his left eye. His eye was still there, but the most serious wound was to his leg. Also, Norman's right toe was nearly severed, saved only by his new, and now ruined, steel-capped Australian para boots.

The battle was raging too fiercely for a G-car to get in to pick up the wounded, so Norman and the other wounded soldiers had to wait for more than an hour before a G-car, Pink 5, arrived to take Norman, now very weak from loss of blood, straight to the resuscitation unit at

Lake Alexander. Already on board the G-car when it stopped to uplift Norman was the body of a dead SAS soldier.

Robinson could now start the sweep from the south. SAS Stop Groups 4, 5 and 6 started sweeping towards the main area. As the stop groups advanced, the noose tightened and they came under almost continuous fire. Bright-orange luminescent patches stitched onto the ground forces' caps helped the pilots differentiate friend from foe, but they occasionally gave ZANLA marksmen nice bright targets to shoot at. It took the death of an SAS soldier for them to realise the problem. Trooper Frans Nel was shot in the forehead by a female guerrilla. Barbara Cole tells the story in her book *The Elite*: 'As one SAS group advanced ... the enemy opened fire. Corporal Trevor Kershaw looked to see if the sweep line was straight, and as he did so, a single shot struck the man next to him between the eyes.'

Under fearsome fire, Nel's brave fellow troopers tried to revive him, but to no avail. Trooper Frans Jacobus Nel, a 24-year-old SAS soldier hailing from Karoi, became the second Rhodesian casualty of the day.

The Rhodesian sweep lines were now very close to the enemy defences, making it ever more difficult for air support to be effective. Much of the battle would now be at close quarters – shoot or be shot.

One of the stick leaders sweeping north towards the triangle with Stop 5 was SAS Lieutenant Darrell Watt. Someone who had enormous respect for Watt was Mark McLean, who described him as 'a short and very muscular guy, with a very thick neck, and as tough as nails. He was also an excellent tracker.'

Watt told the story: 'After organising ourselves, we went north in a sweep line. We came to a deep riverbed that was dry. As I peeped over the edge, I saw a gook pointing his AK straight at me. He pulled the trigger first and shot me through my right thigh, missing the bone and femoral artery.' Watt wasn't to let the injury stop him, and he and his men carried on fighting. 'I was bleeding a lot. But we then got them all.' That was the calibre of the men ZANLA were facing, Rhodesia's crack troops from the SAS and RLI.

Watt eventually accepted first aid to stem the blood, yet because of the intensity of the enemy fire, he also had to wait more than an hour before a casevac helicopter came to lift him out.

Anti-aircraft fire was still coming from the triangle, even though the Hunters and Vampires had attacked most of the gun emplacements.

Eventually, it was the ground troops sweeping towards the triangle who managed to silence the guns. Stop 3, led by Captain Colin Willis, spotted a heavy-calibre weapon manned by eight ZANLA guerrillas – a lot of personnel for a gun. ZANLA had big teams manning its numerous guns, and was able to get many of its guns firing again soon after the jet strike. Willis's men flanked the position and killed all eight crew.

Bob MacKenzie's Stop 4 also put paid to a troublesome 12.7-mm anti-aircraft weapon:

> Leading a 15-man patrol back into the forest towards our next objective, the ZANLA intelligence centre, my point element signalled there were enemy ahead. The patrol deployed on line and advanced cautiously toward a large clearing. In the middle of the clearing stood a 30-foot tower with a DShK 12.7-mm anti-aircraft machine gun, its crew frantically blasting away at every plane in sight.
>
> Preoccupied with aerial targets, neither of the four gunners nor their security party on the ground saw the SAS patrol creeping to the edge of the clearing. Silhouetted against the hazy sky, the crew were perfect targets. On command, my troopers opened fire. Bodies tumbled off the tower onto the group guarding the base of the tower, who were shot before they could return fire.

A moment later, MacKenzie's group came across a far more formidable anti-aircraft weapon, a Chinese twin-barrelled 37-mm cannon, obviously a new acquisition, as it was still covered in gun grease. 'Happily for the air force, it had not been put into action. A few pounds of plastic explosive soon ensured it never would be.'

To the north, the RLI helitroops were meeting fierce resistance from the Takawira complex, housing semi-trained guerrillas ready to be dispatched to other countries for training, and in particular from the Pasidina 1 complex, which housed limbless guerrillas. The K-cars helping the RLI also came under heavy fire.

Dave Jenkins was amused by the call from one of the K-cars: 'I think it was Baldy Baldwin or Gaps Newman, but it went something like this: "Christ there are thousands of the bastards here, all with automatic crutches, shooting the shit out of us."'

Norman Walsh brought the Hunters in to help, ordering Vic Wightman's White Section to hammer the area from Takawira to Pasidina 1.

Mark McLean's helicopter, Alouette serial number 5037, now resembled a flying sieve; it had taken 12 hits. 'You know when you have taken a hit, it's a "ting" sound. A crack is just a near miss.'

Mark remembers that his technician, Finch Bellringer, was still sporting fresh wounds in his back from his last Fireforce action before Dingo, which made him 'aware of his mortality, not overly nervous, but aware'. Then, just after 13:00, one round got much, much closer: a bullet passed right through McLean's helmet. 'I was in my left-hand attack orbit, and then I woke up to hear Finch Bellringer shouting, "Are you all right; are you all right?" By then, we were in a right-hand orbit. We must have flipped over into a right turn during the moment I was unconscious, or at least stunned, and Finch didn't know what the hell was going on. He must have thought his pilot was dead.'

A bullet had entered the front of McLean's helmet just above his right eye, smashing the visor and exiting above and behind his right ear, grazing his right temple. The bullet brought the total number of holes in the helicopter to 13, excluding the two holes in the pilot's helmet. McLean recovered his wits enough to stabilise the helicopter:

> It felt like I had been smacked by a prizefighter. I can only think that the resistance of the fibre in the helmet must have snapped my head to the right. It certainly gave me a savage headache, which lasted for the rest of the day. I remember the headache being worse the next morning, but that was probably more to do with the amount of beer I drank at Grand Reef that night.

Mark McLean, sporting a huge AK-47–induced lump over his right eye, and his recently wounded technician, Finch Bellringer, bravely continued with the task of eliminating ZANLA resistance without any thought for their own discomfort or safety. McLean carried on flying his K-car, clocking a total of six hours, 40 minutes in the air that day.

Soon after McLean's incident, another K-car had a lucky escape. Ian Harvey was engaging the enemy when their 20-mm cannon jammed. Mark Jackson, Harvey's technician/gunner, confirmed that a round was stuck in the super-hot barrel. 'Get it sorted, quickly' was all the world's most experienced Alouette pilot said. Jackson had to first remove the hot barrel and insert the spare. But heat-swollen barrels are not easy to remove and Jackson struggled to loosen it. Eventually, he had no choice but to undo his safety harness so that he could lean well forward to get the required leverage. As he was doing this, their K-car took hits from ZANLA ground fire. A bullet smashed into the pilot's door handle, spraying Harvey's right elbow with shrapnel. Another bullet passed through the upper part of Jackson's seat – exactly where he had been sitting moments before moving forward to change barrels.

The fierce volume of ZANLA's ground-to-air fire that day ensured that most K-car crews had similar experiences – every single K-car was holed at least once.

As the noose tightened, the battle became a series of skirmishes as the fight was slowly but surely knocked out of ZANLA. The sweep of the outer perimeter was done, and Robinson transmitted 'Short Leg' to General Walls. Another milestone was ticked off. But time was dragging on and there was still much to do, in particular clearing hundreds of buildings, recovering or destroying weapons and equipment, and getting the men of Special Branch in to look at bodies and documents.

Recovering 184 men and their equipment back to Rhodesia was the planners' biggest headache. They would be evacuated by helicopter, four at a time. The recovery plan stipulated that at 13:30, the G-cars would begin the extraction. First, they were to recover the 144 used parachutes, followed by a phased extraction of the troops. According to the plan, the last troops were to leave the target at 16:10. Clearly, this was not going to happen, as it was already 13:35 and the sweeps were still advancing.

Brian Robinson called General Walls: 'Request permission to remain in target area to 16:00 then recover back to admin base. Recovery from admin base tomorrow.'

This was a big change to the plan, leaving a large force in hostile foreign territory overnight. Peter Walls knew the battle was going well. He also knew that the risk of a ZANLA counter-attack or of FRELIMO intervening now seemed distinctly unlikely, which significantly lowered the risk of remaining in Mozambique. But he was well aware of the political sensitivity of Operation Dingo being seen by the outside world as an invasion of a sovereign nation. Staying overnight increased this prospect. The telex machine in the command Dak was kept busy updating Prime Minister Ian Smith in his office in Milton Building as the day wore on. Walls sent an evaluation of the risks and rewards of extending the stay in Mozambique for the night. The prime minister agreed.

Robinson was given permission to stay longer. Walls had also taken into account that the weather over Lake Alexander, the next staging and refuelling stop inside Rhodesia, had deteriorated, which meant they might have no option but to stay in Mozambique overnight.

37

Pit-stop bingo

All things being equal, the Hunters attacking at low level could remain airborne for just under two hours. The trip back to Thornhill from Chimoio would take 25 minutes and consume about 1 200 pounds of fuel at high altitude. In his pre-sortie planning, Rich Brand had added a further 600 pounds to this for the approach, landing, taxiing and contingencies for 'joker' fuel. This is an RAF term signifying that the fuel level has reached the minimum to get to one's destination safely. The first pilot to reach this level calls 'joker' over the radio, and everyone understands precisely what it means: time to head for home. There is another fuel level after joker has been reached – known as 'bingo'. This is the critical fuel point, another way of saying 'oh shit!' In the case of the Hunter, bingo is reached when there is only enough fuel, when flying at low level, to stay airborne for 17 minutes. This flying time can be extended to nearly 30 minutes by flying at a high altitude where the thinner air provides better efficiency for a jet.

In the thick of battle, with all sorts of distractions, it is easy to pay scant attention to the fuel level, and in some cases miss joker completely. To get the pilot's attention, the Hawker Hunter has a pair of prominent amber lights, called bingo lights. These are activated when the aircraft reaches the critical level of 650 pounds of fuel. As soon as the bingo lights flicker on, it is imperative the pilot drops everything and heads for home, immediately.

Bingo has no fat built in. It assumes there will be no delays whatsoever, and leaves no room for error. If, for example, one of the Hunters has a problem on landing and blocks the runway – there is a high probability of this when you have just been shot at – it leaves those still needing to land with no option but to land on whatever part of the runway is available. The luxury of diverting to another airfield is no longer an option.

Fuel was not an issue for the White and Blue Hunter sections; ammunition was their limiting factor. Wightman and Geraty ran out of rockets and cannon after only 15 minutes, returning home immediately to rearm. But Red Section remained high over the target, attempting to conserve fuel, providing top cover and a reaction if FRELIMO decided to intervene. At 08:25, Rich Brand spotted the first glimmer of one of his bingo lights. He immediately called: 'Red Section, pogo pogo go.'

'Pogo' was a code word the Hunter pilots recognised instantly; it was an instruction for them to flick to an unused radio frequency to talk, thus avoiding clogging up the battle frequency. On the private frequency, Brand told his section he was on bingo: time to head for home. The other two Hunters followed Brand in trail (loose line astern). As the Hunters left Chimoio, the 'jammers', the Vampires of Voodoo Section, moved in to replace them.

Passing through 20 000 feet, Brand radioed air traffic control at Thornhill, requesting a 'priority approach and landing', which meant air traffic control would clear the airspace and ensure the runway was clear of other traffic. After descending and nearing the base, Brand slowed the Hunter down to 180 knots after 26 minutes and selected gear down; the action was shortly followed by a gentle thump and three green lights came on as the undercarriage locked down.

Three green lights is a good thing. In a sortie a few months earlier, Brand's Hunter had been damaged by ground fire. That time, only two green lights, left and right, came on. 'I tried all the usual tricks to get the nose wheel down, but it was stuck. I landed on the main wheels, holding the nose up as long as possible. The aircraft scraped along gently on its nose, the only thing needing replacing after the incident was the nose-wheel door.'

This time, all was normal. He selected full flap and initiated a continuous left-hand turn onto the final approach. The barn-door flaps and extended undercarriage increased the drag, slowing the aircraft. Brand rolled the aircraft level just as he crossed the threshold, allowing the Hunter to gently kiss the Thornhill runway at 130 knots. Being so light on fuel, Brand did not need to deploy the brake chute – the wheel brakes would suffice. Behind him, Dave Bourhill was already on short final, and John Annan was turning in from a short base leg.

Fortunately, there were no landing-gear problems, burst tyres or other battle-inflicted damage to spoil the landings. As Red Section touched down, Wightman's Whites were waiting at the runway holding point, rearmed, refuelled and keen to return to Chimoio.

Eagerly waiting to receive Red Section was the ground crew, like the pit crew in Formula One racing, ready to refuel and rearm the aircraft. Brand hopped out of the cockpit, had a quick word with the crew chief and then did three things in strict order of priority: he had a pee, grabbed a Coke and Cornish pasty, and then went off to call Air HQ Ops in Salisbury to give them a sitrep. This routine took Brand just 10 minutes, by which time the armourers had replaced the gun pack and recharged the Matra rocket pods. The slowest task was refuelling, which would take another seven minutes – in total, a remarkably quick turnaround time of 17 minutes.

Some 20 minutes after stepping out of their cockpits after the first sortie, Brand, Bourhill and Annan were strapped in their Hunters again, and Red Section was ready to head back to Chimoio. The aircraft took to the sky just as Norman Walsh and Brian Robinson were lifting off from the admin base in the repaired command helicopter.

The Hunters would return to Chimoio three more times before the day was out. Four of the seven Hunters would take hits and need repairs. Rich Brand's favourite Hunter 8116 took a hit in the rear fuselage; John Blythe-Wood's machine suffered a hit in the starboard windscreen; Vic Wightman got a hole in the air intake; and Spook Geraty a hit in the gun pack.

38

Centre Wicket

The Centre Wicket phase of the operation signified the start of a thorough search of the camp area. The task was to clear the buildings, recover intelligence material, destroy or recover arms and ammunition, and destroy infrastructure in the Chimoio base. To achieve this, the RLI and SAS men fanned out. Bob MacKenzie's SAS group was assigned the task of clearing Chitepo College and the ZANLA intelligence centre. He tells the story: 'Sweeping through another 150 metres of woods, during which 15 to 20 more terrorists were flushed out and killed, my patrol reached ZANLA's intelligence centre. It comprised 18 grass huts which served as offices, classrooms and storerooms, and although sur- rounded by more trenches, they had been abandoned.'

A group of MacKenzie's men called him over to an open-air class- room beneath the forest canopy, which had taken a stick of bombs from a Canberra, killing, it seemed, all 60 student political commissars. This was part of Chitepo College, the central unit for training ZANU's commissars to operate in Rhodesia. Only the brightest military-trained cadres were selected for the intensive preparation here.

'Blackboards blown over by the blast carried drawings of AK-47 rifles and terrain sketches, and the students' notebooks were filled with the wisdom of Chairman Mao.' The air strikes had clearly caused heavy damage throughout Chimoio. MacKenzie praised the air effort: '[T]ogether with those killed by rifle fire, some 600 dead guerrillas were counted in the headquarters area alone.'

Then MacKenzie had a lucky escape. Brian Robinson ordered him to take a patrol to the ZANLA vehicle-maintenance depot, about a kilo- metre away. There they found several vehicles, including buses, Scania trucks and luxury cars for Mugabe and his commanders. After taking a pickup truck to use as transport, the SAS men blew the garage and its contents to bits. Armed with the nice white ZANLA Peugeot pickup truck, MacKenzie and his patrol toured the anti-aircraft sites to recover the DShK 12.7-mm guns, which would prove useful in Rhodesia.

Acutely aware that they might be mistaken for ZANLA in the white patrol vehicle, MacKenzie called as many pilots as he could to let them know that the white pickup was friendly. The message clearly did not reach everyone:

> About halfway along, I was alarmed to hear two Hawker Hunter pilots talking on the net about a group of terrs escaping in a white truck; they were about to turn in and 'fire them up' ... I was anxiously shouting 'stop, stop, stop!' into the handset and getting ready to abandon the truck, when a powerful transmission broke into the net, ordering the Hunters not to attack.
>
> The new voice belonged to General G.P. Walls, ComOps commander, who was monitoring the battle from a specially equipped command C-47 Dakota orbiting inside Rhodesian airspace. I felt a strong surge of relief, then another of warmth and respect for the general, who obviously was paying attention to the details of the battle into which he had sent his men.

As the battle subsided, it was time to bring in the SB men to identify the bodies of senior ZANLA commanders and sift through vast amounts of documents to see what was worth taking back to Rhodesia for deeper analysis. Keith Samler, his boss, Mike Edden, and Ken Milne were taken from the admin base in a G-car escorted by a K-car, obviously in deference to Mike Edden's senior rank of assistant commissioner.

They were dropped on the road just west of the HQ, from where an RLI callsign escorted them to the main complex. Samler had interrogated a number of guerrillas captured inside Rhodesia, which had given him a good mental picture of the layout of the area. But he did not expect what happened next:

> We were approaching a clearing in the bush when somebody said 'down', then I heard a sound I will never ever forget. It was horrific. It sounded like a dozen people tearing up a dozen sheets at the same time, an awful ripping sound. I had no idea we were being shot at by a K-car equipped with four Browning machine guns. One of the soldiers reversed his cap to reveal the day-glow patch, while another yelled 'stop, stop!' over the radio. Thank goodness it stopped immediately. We recovered ourselves and continued walking to the HQ building area.

The first place Samler searched was a brick hut brimming with sophisticated medical equipment, including scanners, X-ray machines and all sorts of electrical equipment donated by the UN, Oxfam, and the like. Samler recalled:

> I found this totally incongruous in the middle of the African bush, where there was no electricity. As I walked out, I saw Jeremy Strong. He recognised me and yelled, 'Hey, Samler, what the fuck are *you* doing here?' I shouted back that I was minding my own business and asked him what the fuck *he* was doing there. We knew each other well, and had a convivial discussion and then got on with our work, firstly blowing up the medical hut.

Major Jeremy Strong, a Sword of Honour recipient from the Royal Military Academy Sandhurst, commanded the RLI's No. 3 Commando, and had jumped in with Stops 1 and 2. He was second in command of forces on the ground during Op Dingo.

From the medical hut, Samler made his way to the HQ building, to seek out and identify bodies of the ZANLA hierarchy. As he approached the HQ, he took colour footage with his Super 8 movie camera, a brilliant record of New Farm after the initial attack. The main HQ building, the red-roofed former farmhouse, was still standing, but badly damaged internally by Rich Brand's 30-mm cannon fire at H-hour. In the swept gardens nearby, Samler filmed an unexploded Alpha bomb, a clear indication Chris Dixon had also hit his target accurately from his Canberra.

The puzzling thing was a distinct lack of dead bodies in the immediate HQ area – nothing like the scale of death nearby and south of the road in the triangle area. As Samler entered the building, an RLI trooper shinned up a tree outside the HQ and hoisted the Rhodesian flag on a branch, shouting 'just to show who is in command here'.

There were signs that gave the SB men hope that some ZANLA commanders were around. Near the HQ, they found a briefcase belonging to Rex Nhongo, Tongogara's deputy. It was an important item, so much so that Flight Lieutenant Ian Harvey, then the world's most experienced Alouette pilot, was tasked to retrieve the briefcase and personally ensure it got back to Rhodesia. Astonishingly, a rumour that they had got Rex Nhongo swept through the camp faster than the Hunter strikes. But his body was not there.

Inside the HQ building, Samler found a suitcase belonging to Herbert Ushewokunze, a medical doctor, who had recently joined ZANLA. It was stuffed with Rhodesian dollar bills. 'Ushewokunze was the ZANU paymaster, and, thanks to him, I could afford a new set of golf clubs when I got back to Salisbury. The rest went to funding a huge party for the RLI troopies on the operation,' recalls Samler.

The SB team, and everyone else for that matter, were in for a big disappointment, though. There were no bodies or prisoners resembling any of the ZANLA hierarchy – just the cases. 'We proved that Nhongo and the other senior ZANU members were not in the camp when the raid started,' says Samler.

It was Mugabe's lucky day. He and his Dare reChimurenga had switched their routine meeting from Chimoio to Maputo, the Mozambican capital.

Edgar Tekere wrote: 'Later, it became clear that someone had informed the Rhodesians that all the people meeting in Maputo would actually be at Chimoio.'

Had the Dare members been in their conference room, or reviewing the parade from the balcony that morning, Brand's precision strike would undoubtedly have changed history.

One thing became very apparent to the Rhodesians: ZANLA loved the formality of paperwork. Hundreds of thousands of documents were now flying around in the convection breeze caused by the burning huts. Although the SB men found many very important ZANLA documents, there was one that particularly aroused Samler's interest: a report on the findings of a FRELIMO board of inquiry into the Selous Scouts' raid on Nyadzonia. This report confirmed what was well known – Nyadzonia was indeed a ZANLA camp, housing trained and trainee guerrillas.

Their work now complete at the HQ area, the SB team were choppered to the Chitepo College and intelligence complex, where Captain Bob MacKenzie had piles of documents waiting for them. It was already 16:00, yet there was so much still to do.

Norman Walsh ordered Petter-Bowyer to be flown into the target area to assess the effectiveness of the air weapons, particularly the Alpha bombs. Although the troops had accounted for the majority of the enemy killed, the Alpha bombs had wreaked havoc where ZANLA personnel were caught in the open, especially among those who were bunched together. The weapons developer and admin base commander was in for a shock. PB recalled: 'An airman's war tends to be detached. Even seeing CTs [communist terrorists] running and going down under fire seemed remote from the air. Counting holes in dummy targets at Kutanga Range was one thing. To see the same weapons' effects on human beings is quite another. I saw more than I bargained for and the experience shook me to the very core of my being.'

PB was much relieved when it was time to pull out – an airman feels like a fish out of water on the ground with bullets flying about.

Back in Salisbury at New Sarum Airbase, all the jets but one were back under covers. Squadron Leader Steve Kesby reflected on the long day: 'It was a very hectic and sad day for the Vampires.'

39

Sleepless in Chimoio

Time seemed to fly at supersonic speed for Norman Walsh and Brian Robinson. It was already approaching 17:00 and three of the remaining milestones stood no chance of being ticked off: Leg Break (thorough search of camp); Fast Ball (withdrawal of troops from target area); and Off Spin (all troops clear of Mozambique).

Robinson had obtained permission from Peter Walls to withdraw half of the troops and leave the remainder in a defensive ring at the centre of the target area for the night. The thorough search could then recommence at first light.

At the admin base, all 32 helicopters were on the ground, ready to fly back to Rhodesia. Having all the helicopters on the deck in Mozambique at the same time, including the Polo helicopters borrowed from South Africa, was something ComOps had prohibited. The original plan had been changed, however, to cope with events, and as it was pretty clear that ZANLA had been well and truly beaten at Chimoio, the risk of a counter-attack was low. Some helicopters stayed at the admin base. The rest of the armada departed as night approached, ducking low cloud to land at Lake Alexander for refuelling and then on to Grand Reef, near Umtali.

Second Lieutenant Neill Jackson of the RLI Support Commando, which had been on standby at Grand Reef to provide Dingo reinforcements, remembers seeing the helicopters return:

> Later that afternoon, as the action at Chimoio was winding down, I was sent to Umtali to buy cold beer for the returning SAS and RLI troops.
>
> I remember being in the bar of the hotel on the Harare side of Christmas Pass when one of the local barflies called everyone outside onto the veranda to witness an amazing spectacle unfolding on the horizon. As we tumbled out of the bar to see what he was so excited about, he pointed to a long row of twinkling red lights moving from right to left. Much speculation ensued as to what these strange lights could be, with the usual suggestions of UFOs, monster

fireflies, and the like. I felt that I had to put the poor fellows out of their misery, and explained that they were actually helicopters returning from Lake Alexander to Grand Reef after an operation. 'Nonsense!' proclaimed the initial spotter. 'We don't have that many choppers in our entire air force!'

The sight of the helicopter fleet, red strobe lights flashing in the twilight, was something to behold. Those on the ground at Grand Reef would never forget it, and it even brought the odd tear to the eye. But Zulu 1 was not over yet. There were troops spending an uncomfortable night in the heart of the ZANLA complex and more at the admin base. This meant that the priority for Norman Walsh and Brian Robinson that evening was to come up with a plan for the next day.

As the sun sank below the Rhodesian Highlands in the distance, activity at Chimoio started to slow down and the men thought about night positions. The officers now focused on bringing order to the situation and getting their men together.

Everyone knew that quite a few guerrillas had escaped the envelopment, either through the eastern side of the box or under the descending paratroops. There was the obvious threat that the ZANLA remnants might come back to their smouldering camp in an organised manner. The officers chose a heavily treed area near Chaminuka Camp, at the centre of the triangle, to set up an all-round defensive perimeter. The RLI would guard one half of the circle, and the SAS the other. Once settled, the exhausted soldiers tucked into their ratpacks (food ration packs), wolfing down bully beef and hard biscuits. The guard would be rotated through the night, allowing the men time to get much-needed sleep.

One RLI machine gunner recalled: 'It was a dark night, and during my guard shift I heard a cry from the SAS side. It was a sleeping SAS soldier. One of three gooks passing by had stepped on his head. The SAS sentry fired his RPD immediately, killing two gooks; the third escaped. I was very alert for the rest of my guard shift.'

Not far from this incident, Bob MacKenzie was falling asleep. Earlier that afternoon, he had found a locked Samsonite suitcase, which he believed was the suitcase full of money already discovered by Samler, but at the time he was too busy fighting ZANLA to think about opening it. 'I drifted off to sleep dreaming of a suitcase full of money, often interrupted by gunfire from all around Chimoio as surviving guerrillas battled each other, or shadows. I would find that case first thing in the morning.'

The defence perimeter was very effective. During the night, another 60 ZANLA perished, mostly on the RLI side of the perimeter. The main priority of D-day + 1 was to move the men out of Mozambique. General Walls wanted that completed by midday at the latest.

The G-car helicopters of Pink Section would leave Grand Reef at first light to be in position at the admin base and begin the final troop withdrawal. Norman Walsh ordered a pair of Canberras and three Hunters to be over the target by 05:15 to provide top cover and respond should FRELIMO decide to send tanks and troops up from Chimoio Town. At Thornhill and New Sarum, the ground crews were up at 03:30 to prepare the aircraft. Rich Brand decided to hand the leadership for the day over to his deputy, Flight Lieutenant Vic Wightman.

Wightman would lead Red Section with his faithful wingman, Spook Geraty; John Annan made up the trio. Wightman set the walk time for 04:20, when it was still pitch dark in Gwelo. At 04:40 precisely, just as dawn was breaking, he applied full throttle, and the FGA9 started accelerating down the runway. Red Section joined the Canberra pair of Green Section over the target at 05:45. The mere sight of these warplanes would make any ZANLA guerrilla think twice about attacking the Rhodesians.

The main area of the ZANLA camp was quiet, so the early-morning focus switched to the recruits' camp, seven kilometres away, where stragglers were firing at the aircraft. Walsh ordered Red Section to attack with frantan and rockets, followed by a Canberra attack over the heavily wooded area along the Mombezi River.

A sweep through the recruits' area, performed later by Captain Grahame Wilson's group, revealed that 70 were dead out of a total in the camp of 700, and many were heavily wounded, judging by the trails of blood. On D-day, only Vampires and K-cars had attacked this target, as it was a second priority. Unfortunately for the Rhodesians, at least 80 per cent of the ZANLA trainees in the camp would survive to fight another day.

Bob MacKenzie took a small patrol to find the pile of documents his men had stashed away and, of course, the mysterious suitcase.

Declaring to his men they were about to be rich, MacKenzie opened the first latch with his bayonet: 'I paused for a second, then lifted the lid. "Bugger! Nothing but bloody papers," I said, shaking the case ... With the shake, though, a new Rolex watch bounced out and into my hand ... only a low-end Rolex. It nevertheless brought more than a month's pay when I sold it in Salisbury a few weeks later.'

Little did MacKenzie know that Samler had already found the suitcase full of money that belonged to the ZANLA paymaster, Herbert Ushewokunze.

The rest of the morning was spent gathering documents and destroying vast quantities of arms, ammunition and other supplies. The best equipment, such as AK-47 rifles, RPD sub-machine guns and 12.7-mm anti-aircraft guns, was taken back to Rhodesia. But there was only so much the helicopters could carry; the rest had to be destroyed, including more than 500 semi-automatic SKS rifles.

All this took time, and, once again, the plan was flexed, with the last helicopter crossing the border back into Rhodesia just after 16:00 on 24 November 1977. But it wasn't quite over: Captain Bob MacKenzie had laid down radio-activated marker flares for a Canberra to drop bombs on the complex that night, some with delayed fuses. The Canberra run effectively brought a close to Operation Dingo, Zulu 1.

General Peter Walls summed up Zulu 1 in a call from the command Dak as it headed back to Salisbury: 'At worst, the job was worthwhile; at best, it may have been bloody excellent.'

But there was no time to celebrate. An even more difficult task lay ahead: attacking ZANLA's Tembue base deep within Mozambique, almost on the Malawian border. This was Operation Dingo, Zulu 2.

Part 3

Zulu 2: Tembue

40

Lightning over the Saudi desert

'Mayday, Mayday, Mission 262 ejecting.'

Former Royal Rhodesian Air Force pilot Charles 'Vic' Wightman had lost control of his English Electric Lightning supersonic interceptor over the Saudi Arabian desert. He was demonstrating an intercept on another Lightning, watched on radar by a senior Saudi government minister at the Khamis Mushayt Airbase. Wightman recalled:

> After take-off, I noticed the ventral tank was not feeding, probably a fuel-no-air valve sticking. So I applied positive and negative G to unstick it, plus a few slow rolls. This didn't sort the ventral feed, but seemed to induce, first, a hydraulic 1 failure, followed shortly by hydraulic 2, and on came the clangers and lights of the central warning system. The elevator accumulators exhausted almost immediately, but pitch control was possible using differential engine power, so I continued the climb to gain space and time to sort the problem. At about 26 000 feet, the aileron accumulators exhausted and the aircraft rolled over into an uncontrolled, rapidly accelerating dive.

With the airspeed indicator rising sharply, Wightman knew he risked very serious injury if he ejected at supersonic speed, so it was not a difficult decision: pull the ejection handle now.

> It all happened so fast. There was a terrible rush of cold wind, then I was free of the aircraft, but the seat and I were in a rapid spin, making me feel awfully nauseous. I tried to stop the spin, and even opened my visor to overcome the overwhelming feeling of wanting to vomit. All of a sudden, the chute opened. Below was a wonderful view of the Saudi Arabian desert, and the long canopy ride down to terra firma gave me ample time to work out what I would say to the board of inquiry.

As Wightman was nearing the ground in his inaugural parachute ride, he was alarmed to see that the numerous darker patches in the desert sand were in fact jagged rocks.

There was a strong wind and I was swinging like a pendulum below the chute. I was so worried about the rocks that I forgot all my training and landed with my legs wide apart, slamming my face into the ground, causing a bloody nose. But I felt euphoric – I had survived.

As I stood up, I saw a Saudi woman, looking like a full bottle of Guinness in the middle of the desert. When she saw me, she got such a fright that she threw her hands in the air and ran off shrieking. I think she must have thought I was the second coming of someone or another.

I walked up to the top of the nearest mound to set up my search and rescue beacon. When I turned to go back down and collect my other survival toys, I realised I could not walk; my ankles were damaged. So I sat there like a dummy. I wasn't even able to put a mosquito net over my head! Then a man in a truck arrived and offered me a lift, which I declined, telling him, 'No problem, all my shamwaris will be here soon.' But it was a quite a while before my shamwari Farouk arrived in his rescue helicopter. He couldn't land next to me, so crew members had to pick me up and lug me to Farouk's helicopter, where they unceremoniously dumped me inside.

Vic's ankles, nose and pride healed and he continued flying the 'frightening Lightning' until, a few years later, his wife, Shirley, unexpectedly fell pregnant with their fourth child. Saudi was not a great place to be for childbirth, so Vic resigned from the Saudi Air Force and later that year, 1973, the Wightmans decided to head back home to Rhodesia.

Vic had joined the RRAF in 1958. He was posted to No. 11 Short Service Unit with the likes of Ian Harvey, Rich Brand and Tol Janeke. In many ways, Vic was not a typical air force pilot. He liked challenging the system, hated wearing shoes, disliked routine and got airsick. But he got his wings, and after the two-year contract was over, he left for England to join the RAF, where he spent time flying Canberras and Gnat trainer aircraft before volunteering to teach Saudi pilots to fly the Lightning.

Vic rejoined the RhAF and flew Hawker Hunters in No. 1 Squadron. Two years later, he spent time instructing 'snotty-nosed students to fly the Impala and Vampire'. Just before Operation Dingo, Wightman returned to No. 1 Squadron as Rich Brand's deputy. He would be the first pilot to deliver a new weapon on an external target – an anti-personnel bomb called flechettes.

Flechettes

Peter Petter-Bowyer had studied a French anti-personnel rocket system that delivered thousands of small darts (*fléchettes* in French) at high speed. This weapon was eventually banned by international treaty, mainly because the darts tended to tumble, making awful exit wounds. 'What never made sense to me,' recalls PB, 'was that ordinary rifle bullets caused more damage and were just as lethal – yet they were not banned.'

PB experimented unofficially with a locally made version of the flechettes in 1964, launching a canister armed with the darts from a Provost, but the project was shelved. Twelve years later, having completed his work on the highly effective Golf bomb project, PB applied himself to completing the new weapon.

With his usual passion for simplifying things, PB had the darts made from headless six-inch nails, onto which were fitted moulded fins made from recycled plastic. They were packed into a single dispenser that held 4500 darts. Being dropped at high speed – 450 knots was ideal – increased the weapon's effectiveness. There was only one aircraft capable of achieving this speed: the Hawker Hunter.

PB had tests done from a Hunter in the typical gun or frantan profile, a 30-degree dive. 'The tests proved that the new weapon was accurate and highly effective. Released in pairs at 450 knots resulted in an immensely dense cloud of flechettes flying a shallow trajectory, which made survival of those exposed within the 900 metres by 70 metres strike area impossible.'

The effect was equivalent to 340 Browning machine guns firing simultaneously. PB had developed yet another remarkable weapon.

Norman Walsh was not keen for the new weapon to be used during the Chimoio raid, however, because the UN High Commission for Refugees was bound to visit the complex after the raid. Because Tembue was so far off the beaten track, however, such a visit was unlikely, so Walsh approved their use for the second raid, Zulu 2. Vic Wightman would deliver the first flechette canisters on a ZANLA target in Mozambique.

41

Tembue by train

The ZANLA Tete Province HQ at Tembue comprised three complexes along the Luia River, at the base of the Angonia Plateau of northern Mozambique, near the picturesque hamlet of Catane. The hamlet sported its own 900-metre grass runway, registered as Tembue airstrip, not to be confused with Tembue Town, also known as Chifunde, which is 12 kilometres to the north.

The Rhodesians knew Catane well, having visited it many times to liaise with the Portuguese military in the pre-FRELIMO days. It was only 25 kilometres from Bene, another place often frequented by the Rhodesian military in the days of Portuguese rule. Bene was known for the stench of the open latrines; it was also where the Rhodesians had first set eyes on a K-car belonging to the Portuguese. The Tembue airstrip is easy to find by air, as it lies near Serra Techecunda, a near-perfect conical mountain known by some as the Tembue Tit.

The three ZANLA camps at Tembue were made up of 400 mud-and-thatch buildings situated between the Bene–Tembue road and the Luia River. Camp A, a basic training camp for recruits, was isolated, lying six kilometres north of the other camps, not unlike the recruits' camp at Chimoio. Camp B was where ZANLA taught specialist skills to already trained guerrillas. Camp C, just less than three kilometres to the south of Camp B, housed fully trained guerrillas ready to deploy into Rhodesia. Each camp had a series of anti-aircraft pits surrounded by thick timber walls; these were dotted around a vast number of defensive trenches and bomb shelters.

In the aftermath of the Chimoio raid, it was not inconceivable that FRELIMO would decide to react this time, although Tembue was much more remote and isolated than Chimoio. The nearest threat to the Rhodesians was a platoon at Bene, 20 minutes away by road, and a company of 150 soldiers at Tembue Town, 30 minutes away. Any other potential FRELIMO reaction would take longer. There was a battalion at Fingoe, three hours away, and a FRELIMO company at Farancungo. The biggest threat was a reaction from the FRELIMO brigade HQ at Tete, six hours away by road. As a precaution, the roads leading to the target would be mined, ambushed and a mortar site set up within range.

The problem posed by Tembue was its distance. At 200 kilometres from Chiswiti, the final staging post inside Rhodesia, it was well out of range for a fully laden Alouette. Besides the admin base near Tembue, another refuelling site was needed on the way, ideally about halfway between Chiswiti and the target. The halfway mark, however, was bang in the middle of the widest part of Lago de Cahora Bassa (Lake Cahora Bassa), a large hydroelectric reservoir and dam holding back the Zambezi River.

Norman Walsh pondered the options. The lake's shoreline was very rugged and too close to habitation. Landing beyond the lake was out of the question because that would push the Alouettes beyond a safe fuel reserve, not a good idea over dry land and even less attractive over water. A secure open piece of ground south of Cahora Bassa was needed. Walsh knew the area well from his earlier days as boss of No. 7 Squadron, when he often flew into Mozambique for meetings with the Portuguese and to fight FRELIMO. He needed a secure area away from populated areas and roads, but within an hour's flying time of the target at Tembue. Walsh pored over the aerial photographs and maps, and soon realised exactly where the best place was.

About 40 kilometres north of the Rhodesian border in Mozambique was an ancient plateau, rising 700 feet above its surrounds. This tabletop feature ran broadly west–east, and measured 26 kilometres from end to end. Over the ages, it had eroded into an irregular shape, resembling a long-necked cat when seen from directly above at high altitude. When viewed from the ground in Rhodesia, the feature resembled a giant train heading west. The two parts forming the cat's tail were the engine and coal tender, followed by irregular carriages ending with the cat's head, resembling the guard's van. Rhodesian pilots flying in the north-east on a clear day would often use the 'Train' as a navigation aid.

Being flat-topped, the plateau should make a good helicopter refuelling point, thought Walsh. It was exactly one hour from Tembue for a loaded Alouette, and only 21 minutes from the home staging base at Chiswiti. Another important factor was that the Train was inaccessible by land vehicle, making it a safe haven in the heart of hostile territory.

'That's where my first admin base will be,' said Walsh as he planted a mapping pin, giving the cat a left eye, or, when looking at it from ground level, forming the roof of the guard's van.

Walsh chose Wing Commander Rex Taylor as his 'train driver', or, more accurately, as the 'guard'. Taylor had joined the second SSU as a cadet pilot in March 1952 along with Frank Mussell and 10 others. After the two-year contract was over, Taylor, together with Vic Paxton and Barry Stephens, joined the Kenya Police Air Wing. Both Taylor's colleagues would perish in air accidents in Kenya. Taylor rejoined the RRAF in 1957, later becoming a founder member and instructor of No. 7 (Alouette) Squadron in 1962.

Rex Taylor loved the outdoors, nature and fishing. He also liked a bit of comfort in the bush. 'In the late 1970s, I was "retreaded" out of a cosy office back to the cockpit of an Alouette III and fed into the Fireforce operating out of Grand Reef.'

After deploying a stick of troops during Fireforce operations, the G-cars would land nearby and await developments. But there was no tea served in the middle of the bush, so Taylor came up with a plan:

> Legend has it that the army marches on its tea, but I was sure that I could make a brew which could be drunk, not marched upon. I acquired a gas stove and a cardboard box. From our caravan camping kit I borrowed the aluminium teapot and four plastic cups. The ration packs yielded tea, sugar and milk powder. The box shielded the gas stove and teapot from the wind, and the cups were painless to drink from, unlike the metal ones in issue.

It was no surprise that the Fireforce pilots and reserve sticks of infantry-men would gather around Taylor's helicopter for tea. 'Our tea tin shared the rigours and dangers of a gentleman's war, camaraderie, banter and real bullets too.'

One of the first things Rex Taylor loaded into the Alouette about to ferry him from Mount Darwin to the Train was the Tea Tin Mark II and some fresh milk. Five Alouettes took off in the late afternoon, on the eve of the raid, bound for the Train, carrying Taylor and stopping at Chiswiti to pick up the RLI protection troops. Their role was to prepare the base for helicopter landings and a fuel drop early the next morning. There would, unfortunately, be no time for tea that evening.

'The photographs had shown the landing zone to be a flat area covered in grass,' recalled Taylor. 'My first jolt came as we approached to land. In the fading light, the LZ seemed too good to be true, but as we got closer, what had seemed like grass suddenly became a grove of thick saplings. None of the choppers were able to land, and the whole company, plus a trembling, grey-haired airman, deplaned by jumping the last six feet into and among the stiff trees.'

Fortunately, no one was hurt, and Taylor and the RLI troops got down to clearing three hectares of bush as the full moon was rising. 'I paced out the smallest individual landing circles that I dared, while my army colleague split his men into small groups to cut the clearings with pangas.'

The bush was thick, making the going tough. It took the men, including Taylor, until three in the morning to cut sufficient clearings for the helicopter fleet. Taylor's 'army colleague' was none other than Major Simon Haarhoff, who had successfully formed the north side of the box with his 2 Commando heli-borne troops at Chimoio two days earlier.

Haarhoff saw the bush-clearing effort in a slightly different light than Taylor: 'As soon as the troops started to clear the LZ, it became apparent that our equipment was woefully inadequate for the task. Army-issue pangas with blunt edges were just not able to cut the branches of the bushes, let alone the trees.'

Eventually, Haarhoff ordered his men to use a well-known panga substitute, the FN infantry rifle. He explains: 'The 7.62-mm FN "chain-saw" was brought into action, and a number of the larger trees and bushes were cleared using this cunning device.' Then it was time to sleep. Taylor recalled:

Each man found a hollow where he could crawl into his sleeping bag. I found what seemed like a game trail and spread my tense body into it, making a little scrape for my hip, as I had been taught in my scouting days. The advice was not sound – my hip seemed to find only jagged stones on the edge of the hollow! We were all probably too tired to sleep, but maybe those battle-hard toughies were made of sterner stuff and slept like the babes they really were. Ominous clouds had been threatening our little detachment and it wasn't long before the heavens opened. Luckily, the storm just missed us, but my game trail revealed itself as a natural drain. I shifted out of the trickling water and fell asleep again.

After barely an hour's sleep, the exhausted 'train gang' were up and about at the first hint of dawn, ready to receive the fuel drop. At Mount Darwin, Brian Robinson and Norman Walsh were anxiously waiting to hear the code word 'Knock-Down', confirming the base on the Train was operational. Taylor duly obliged: 'My first act of war was a one-word transmission confirming that the weather was clear and we were ready for the fuel drop.'

Taylor barely had time to boil the water for tea before the sound of radial engines broke the early-morning silence. The fuel drop was very accurate. As Taylor observed:

> We didn't have time to admire the accuracy of the drop because, by my watch, the choppers were now starting engines and engaging their rotors. The eager RLI beavers rolled and wiggled two drums to each LZ and stood them up just off centre and forward of each clearing's midpoint. The distance was such that if each Alouette landed with its starboard wheel alongside the drum, its vulnerable tail rotor would be within the safety of the clearing. More than that, the tech would simply have to open a drum, slip in the refuelling hose, and before the rotors had come to a halt, the chopper would be nearly full.
>
> The defining tactic was that one soldier in each section donned a shiny, starched white dustcoat and stood in the middle of each clearing. In the gloom, the chopper pilots were able to pick up an LZ and land after homing onto our white-coated 'pointsmen'.

Taylor's eye for detail would make a big difference on the Train.

First Round

The nine cricket code words marking the major milestones on Zulu 1 were substituted by 10 boxing terms for Zulu 2, the extra milestone being the Train. The Zulu 2 milestones were First Round, Knock-Down, Square Ring, Last Leg, Punch Leg, Tight Rope, Corner Seat, Seconds In, Fat Lip and Broken Nose.

For Zulu 2, the Hunters would operate from Salisbury, which was 112 kilometres, or 16 minutes, closer to the target than Thornhill. The reconnaissance Lynxes and all helicopters would leave from FAF 4, the air force base at Mount Darwin. After the paradrop, the Dakotas would land at Mount Darwin to be on standby to drop reinforcements, should the need arise.

The first of three helicopter refuelling stops, the equivalent of Lake Alexander for the Chimoio raid, would be set up at the Chiswiti army base airstrip, 18 kilometres from the Mozambican border. The base lay below the edge of the Mavuradonha Mountains, the eastern end of the great rain-creating Zambezi Escarpment, beyond which the ground falls away gradually into north-western Mozambique. The single 700-metre dirt runway would allow the helicopters to land on either edge of the airstrip to refuel, although the arrivals would be staggered to avoid congestion.

A load of 240 drums of Jet A-1 helicopter fuel would be trucked to Chiswiti the afternoon before the raid. No. 7 Squadron technicians and spares for the helicopters would arrive by road in the afternoon, accompanied by RLI protection troops, who would secure the base and surrounding area from potential attack by local ZANLA forces.

The first milestone was reached at sunset on P minus 1, the day before the raid. The RLI officer in charge of Chiswiti sent a radio signal to Brian Robinson, now in Mount Darwin: 'First Round' was complete. With satisfaction, Robinson ticked off the first of the 10 milestones.

42

Mount Darwin, P minus 1

Mount Darwin is a small town 156 kilometres north of Salisbury. The actual mountain, named after Charles Darwin, lies 10 kilometres south-east of the town. It was widely believed that this was where the Portuguese Jesuit priest Gonçalo da Silveira converted the Monomotapa king to Christianity in 1561, and was subsequently garrotted when Muslim traders persuaded the monarch that the priest was a witch.

In the twentieth century, Mount Darwin grew into an agricultural and mining centre. The town took on a military function after the outbreak of war in 1972. It was from the airbase there, known as FAF 4, that the Fireforce, working closely with the Selous Scouts, dealt a massive blow to ZANLA as Operation Hurricane got into full swing in the area.

FAF 4 would now be the launch pad for an armada of helicopters mounting the largest ever attack on the source of the Hurricane guerrillas, ZANLA's HQ in Tete Province.

On the afternoon of Thursday 24 November, or P minus 1, New Sarum was again a hive of frenetic activity as the helicopters that had positioned in Salisbury prepared to fly to Mount Darwin, while the remainder came from FAF 5 at Mtoko. The first section of four K-cars, led by Squadron Leader Harold Griffiths, left Salisbury at 17:50, followed five minutes later by the remaining four, led by Flight Lieutenant Ian Harvey, with Norman Walsh tagging along in his command heli. The remaining helicopters followed at five-minute intervals in groups of five or six, each flying a slightly different route.

A news blackout meant that people in and around Salisbury were blissfully unaware that the Chimoio attack had even taken place. But anyone near Salisbury Airport would know something big was happening: it was impossible to hide so many departing helicopters. Where were they going? Zambia perhaps? Nobody knew.

As the last gaggle of G-cars, led by Geoff Oborne, lifted off and headed north, Rich Brand's Hunters were approaching Runway 06 at Salisbury from the south, completing their 16-minute positioning flight from Thornhill. The seven Hawker Hunter jets nosed their way through the perimeter gate and parked on the apron. The camouflaged aircraft added a menacing look to New Sarum. The Hunters would operate from here until Zulu 2 was over.

FAF 4 was a big forward airfield equipped with a 1 200-metre bitumen runway and lots of hard standing space for aircraft parking, as well as accommodation for the crews. However, the base had never hosted more than eight helicopters at one time, and 32 machines coming through would strain the system. In typical RhAF fashion, a plan was made to ensure there was enough fuel, food and, importantly, a good supply of ice-cold beers.

Just before 18:00, the first helicopters began to arrive, and they kept landing until all were parked according to the marshals' directions. Five helicopters of Yellow Section refuelled immediately and took off to drop Wing Commander Rex Taylor and the 16-man RLI protection force on the Train.

It was originally planned that this deployment would be done at first light on P-day, but after the experience of Chimoio, Norman Walsh decided that the advantage of extra time to prepare the LZ outweighed the risks of deploying men in Mozambique on the eve of the raid.

It was a wonderful late-November evening in Mount Darwin. The deep-red sun was setting spectacularly in the west as the full moon just started showing itself in the east. Many crewmen, having finished their preparations, were relaxing outside, sipping beers in the brightening moonlight. Soon, slightly to the right of a large, bald, mineral-rich hill, a landmark north of Mount Darwin known as Chitse, appeared the dancing, red flashing lights of the returning Yellow Section helicopters. Gradually, the whine of the jet turbines could be heard, resonated by the chopping of the main rotors and the buzz of the tail rotors.

In the very far distance, lightning illuminated massive cumulonimbus clouds as a storm broke somewhere over northern Mozambique. It all looked and felt surreal, but there was serious work to be done early the next morning. By 21:00, the bar was closed and the base had gone quiet; everyone was trying to get as much sleep as possible.

43

P-day

Squadron Leader Harold Griffiths – and his helicopter – started early on P-day at Mount Darwin. At precisely 05:55, two hours and five minutes ahead of H-hour, Griffiths led the eight K-cars and the command heli to the assembly point at Chiswiti, the first refuelling stop. The G-cars of Pink Section followed them.

There was low cloud on the uplands north of Mount Darwin, but this time, Griffiths skirted it easily. The flight took 20 minutes. The helicopters landed in two long lines on either side of the runway, each next to neat stacks of upright fuel drums. Chiswiti was soon a maelstrom of dust as the Alouettes landed and taxied to their allocated points under the guidance of marshals. The sound of dozens of put-put fuel pumps filled the sound vacuum left after the engines were shut down. Half an hour later, Griffiths signalled the start of the next leg for the K-cars and command ship – to the Train.

After the helicopter armada had skirted the eastern edge of the Mavuradonha Mountains, the ground fell away and the bush became khaki and sparse – this was the dry side of the escarpment. The sky was clear, and in the distance the Train dominated the horizon. To the left was the pronounced engine and coal tender of the plateau, and to the right was the guard's van, where Rex Taylor and his men were eagerly waiting to receive the helicopters.

Meanwhile, back at New Sarum, paratroopers were boarding the Dakotas. Neill Jackson remembers:

> There were 48 men from Support Commando, divided into two stop groups. Major Nigel Henson commanded Stop 1, and I was in command of the 24-man Stop 2. I distinctly recall General Walls helping me with one of my parachute straps and murmuring a quiet word of encouragement before he moved off among the rest of the men, stopping to lend a hand here and have a short chat there. It was encouraging to know that the supreme military commander cared enough to be mingling with his men as they kitted up for an external parachute drop.

Soon Bob d'Hotman was again leading the six Paradaks of Silver Section down the runway at Salisbury. It was 06:30; the flight time to the target was one and a half hours, a long ride for the paratroops. Once again, the command Dak followed Silver Section.

The sequence of events would be similar to Zulu 1, except there would be no DC-8 jetliner as a decoy, and the Hunters would be the last aircraft to leave Salisbury, at 07:25. Rich Brand would again open the attack at H-hour, but this time there was no HQ building housing VIPs, so Red 1 and Red 2 would attack anti-aircraft sites at Camp B, while Vic Wightman and Spook Geraty hit the parade square at Camp C with Petter-Bowyer's new weapon, the flechettes.

Blue Section would pounce on Camp A, the recruits' camp six kilometres north of the main targets, while Red 3 remained overhead as top cover. The Canberras would attack 30 seconds later from the west, across the Luia River. Steve Kesby's Vampires would join the Hunters in silencing anti-aircraft guns, attacking buildings and providing fire-power support for the paratroops.

Everything went to plan – except for the Vampires. Steve Kesby could not start his FB9 Vampire, despite the huge efforts of the ground crew. He recalled the tense moment: 'I passed the lead to Varky and said that I would catch up by using the standby aircraft. The strike formation taxied out and I hurriedly strapped in and started the new aircraft. As I was taxiing out, I saw the other aircraft taking off. This whole episode caused a time delay.'

The ancient jets were four minutes behind schedule. This worrying news was relayed to the command heli via the command Dak. Norman Walsh and Brian Robinson decided not to flex H-hour. The attack would go in as planned, with Blythe-Wood's Blues restriking Camp A with their 30-mm cannon and rockets until the Vampires arrived, or when their Hunters ran out of ammo.

Varkevisser pushed hard and managed to reduce the delay to just less than two minutes, and the Vampires got stuck in as soon as they arrived at Tembue. But it wasn't Kesby's day.

'Venom Lead, Alpha 2, do you read?' This was Kesby, still chasing the Vampire pack, trying to establish communications with Varky, the stand-in leader. Kesby could hear other pilots talking, but no one would talk to him. He wiggled the radio jack plug behind his shoulder, recycled the radio and called a few more times. He then knew what he didn't want to know: the standby machine had a total radio transmission failure. A highly frustrated Kesby was forced to abandon his attack and return to base. Losing one of his pilots two days earlier and now this mishap made for a very unhappy squadron leader.

But Kesby wasn't the only one to have difficulties: one of the K-cars had a problem starting at Chiswiti, which delayed the departure by just over 10 minutes. However, Rex Taylor's preparation of the Train would enable the helicopters to refuel quickly, which more than made up for the lost time. The armada left the Train on time for the long haul to Tembue.

Peter Petter-Bowyer paid tribute to Taylor's efforts: 'Rex and his men had positioned the previous day to receive a large supply of fuel by paradrop. With plenty of time to spare, the fuel drums had been set out neatly throughout the open ground of the staging base, and all parachutes were stacked out of harm's way. Everything seemed unhurried as the helicopters refuelled in the crisp early-morning air.'

PB, however, would not have the luxury of time. Once again, he had to set up an admin base close to the target as the DC-7 was arriving with fuel and protection troops.

At 07:05, the eight K-cars, Norman Walsh's command helicopter and PB's admin base helicopter left the Train for the target. They reached it after nearly an hour, just as the jet strikes and restrikes were complete. The G-cars of Pink Section would leave a few moments later and fly straight to the admin base. There were no troops to carry to target, so Pink's role was primarily ferrying additional supplies to and extracting men and equipment from Tembue. The South African Polo helicopters of Yellow Section would ply the Chiswiti–Train route, carrying additional supplies to the Train and bringing men and equipment back to Rhodesia.

Keith Samler and Ken Milne, again with their boss, Mike Edden, boarded a G-car at Chiswiti and flew to the Train as part of a loose formation of 12 helicopters. Samler, armed with his Super 8 movie camera, recorded some great footage, especially of Alouettes arriving at Chiswiti in swirling dust in the early-morning light, and some dramatic shots from his starboard side of eight Alouettes in line abreast, rising and falling in the gentle early-morning turbulence.

Barely eight minutes after leaving the Train, the helicopters reached the shores of Lake Cahora Bassa. Although much smaller than its upstream cousin, Lake Kariba, in terms of surface area, Cahora Bassa's hydroelectric capacity is greater. Commissioned in 1975, two years before the operation, the lake was still filling. After the long, dry winter, the level had receded by about 10 metres, exposing huge eroded banks and stark islands leached of all their topsoil and flora, which appeared almost white in the morning sun. The most striking feature of the new lake was the vast quantity of partially submerged forests, which would petrify over time and stand as a stark memorial of a bygone era when the Zambezi was just a river here.

This was the first time quite a few men on the Tembue raid had seen Cahora Bassa. It reminded the older ones of when Lake Kariba was first filled in 1960. As the Zambezi River swelled to form Lake Kariba, animals from rhino to lion, antelope to warthog, jackals to tortoises became marooned on shrinking islands, provoking a massive wild-animal rescue programme called Operation Noah, led by Rupert Fothergill. Over 5000 animals were saved and relocated. Here in Mozambique, the last thing on the new FRELIMO government's mind in 1977 was saving animals.

The armada of helicopters, their Matra cannons poking out of open port-side doors, looked menacing and spectacular, reflected in the mill-pond that was once a raging river. As they crossed the lake's northern bank back over land, the calming effect of the water vanished and the serious mood returned. The helicopters had 30 minutes to run to target. High up it was overcast, and there were a few low-level cumulus clouds scudding about, a sure sign that the air was saturated, which virtually guaranteed afternoon thunderstorms.

At the same time, the six Dakotas were just crossing the southern shore of the lake, gaining rapidly on the helicopters. Flight Sergeant Kevin Milligan, this time the parachute jump instructor in charge of the lead Dakota number 7053, flown by Bob d'Hotman, saw Cahora Bassa close up for the first time: 'I moved up to the cockpit and stood behind the pilots, watching as we flew in formation, extremely low over Cahora Bassa. It was a wonderful sight.'

Soon D'Hotman pointed to the helicopters ahead, but Milligan wasn't looking; he was already making his way back to the door area to prepare the paratroops for action. Five minutes later, and looking out of the open Dak door, Milligan saw the Canberras of Green Section whizz by.

Keith Samler, flying with the helicopters of Pink Section, filmed the brown camouflaged Dakotas passing them in a valley. He could clearly see the dispatchers standing in the open doors.

Squadron Leader Rich Brand chose a route for the Hunters that would skirt the Serra Macuacua granite range, which was sufficiently west of the target for them to avoid detection. Brand smiled as he saw the small settlement of Vila Vasco da Gama pass by on his left. Someone in the squadron had given the great navigator's name to Brand as a nickname, a tribute to the squadron leader's navigational skills. A few minutes later, the Hunters headed east, crossing the Rio Capoche as they approached the initial point, a small feature 38 kilometres, or three minutes, north of the target.

At 07:57, Brand broke radio silence as he turned tightly onto a southerly heading: 'Red 1 at IP.' The new track took him straight towards the well-known Tembue Tit landmark, the prominent conical feature that stood 53 seconds north of the target.

As White Section passed the IP, three seconds behind Red Section, Vic Wightman made a terse call: 'White, seven-eight rpm' – a signal to his wingman, Spook Geraty, that he was about to push the throttle forward to 7 800 rpm, almost full power, to accelerate to a higher speed so that they could drop the flechettes at 450 knots, the ideal speed for dart dispersal. Wightman adjusted his course five degrees to the right, checking one final time that the gun sight was set to 'bombs'. By the time they passed the 'Tit', White Section had almost caught up with the Hunters of Red Section, which was now 200 metres to their left. Wightman heard Brand call 'Red 1 target visual' 24 seconds later. Operation Dingo Zulu 2, the attack on ZANLA's Tete headquarters, was about to commence.

White Section's target was Camp C, housing the fully trained guerrillas, which lay three kilometres south of Red Section's target. The expectation was that the insurgents would be lined up on the parade square, an ideal target for the flechettes, provided they were dropped accurately. Wightman scanned his stopwatch. Eleven more seconds, ten, nine, eight ... pull.

'My two great fears,' said Wightman, 'just before pulling up to the perch were, what sort of reception awaits us here and will I see anything I recognise from the photos, the intelligence or the maps? We felt quite invincible in our chariots, so I do admit the latter was the greatest fear – the shame of getting to the target area and then not finding the target, and cocking it all up for the others, was too terrible.'

The fear of 'cocking it up' added adrenalin, sharpening Vic Wightman's focus. As the Hunter rose into the sky, he recognised the target immediately, adjacent to a distinct kink in the Luia River. 'The secret to a good attack is to have the height, speed, power setting and distance from the target all correct at the perch,' says Wightman.

The parameters were all good as he rolled his Hunter left, with Geraty mirroring his leader's move. Soon both Hunters were in an attacking 30-degree dive, heading straight towards the neatly swept parade square set out among the clusters of buildings.

Taking note of the size of the fixed cross in the sights relative to the target, and drawing on his experience, Wightman judged the right moment to stab the bomb-release button on the stick, releasing both canisters of flechettes. He immediately pulled up, back to the perch, quickly switching the sight to 'guns' and checking that two of the four guns were selected. Geraty followed suit, dropping his flechettes on the southern half of the parade square.

The four flechettes were bang on target, sending 18 000 lethal darts, covering an area of 900 metres by 70 metres, across the parade ground – equivalent to the firepower of over 700 Browning machine guns firing simultaneously.

As Wightman rolled his Hunter over to arrest the climb at the perch, he glanced quickly at the target: 'I could see anti-aircraft tracer directed at someone, but the parade ground looked quite deserted.' It was.

Squadron Leader Chris Dixon and his Green Section Canberras already had their bomb doors open, and were closing in fast on Camp C, attacking west to east across the Luia River. Alpha bombs soon bounced over a wide area, and many went beyond the target, which was unavoidable owing to its narrow profile. The after-battle debriefing would conclude that it would have been more effective had the Canberras run south to north. The Hunters dived back and attacked the anti-aircraft positions with cannon or rockets as the Canberras passed through.

John Blythe-Wood and Martin Lowrie pounded the daylights out of Camp A, the recruits' section, which was not a Canberra target. They attacked first with cannon and then switched to rockets, attacked, rose and attacked again, until Justin Varkevisser's Vampires arrived to take over. Herds of trainees were seen running into the thick cover of the Rio Chamacheto, a tributary of the Luia.

Four minutes into the battle, Harold Griffiths called, 'Red Section from K 1, break off, K-cars approaching overhead.' This was the signal for the next phase of the battle; the K-cars would engage their targets as the Paradaks positioned for the drop.

Kevin Milligan recalls: 'The Daks split into three pairs, each pair covering one of three sides. The bombers and strike aircraft were in there doing their deadly work. The green light came on and we began the dispatch. The camp was already in flames from the vicious strikes that had gone in on target. Directly across from us, I could see another Dak with parachutes blossoming below it parallel to our drop.'

The target was long and thin, so the paratroops would have to envelop both Camps B and C. Therefore, 48 men were dropped to form each of the three sides of the box. The base of the box ran north to south along the banks of the Luia River, now just a series of streams waiting for the imminent summer rains. The other two sides of the box would bracket Camps B and C.

One hapless paratrooper, SAS Sergeant Dale O'Mulligan, had a shock when he came to the 'check canopy' drill after jumping from the Dakota. His parachute was badly malformed, and looked like it had deployed through some lines, known as a lineover. O'Mulligan knew the ground was close, and he reacted instinctively and fast. He looked down, found the reserve parachute ripcord handle on his chest and pulled it with all his strength, using up his second – and last – chance. The reserve chute is a small auxiliary chute designed to open quickly and save your life – not much more than that. A hard landing under the small chute can be expected. O'Mulligan, now barely 200 feet from the ground, was horrified to see that the reserve chute, instead of billow-ing out above his head, was lazily flopping out of his chest pack.

He was in an awful position, falling too fast, yet too slowly. He was descending way too fast for a safe landing with the malfunctioned main chute, but too slowly to deploy the reserve. A total malfunction of the main chute would have been preferable in the circumstances, but he had no options left. The ground was rising up frighteningly fast and O'Mulligan braced himself for impact.

It was Dale O'Mulligan's lucky day. The malfunctioned chute crashed into one of the very few big trees in the area, arresting his fall and leaving him dangling a few feet off the ground completely un-harmed. Derek de Kock's preference for landing zones with trees had again proved its worth.

Second Lieutenant Neill Jackson, jumping in the middle of his 24-man stick to have better control of his men, vividly recalled the parachute ride down:

> The first thing I recall once my parachute (and my eyes) had opened was the awesome sights and sounds of the Hunters attacking the camp about two kilometres away to our west, diving in steeply from their perch height and firing three- to four-second bursts from their 30-mm front guns into an already burning and smoking camp area.
>
> I saw the large thatched barrack blocks simply disintegrating under the weight of these long single bursts of cannon fire. I could hear the ripple of the explosions and observe the twinkling flashes as the cannon shells found their targets, followed half a second later by the matching sound of the discharge from the guns. Then the unmistakable warbling scream of that famous blue note as the attacking Hunter pulled up and away from the target at full power and incredible speed. They caused an immense cacophony, and it gave me a huge confidence boost to know that these deadly aircraft were on our side.

44

Square Ring

The Tembue admin base was a lot closer to the target than was the case at Chimoio. It was barely eight kilometres from the southern edge of Camp C, the main target, across the Luia River, and only 16 kilometres from Bene.

'My helicopter broke away from the others as they passed the admin base area. This site had short grass and some small trees, but there were plenty of openings for individual helicopters,' recalled Petter-Bowyer.

As his helicopter approached the admin base, there were clouds of white smoke rising from across the Luia River. Everything looked like it was going to plan. Even the DC-7 was not misbehaving with premature drops, although after the frank debriefing following what had happened at Chimoio, PB expected no further problems. As soon as the rotors stopped, PB clambered onto the roof of the helicopter to spot the DC-7 over the trees early enough to give the crew directions. He talked the DC-7 in: 'Red light on … five degrees right … steady … green light.'

'George [Alexander, the co-pilot] was listening this time. Troops and then pallets descended right where I wanted them. But there was a tense moment when one pallet appeared to be dropping directly onto me. Happily, it drifted away and crashed through a tree next to the helicopter.'

One of the parachutes 'candled', meaning it streamed, but failed to billow open, resembling a Roman candle, and the drums burst on landing. Otherwise the operation went like clockwork and it wasn't long before PB was able to transmit 'Square Ring complete' to Norman Walsh in the command heli, which signified that the base was ready for business.

The only dramatic event at the admin base that day was when a K-car took a bullet in the engine. The machine flew back safely, but would not start. The technicians of No. 7 Squadron again showed their incredible skill. By standing on empty fuel drums, they managed to remove the damaged engine by sheer physical effort and replace it with a new one flown in from Chiswiti via the Train.

45

The battle

The Tembue raid was a lot quieter than the Chimoio operation. Far less fire was directed at the aircraft and paratroops. Within just 15 minutes of H-hour, Brian Robinson asked the stop groups to throw smoke in preparation for the sweep. Codenamed 'Last Leg', the sweep started at 08:25. As the stop groups began tightening the noose, Robinson warned, 'Watch out for trenches, plenty of CTs in trenches.'

There was indeed an enormous labyrinth of trenches, particularly in Camps A and B, many of which had not been picked up on the aerial photographs, probably because there was heavy tree cover in the camps.

Despite the vast network of trenches, however, many of the ZANLA guerrillas chose to run to find cover in thick bush along the banks of the Luia River. In her book *The Elite*, Barbara Cole tells a story of three soldiers, A-Troop Commander Bob McKenna, Sergeant Les Clark and Trooper Gerry McGahan. They were confronted by a large group of ZANLA guerrillas fleeing into a gully: 'Standing back-to-back, the three soldiers blazed away while the enemy fled into the bush and dived for cover. Fortunately for the Rhodesians, Bob and Les carried automatic rifles, and Gerry an RPD light machine gun. In the whole of the war, the three men had never fired so rapidly or changed magazines so quickly.' Within three minutes, scores of ZANLA lay dead in the gully.

Only 48 minutes after the attack had begun, General Peter Walls, sitting at his desk in the command Dak, could no longer contain his curiosity: 'Niner, this is Zero. Can you estimate CT casualties yet?' Brian Robinson replied rather curtly to the supreme commander, 'Not yet.' He and Norman Walsh were extremely busy controlling the battle. Walsh was relieved that, so far, only one aircraft had taken a superficial hit – a Vampire, now with a neat hole through its fuel drop tank, which it incurred while attacking Camp A.

Brian Robinson ordered Neill Jackson's Stop 2 to sweep westwards, where they came across a 75-mm recoilless rifle, fortunately abandoned, which Robinson told them to destroy. Jackson explained: 'Under instructions from the airborne commander, we continued with our advance, and soon began making contact with the camp defenders. We fought our way westwards through the outskirts of the camp, killing about 40 to 50 terrs as we went, most of them in trenches or hidden under bushes.'

It didn't take long for the Rhodesians to suppress the initial ZANLA fire. Then the battle moved into its most dangerous phase, codenamed 'Tight Rope', which entailed searching and clearing the camps. Barely two hours after the attack had started, Norman Walsh radioed PB at the admin base, asking for a helicopter to bring in the Special Branch men to interrogate prisoners and search for documents. Pink 4, one of the G-cars at the admin base, carried the SB men into Camp C.

Shortly after landing, Keith Samler and Ken Milne entered a hut complex, looking for intelligence. Samler tells the story:

> It was a typical African pole-and-dagga hut, with a low door, and a thatch roof almost to the ground. While I was inside, I heard this noise of people scrabbling around outside the back of the hut, which gave me a fright – I thought some gooks were there. I went out of the hut quickly, weapon cocked, and advanced around the curved building – and, lo and behold, doing the same thing was Frank Hales. Behind Frank were Bob MacKenzie and Jock Hutton. Frank said to me, 'What the fuck are *you* doing here?' I replied by asking what the fuck *he* was doing there, as he should be in an old-age home. Anyway, I had found a crate of Cerveja Manica in the hut, so we cracked open a few bottles of the warm beer and then went our separate ways.

Samler continued searching the huts. As he entered a particular one, he saw movement in the corner of his eye. It was an armed guerrilla hiding under the bed. Fortunately for Samler, his reaction was quick, and he killed the man with a burst from his Uzi sub-machine gun, adding his contribution to the bigger picture, as Samler put it.

The firing died down in the battle and things became quiet. Mark McLean remembered two pilots nearly getting into a fight at the admin base. A K-car was orbiting some huts, and a man in a white shirt was sitting outside. 'It was odd,' said McLean. 'Among all the air strikes and with all the noise, there was this man just sitting there. To establish whether he was hostile, they put a few shells into one of the huts to set it alight. The man didn't move, so they put a few into the next hut.

He then went inside the burning hut and dragged out his belongings, so they took pity on him and let him be, thinking he was some poor individual caught up in the war.'

When the K-car needed refuelling, another replaced it. Later, the original crew asked the second crew if they had seen the man in the white shirt. '"Yes, we shot him" was the reply. The merciful pilot of the first K-car was shocked. "You bastard," he screamed, and tried to punch the other pilot. This is the sort of thing that happens in warfare.'

Another ZANLA man was more fortunate. He had been captured by Stop 2, and was indicating the anti-aircraft sites. Neill Jackson was so engrossed in helping dismantle three 12.7-mm anti-aircraft guns that he forgot about his ZANLA captive:

> I turned my back on him while struggling with the heavy weapon in front of me. I heard him calling softly to me, but recall telling him a couple of times to keep quiet, as I was too busy to deal with whatever his problem was. Eventually, I responded to the urgency in his voice and turned around to see what the man wanted. He beckoned me over to where he was standing, about five paces from me. As I walked over to him, he pointed at an object lying in the grass at his feet and said, 'I think you must pick this up and take it away.'
>
> It was an AKM assault rifle, with a full magazine and, as it turned out, loaded and cocked, with the safety catch set to 'fire'! I went completely cold as I looked down at the weapon at his feet, and then up into his eyes. He stared back at me, not saying a word. I picked up the weapon and told him to sit down where he was and not to move. I was shocked and shaken as I contemplated how easy it would have been for him to pick up the AK and shoot me in the back, before turning it on the other men in the stick.

Jackson put on a brave face and continued dismantling the captured weapons, his mind racing with conflicting thoughts:

> Eventually, I realised what I had to do. Before calling in the helicopter, I went over to the man who had spared my life. Telling him to stand up, I turned him to face in a southerly direction, where I knew there would be no stop groups in his path. I instructed him to walk slowly, not to run, next to the river, for two kilometres,

and then to cross the river to the western bank; then, and only then, was he to run as far away as he could. He said nothing, but looked me in the eye, looked at the troopies standing behind me, and started walking. My MAG gunner sidled up to me and asked expectantly, 'Can I pull him now, sir?'

'No,' I replied. 'Let him go. He has earned his freedom.'

And so the ZANLA man walked free, saved by the reciprocal compassion of an RLI officer.

46

The mystery of the empty parade square

Norman Walsh again ordered Petter-Bowyer to go forward to inspect the effects of the air weapons, in particular the flechettes. 'The entire parade ground was crowded with the darts' partially embedded pink tail fins, which had separated from the steel shafts, now buried below the surface. Nobody, but nobody, would have survived the daily parade had it been held at the routine time,' said PB.

Later, during the interrogation process, it became abundantly clear why the resistance was less than expected and why the parade square at Camp C had been empty when Wightman's Whites had dropped their flechettes. Most of the trained guerrillas, 1 500 of them, had moved out the previous night. About 1 000 had gone to a new camp further north, and 500 to Bene on the first leg of being deployed into Rhodesia. A captured guerrilla knew exactly where the new camp was, pointing on the map to a place called Usata, quite close to Tembue Town. The new complex had huts and other structures, recently built around a neat parade square. This information was quickly relayed to the command helicopter.

Brian Robinson and Norman Walsh knew that everyone for miles around would have heard the explosions and seen the attacking Rhodesian aircraft, virtually guaranteeing that the guerrillas would long since have legged it into the bush and into the nearby hills. This likelihood, and the late hour, meant an infantry attack was not feasible, so Walsh asked General Walls for permission to attack Usata with Hunters and Canberras. 'Delta Zero, you have permission,' said the general.

Later that afternoon, Blythe-Wood's Blues put rockets into the new complex to mark the target for the Green Section Canberras. The attack was successful, setting more than half the new huts on fire. Intelligence received later surprisingly revealed that ZANLA had suffered many casualties at Usata – one would have expected them to have fled after the Tembue raid. Nevertheless, the casualty rate would have been much higher had the occupants remained in Camp B.

It was a huge disappointment for the Rhodesians that 1 500 ZANLA guerrillas had slipped through the net. Had the attack been launched

24 hours earlier, the outcome of Zulu 2 would have been very different. The feeling among the Rhodesians was that news of the Chimoio attack had prompted the evacuation. That may have been so, yet the fact that the camp at Usata had just been completed points more to luck more than a deliberate plan.

Ron Reid-Daly added an element of controversy to Zulu 2. He believed the attack should have been aborted. 'Lieutenant Schulenburg of the Selous Scouts was actually close to Tembue at the time, observing the place with, I think, Martin Chikondo. Schulie had come through the night before on Morse code, advising he was not convinced that the numbers expected were actually in the camp. I relayed this to ComOps, but the attack still went ahead.' Reid-Daly felt that the SAS had deliberately avoided communicating with Schulenburg directly, as they 'did not want the Scouts to be involved'.

Back at Camps B and C, the K-cars were still trying to flush out what few guerrillas remained, and sometimes the pilots became frustrated with the process and lack of targets. Mark McLean, flying his K-car near Camp B, was told to go and check out an area that he had already checked:

> I got a message relayed by another helicopter pilot to go back and check this place, so I said that I had already checked it and nothing was happening. In fact, I started arguing over the air with the guy, when, suddenly, a clear voice came over the air saying, 'Kilo 6, just do it.' It was Peter Walls talking from the command Dak. I whispered into my mike: 'It's the voice of the Lord.' After that, I didn't argue any more. When the general spoke, you jumped.

The rain started falling in the late afternoon in Tembue, disrupting the process of lifting men and equipment out. It soon became apparent to Robinson and Walsh that they would have to ask Peter Walls once again for permission to leave men in the camp for the night.

News of the overnighter did not surprise Captain Bob MacKenzie: 'First in, last out is what I do,' the American observed wryly. Arms and ammunition caches were dotted all over the camps, so the SAS teams were kept busy until dusk, and again at dawn, blowing up what could not be airlifted out.

A huge line of storms on the escarpment acted like a dark curtain covering the late-afternoon sun and bringing early twilight. The helicopters evacuating troops from Tembue to the Train would have to hurry up. Neill Jackson's Stop 2 was one of the first to be lifted out. Jackson and three of his men boarded their Alouette. As the six helicopters were crossing Lake Cahora Bassa, Norman Walsh got a call: 'Pink 4, red light on, I need to land.' Walsh told the pilot, Dave Rowe, to land on one of the larger islands in the lake and wait for fuel.

Neill Jackson was not wearing headphones, so he remained blissfully unaware that there was a serious problem, made worse because they were over water. 'As we were crossing the wide expanse of Cahora Bassa,' recalls Jackson, 'our pilot indicated that he was flying on red light, meaning that our fuel was running dangerously low. Once again, our adrenalin levels were raised as we wondered what was going to happen next. The pilot spotted a tiny island ahead of us, and landed safely on its highest point, while the rest of the helicopters continued on their way back to safety.'

Tony Merber, the helicopter's technician, recalls: 'We had gone on the raid as a gunship, but for the extraction of the equipment and troops, some of the K-cars, including myself, had removed our 20-mm cannons on the first ferry trip out and had then returned lighter and with more space to help the G-cars ferry the rest of the guys out. I guess we cut back on fuel load to have more capacity on the ferry trip out.'

As soon as the Alouette landed, Jackson's stick clambered out of the chopper and spread out into all-round defence, searching the watery horizon for any signs of the approaching FRELIMO navy. Jackson recalled:

> We didn't have long to wait, as we soon heard the drone of approaching aircraft engines and were delighted to see Jack Malloch's DC-7 approaching our little island at low level. Fuel drums were thrown out of the open rear door, and descended slowly under their parachutes to land perfectly on the small drop zone. We retrieved the drums and helped Tony Merber refuel; we then took to the air again and continued with our journey southwards.

But there was more excitement in store for Jackson and his men. The delay on the island had pushed them well into the premature twilight.

They were joined by the last gaggle of helicopters bringing troops out of Tembue. Jackson remembered:

> As the darkness began to creep over the bush, we started climbing gradually up the steep sides of a huge mountain range. It became darker as we climbed, and, at one stage, with the helicopter's landing light illuminating the thick bush on the mountainside, I could clearly see the long grass waving in the rotor wash. For all the world, it looked and felt as if we were hovering for ages in one spot. This, however, was an illusion, and we soon reached the mountain's plateau. We had landed on top of the legendary 'Train' in Mozambique.

Jackson and his men deplaned and, in typical fashion, took up defensive positions around the helicopter. And then something unfamiliar happened:

> Our chopper then lifted off into the hover, only a couple of metres off the ground, the landing light illuminating the ground ahead and below. It remained in that position as the other helicopters came in to land and disgorge their troops. Then those helicopters too pulled up into the formation hover alongside the others.
>
> This procedure appeared to take an absolute age, while we cowered, totally confused, in the long grass, being blasted by the gusts of wind and debris from the whirling rotors, and not daring to venture out of the lit area into the forbidding blackness beyond.
>
> Eventually, all the aircraft landed together and shut down, and a semblance of normality returned, as the techs jumped out of their aircraft, and the familiar faces of Major Simon Haarhoff and his 2 Commando men welcomed us to their admin base and directed us to our sleeping places.

Why the strange procedure of hovering in the dark?

'One of the pilots later explained,' said Jackson, 'that the procedure they had followed was standard practice for a number of helicopters landing together in a confined LZ at night, and was designed to prevent damage to aircraft that had shut down on the ground, by the rotor wash of the incoming choppers. All very frightening and confusing, especially after all we had been through during that long and stressful day!'

Quite a few helicopters managed to leave for Mount Darwin before darkness overwhelmed the Train. The biggest problem the pilots now faced was not simply the fading light, but the storm starting to break along the escarpment. Norman Walsh decided that for safety reasons, the helicopters should fly back independently. The pilots, at least those who had arrived early enough, managed to pick their way through gaps in the storm line; others were less fortunate, including Walsh.

PB was on one of the earlier helicopters and reached Mount Darwin after dodging the storm under low cloud: 'I became really concerned when a fair number of the helicopters, including the command helicopter, were well overdue.'

Some pilots made it to Centenary, where there would be hot water and cold beer, but others were less fortunate, and had to land in the bush for an uncomfortable night.

Norman Walsh could have got back sooner, but he first wanted to ensure that the stranded, fuelless Alouette was safely off the island. In the storm and the darkness, Walsh managed to find Chiswiti, where he and Brian Robinson allegedly drank the army pub dry.

Back at Tembue, a few contacts erupted during the night, particularly along the Bene–Tembue road, which guerrillas were drawn to as they tried to find their way in the dark. Other than that, it was a quiet night until Bob MacKenzie's Stop 4 moved into Camp A at first light. A group of ZANLA guerrillas had formed into a defensive position, putting down heavy fire as the SAS men advanced. After a brief but intense firefight, the few survivors surrendered or bolted. MacKenzie reported that the Hunters and Vampires had done an excellent job the previous day – at least three-quarters of the camp infrastructure had been destroyed by the aircraft.

The scattered helicopters started arriving at Chiswiti after first light, ready to fly back to Tembue via the Train to pick up the overnighters. Hunters and Vampires covered the withdrawal from above.

Just after noon, Stop Group 4 were lifted out, completing the evacuation. Captain Bob MacKenzie was the last Rhodesian soldier on Operation Dingo to step from Mozambican soil into an Alouette helicopter.

At 12:55 on Sunday 27 November 1977, Major Brian Robinson

effectively closed Operation Dingo by transmitting 'Broken Nose' to General Peter Walls – the signal that all Rhodesian forces were back safely on home soil. The general recalled: 'The thing that stands out from Operation Dingo was the magnificent cooperation between ground and air, and the planning, execution and direction from Robinson and Walsh. It was just great.'

The men of the SAS, RLI and RhAF had indeed inflicted a most painful broken nose on Robert Mugabe's ZANU forces in one of the biggest battles in Rhodesian history.

Epilogue

Rhodesia Herald
SALISBURY, TUESDAY NOVEMBER 29 1977
Rhodesians' big raids deep into Mozambique
1 200 TERRORISTS KILLED
Forces smash two camps

Security forces have killed more than 1 200 terrorists in what are acknowledged as their biggest and most successful raids to date against terrorist bases inside Mozambique.

The Rhodesian forces have struck at two camps well inside Mozambique in separate operations which started last Wednesday. The first attack was against the main ZANLA operational headquarters and terrorist holding camp – 90 kilometres inside Mozambique and 17 kilometres north of Chimoio, which used to be called Vila Pery.

The second attack started on Saturday and was directed at the Tembue terrorist base 220 kilometres from the Rhodesian border and north-east of the Cabora Bassa Dam.

Operation Dingo did not end the war. It was not expected to, and many more battles lay ahead. Yet it was pivotal. The raid caused considerable damage to ZANU and its leadership, wiping out 20 per cent of its guerrilla forces and seriously injuring another 10 per cent. The very same spot where Robert Mugabe proudly stood, just three months before Dingo, to acknowledge his election as supreme leader was a pile of rubble. The Rhodesian attack also very nearly cost Mugabe his much-cherished leadership. He was castigated for being complacent about the defences at Chimoio. His detractors once again criticised his total lack of military expertise, the reason why they believed he should never have been elected in the first place.

Operation Dingo came at a time when there was a growing assumption that Rhodesia was fast losing the capability to sustain war, and that almost any settlement could be imposed on the Rhodesian government – not really surprising after Kissinger's meat-cleaver intervention a year earlier. Operation Dingo put the record straight by delivering a strong message to the world: the Rhodesian forces were not down and out; there was plenty of fight left in them. The British foreign secretary, Dr David Owen, said as much – to the intense irritation of Robert Mugabe. The fact that Rhodesia could mount an attack on this scale surprised many; some even claimed that South Africa must have been directly involved in the raid.

The UN secretary general, Kurt Waldheim, said the raid had 'greatly impaired peace efforts'. These were tacit admissions that any plans to bypass Ian Smith's government in the settlement process were doomed. The American ambassador to the UN, Andrew Young, summed up the position succinctly: 'If you want to stop the fighting you have to talk to the people with the guns.' And that is exactly what happened two years later at the Lancaster House negotiations.

Mugabe, the most reluctant signatory to the Lancaster House Agreement, achieved victory with a resounding majority in the elections of 1980, thanks in no small way to the strategic foresight of his general-in-chief, Josiah Tongogara. And yet Tongogara, known to some as the Che Guevara of Africa, would not live to see the election results. He died in a road accident on a dark Christmas night in 1979, en route from Maputo to Chimoio to sell the Lancaster House Agreement to his guerrilla forces. With Tongogara's death, any hope disappeared of unifying the two rival guerrilla political parties, ZANU and ZAPU.

In the aftermath of the Dingo attacks, Robert Mugabe and his spin doctors went into high gear to save face, declaring that New Farm was simply a refugee camp. This is the line much of the international media took.

It is true that there were support staff, hangers-on, family members and their children in the complex. Edgar Tekere's wife, Ruvimbo, was the best-known example (she hid in a pit latrine for two days and survived). But there is no doubt that the camp's primary purpose was military. Mugabe, Tongogara, Tekere and others had their own quarters within the complex; it was naive to the extreme to believe that New Farm would never be attacked.

The Harare government's museums department avoided the spin and properly honoured the fallen; many of them had put up a brave and spirited fight. It built a fitting war memorial, designed by architect Peter

Jackson, at the battle site adjacent to the preserved Antonio family farmhouse, now a museum that still bears the huge holes in the floor where Rich Brand's opening shots tore into the building on that Wednesday morning. The large perimeter sign, written in Portuguese and English, reads:

Chimoio – Zimbabwe Liberation War Shrine
Here lie the remains of freedom fighters who fell during Zimbabwe's liberation war. These brave men and women were killed in a Rhodesian air and ground attack on Thursday [sic] 23 November 1977.
National Museums and Monuments of Zimbabwe

Resembling a small version of the Vietnam War memorial in Washington, the shrine has nearly 1 100 names inscribed on rows of polished stone panels. Had the Dare reChimurenga not switched its meeting to Maputo on that fateful day in November 1977, there would certainly have been some well-known names on those panels.

Don't light a fire
The outcome of the Lancaster House Agreement in late 1979 was significantly better for the Rhodesians as a result of Operation Dingo and subsequent external operations. Mugabe's original standpoint was that there would be no settlement unless his army replaced the Rhodesian forces in their entirety. He also made it clear that the white farmers would have no protection of land tenure, and key industries would be nationalised.

As it turned out, the guerrilla forces were contained in assembly points for a very long time, tenure of white land was secured for at least a decade and no major nationalisation took place. Good examples of just how far Mugabe compromised were the appointment of Lieutenant General Peter Walls as his top military commander and the reservation of 20 per cent of the parliamentary seats for white people, which allowed Ian Smith and some of his key lieutenants to remain in Parliament.

In many ways, the Lancaster House Agreement was a defeat for Mugabe, and probably explained why, despite his massive election victory, he was never comfortable with its outcome. It denied him the total control he craved from a military victory, whereby he could have dismantled the Rhodesian state on his terms and replaced it with a ZANU-Marxist model. Mugabe's frustration would become more and more apparent as time passed. The dark cloud of unfinished business would hang over Zimbabwe for decades, with serious consequences.

At the time of the 1980 elections, the Rhodesian forces did in fact have a highly secret contingency plan to attack the guerrilla assembly points and wipe out the ZANU leadership, in effect a *coup d'état*. General Walls had approved the plan; it would be triggered if the Lancaster House Agreement broke down and Mugabe carried out his threat of 'going back to the bush'.

Intimidation of voters was a big issue, and the British governor, Lord Soames, had the power to annul the elections if he deemed that intimidation was materially affecting the outcome. The Lancaster House Agreement came close to falling apart a few times. Then, at the 11th hour, after reports of serious intimidation in Mashonaland and Manicaland, Peter Walls asked British prime minister Margaret Thatcher to annul the election results because of intimidation. But the electoral process had gone too far, and the British government ignored his appeal. Walls was furious: 'I totally lost it, effing and blinding and cursing the British government and their prime minister.'

Angry as he was, the general still held the fate of the new Zimbabwe firmly in his hands; he had the power to authorise a coup. He recalled:

> I had to weigh up whether we would make a Dingo-style strike with a few men against many thousands and with the countryside swarming with these people, who, by the accounts of the provincial commissioners, were fully on Mugabe's side. Also, I was tipped off that our plan had been leaked to Mugabe's men. Before seeing my commanders to give them my decision, I went off to see Boris Thomas, my Presbyterian minister. I didn't tell him any details, just that I had to make a hell of a decision. He said I would be guided and I walked back to my office. I don't always believe in proverbs, but there is this tiny proverb: 'Don't ever light a fire that you can't put out.'

When Walls was back in Milton Building in Salisbury, the anxious commanding officers of the RLI, SAS and Selous Scouts – Charlie Aust, Garth Barratt and Pat Armstrong, respectively – arrived to hear their commander's decision.

'I have decided,' Walls told them, 'that this will be lighting a fire which we can't put out.

'Charlie Aust, the RLI commanding officer, was shocked. He just wanted to get in there and kill the bastards, as did the others. Pat Armstrong was, I think, non-committal, and Garth Barratt looked as if he was expecting it, but I may be completely wrong. Anyway, Garth said, "So we do nothing?" I confirmed that we would do nothing.'

Having made this historic decision, Walls drove to the Pockets Hill television studios to make an announcement to the Rhodesian forces that their job was to preserve the peace. 'It came as a hammer blow to all the guys waiting to go and attack the assembly points. So I can understand why I was seen as the mongrel of the century, the traitor of the century,' said Walls.

Peter Walls made a brave decision, one that history has probably judged as the right one. Had the coup gone ahead, Rhodesia would probably have lost the very few friends it still had – and the fire would probably have eventually been unquenchable.

By appointing Walls as his supreme military commander, Mugabe shocked his own commanders and surprised the world. It didn't last long, however. Four months later, in August 1980, Walls gave an interview to the BBC and told the truth – that he had indeed asked Margaret Thatcher to annul the elections, although he didn't reveal the contingent coup plan. Walls was either naive or deliberately precipitating a problem. In any event, he resigned his commission, which gave ZANU-PF all the ammunition it needed. Mugabe had a special piece of legislation drafted, enabling the state to strip Peter Walls of his birthright, the citizenship of the country in which he was born. The stateless general and his wife, Eunice, took exile in South Africa. He never returned. Peter Walls died in 2010.

After Peter Walls' resignation and deportation, Rex Nhongo (Solomon Mujuru) became commander of the Zimbabwe National Army, a position he held until going into private business in 1995. He died in 2011 in a fire on Alamein Farm, a 5 000-hectare spread near Beatrice, 70 kilometres south of Harare. Nhongo had forcibly seized the farm and its moveable assets from a white commercial farmer, Guy Watson-Smith, 10 years earlier, at the height of the land invasions in Zimbabwe.

Norman Walsh stayed on in the Zimbabwe Air Force, rising to air marshal and commander in 1981; he played a vital role in developing the new air force. There was an unpleasant time when saboteurs, almost certainly operating from South Africa, blew up four brand-new British Hawk jets, five Hawker Hunters and a Lynx. Walsh's chief of staff and colleague, Hugh Slatter, and five Zimbabwe Air Force officers were arrested and charged with sabotage, an offence carrying the death penalty. Walsh was deeply concerned and went to extraordinary lengths to support his officers.

Slatter recalled: 'Norman's position was precarious to say the least, because although he realised that the charges against us were false and he felt the need to support his officers as commander of the air force, he also recognised that the CIO, Ushewokunze, the Home Affairs minister, and others were watching for one move that would allow them to brand him as part of the sabotage plan and an enemy of the state.'

Walsh was not allowed access to the lawyers of his accused officers; he was under constant observation, with his phone tapped. He got round this by lying in the back of a car under a blanket. It was a huge risk, as he could have ended up in prison on the same serious charges. Slatter later said: 'How many people do you know who would literally put their life on the line like that? I only know of one.'

The High Court found the men innocent of all charges, yet they were promptly arrested again, reflecting the paranoia gripping the Mugabe government. Under intense international pressure, the men were eventually released and deported. But the fact that they, and many other air force officers, were prime suspects just because they were white soured things permanently.

Norman Walsh resigned from the Zimbabwe Air Force that year and emigrated to Australia, where he lived until his death in 2010.

Brian Robinson left the SAS shortly after Dingo, achieving the distinction of being the squadron's longest-serving commander. He was promoted to lieutenant colonel and took over as coordinator of special operations at ComOps involving the SAS and Selous Scouts, a role Robinson carried out until the end of the war in 1980, when he became commander of 1 Zimbabwe Parachute Regiment.

Robinson left Rhodesia later in 1980 to become an international arms-sales broker. He returned to his roots in Durban in 1984 as managing director and shareholder of an automotive company. In 2004 he became a military adviser to the United Arab Emirates until he retired a year later and returned to Durban, where he lives.

Despite the pleas of Rex Nhongo and others for him to stay on, Peter Petter-Bowyer left the air force in May 1980, a month after Zimbabwe was born. He became managing director of three Shell BP subsidiary companies. The Iraqi Air Force heard of his skills and asked him to develop a cluster bomb for high-speed delivery from a fighter jet. PB accepted the challenge, resigned from Shell BP and moved to South Africa, where he successfully developed the CB-470 cluster bomb for the Iraqis. He also developed weapons for the South African Air Force before setting up a trading business and ultimately a manufacturing business of his own. He left Africa for England in 2002 and settled in Norfolk, where he lives with his wife, Beryl.

Rich Brand left the Rhodesian Air Force in 1978, the year after Dingo, and, after a spell in the South African Air Force, emigrated to Las Vegas. He joined the flight department of Circus Circus, one of the main casino groups in the desert city, as an executive jet pilot. He soon realised that he wanted a career in gaming, so he started at the bottom, managing slot machines, and rose to general manager at Silver City Casino, part of the Circus Circus Group. But his passion for aviation never faded. With his considerable skill for building model aircraft – most apparent in the perfect scale-model, radio-controlled replica he built of the Percival Provost, in which he flew his first solo – Brand built some excellent full-scale aircraft, including a Super Eagle called *Springbok*, an Ultimate called *Bateleur* and a Rans S-16 Shekari called *Flame Lily*.

Rich's ultimate achievement was building a Giles G-202, named *Panzer One* after the callsign of No. 1 Squadron, adopted under Brand's leadership. He made over 50 modifications to the G-202, in which he went on to win Reserve Grand Champion at the EAA AirVenture at Oshkosh in 1998. He participated as a pilot in the aerobatic show circuit in the US with his wife, Susan, also a pilot, who took part as commentator.

A good example of Brand's incredible eye for detail, a trait he was remembered for in the Rhodesian Air Force, is illustrated in an article that appeared in the March 1999 edition of *Sport Aviation*. Brand is discussing the application of seven coats of paint and primer to an aircraft he was building: 'The finish is determined not by what you put on, but what you sand off. I went over every square inch of it with a magnifying glass, looking for pinholes before shooting the finishing coats.'

After retiring from gaming, Rich continued to build aircraft. He completed a Lancair Legacy, named *Protea*, in 2011. Its registration is N3QB. The letters 'QB' stand for Quintin Brand, his famous uncle who, in 1920, piloted the first flight from London to Cape Town.

Glossary and abbreviations

aileron accumulator: small tank on an aircraft that stores reserve hydraulic energy for the ailerons

air-strike log: written air force record of an air-to-ground attack

AK-47: Kalashnikov automatic assault rifle

AKM: modernised Kalashnikov automatic assault rifle

ANC: African National Congress

BCR: Bronze Cross of Rhodesia

Black Watch: the Royal Highland Regiment

BSAP: British South Africa Police

callsign: a combination of numbers, letters or words used to identify a unique radio transmitting station (a group of soldiers, an aircraft, a base, etc.)

Can: Canberra aircraft

Capewell: quick-release device to separate a parachute from its harness

casevac: casualty evacuation

Chimurenga: Shona for 'resistance struggle'

CIO: Central Intelligence Organisation

ComOps: Combined Operations

CT: Communist terrorist

Dak: Dakota aircraft

Dare reChimurenga: ZANU's war council

dispersal: aircraft parking and manoeuvring area at an aerodrome

donga: gully or ditch

DShK: Degtyarov–Shpagin Krupnokalibernyj, Russian-made anti-aircraft machine gun

elevator: controls the pitch axis (nose up/down) of an aircraft

ESM: Exemplary Service Medal

FAF: forward airfield

flechette canister: warhead carrying darts known as 'flechettes'

FN: Belgian-made light automatic rifle

frantan: frangible tanks; form of napalm-based ammunition

FRELIMO: Frente de Libertação de Moçambique (Freedom Front of Mozambique)

G-car: troop-carrying helicopter

G-force: gravitational force

gook: slang for insurgent, terrorist

HQ: headquarters

int: military intelligence
IP: initial point
JPT: jet pipe temperature
K-car: command car – helicopter gunship fitted with a 20-mm cannon
LTT: locally trained terrorist
LZ: landing zone
MAG: Mitrailleuse d'appui général, general-purpose machine gun of Belgian manufacture
mark one eyeball: in military contexts, the human eye
MBE: Member of the British Empire
MiG: Mikoyan-Gurevich military aircraft (Russian)
MP: Member of Parliament
NDP: National Democratic Party
OAU: Organisation of African Unity
OCC: Operations Coordinating Committee
OLM: Officer of the Legion of Merit
op/ops: operation/operations
OP: observation post
operations order: written battle plan
PTS: Parachute Training School
RAF: Royal Air Force
recce: reconnaissance
RF: Rhodesian Front
RhAF: Rhodesian Air Force
RLI: Rhodesian Light Infantry
RPD: Ruchnoy Pulemyot Degtyaryova, type of Russian hand-held machine gun
RPG: rocket-propelled grenade
RRAF: Royal Rhodesian Air Force
SAAF: South African Air Force
SAP: South African Police
SAS: Special Air Service
SB: Police Special Branch
Selous Scouts: Rhodesian military unit that specialised in pseudo warfare (i.e. imitating the enemy)
shamwari: Shona for 'friend'
sitrep: situation report – daily report on the enemy's and own forces' tactical situation
SKS: Samozariadnyia Karabina Simonova, type of Russian semi-automatic rifle
Sneb rocket: rocket-propelled warhead fired from an aircraft
SSU: Short Service Unit
stick: group of four soldiers, usually deployed from an Alouette helicopter

stop group/stop: group of soldiers positioned to intercept (stop) fleeing enemy forces

terr: terrorist

TTL: Tribal Trust Land

UDI: Unilateral Declaration of Independence

VHF: very high frequency

VSI: vertical speed indicator

ZANLA: Zimbabwe African National Liberation Army

ZANU: Zimbabwe African National Union

ZANU-PF: Zimbabwe African National Union-Patriotic Front

ZAPU: Zimbabwe African People's Union

ZBC: Zimbabwe Broadcasting Corporation

ZIPRA: Zimbabwe People's Revolutionary Army

Select bibliography

Extracts from the Operation Dingo operations orders, log and air strike reports, located in Box 844, British Commonwealth and Empire Museum, Bristol, by courtesy of J.R.T. Wood

Adams, Mark, and Chris Cocks. *Africa's Commandos: The Rhodesian Light Infantry*. Johannesburg: 30° South, 2012

Chung, Fay. *Re-Living the Second Chimurenga: Memories from Zimbabwe's Liberation Struggle*. Stockholm: Nordic Africa Institute, 2006

Cocks, Chris. *Fireforce: One Man's War in the Rhodesian Light Infantry*. Roodepoort: Covos Books, 1988

Cole, Barbara. *The Elite: The Story of the Rhodesian Special Air Service*. Amanzimtoti: Three Knights Publishing, 1984

Flower, Ken. *Serving Secretly. An Intelligence Chief on Record: Rhodesia to Zimbabwe, 1964 to 1981*. London: John Murray, 1987

Geldenhuys, Prop. *Rhodesian Air Force Operations: With Airstrike Log*. Durban: Just Done Productions Publishing, 2007

MacKenzie, Robert. 'Fast Strike on Chimoio' (Parts 1 and 2), *Soldier of Fortune*. Boulder, Colorado, January and February 1994

Martin, David, and Phyllis Johnson. *The Struggle for Zimbabwe*. London: Faber & Faber, 1981

Meredith, Martin. *The State of Africa: A History of Fifty Years of Independence*. Jeppestown: Jonathan Ball, 2005

Moorcroft, Paul, and Peter McLaughlin. *The Rhodesian War: A Military History*. Jeppestown: Pen and Sword Military, 2008

Petter-Bowyer, P.J.H. *Winds of Destruction*. Victoria, Canada: Trafford Publishing, 2003

Presler, Titus. *The Transfigured Night: Mission and Culture in Zimbabwe's Vigil Movement*. Pretoria: Unisa Press, 1999

Salt, Beryl. *A Pride of Eagles: The Definitive History of the Rhodesian Air Force 1920–1980*. Weltevreden Park: Covos Day Books, 2001

Smith, David, and Colin Simpson. *Mugabe*. Falmouth, UK: Sphere Books, 1980

Smith, Ian. *The Great Betrayal: The Memoirs of Ian Douglas Smith*. London: Blake Publishing, 1997

Tekere, Edgar. *A Lifetime of Struggle: Edgar '2-Boy' Zivanai Tekere*. Harare: SAPES Books, 2007

Wood, J.R.T. *Counter-Strike from the Sky: The Rhodesian All-Arms Fireforce in the War in the Bush, 1974–1980*. Johannesburg: 30° South, 2009

Index

Brand, Richard 'Rich'
  attack on Chimoio (Zulu 1) 159,
    165–171, 201–203, 211, 247
  attack on Tembue (Zulu 2) 224, 227, 230
  background of 16, 145–154, 216
  life after Operation Dingo 251–252
  planning for Operation Dingo 135, 137
Brand, Susan 251
briefcase found *see* suitcases found
briefing for Operation Dingo 116–117,
  130–138
Britain 5, 6, 11, 77–78, 80, 104, 106
British Airways 95
British South Africa Police (BSAP)
  26–27, 45
Bronze Cross of Rhodesia 115, 125
Browning machine guns 144, 205
BSAP *see* British South Africa Police
Buckle, Bill 85–86
Burford, Mr 34
Bush War, beginning of 46–47

Caetano, Marcelo 59
Cahora Bassa 38–39, 219, 228–229, 241
Calvert, Mike 109, 110
Canberras
  attack on Chimoio (Zulu 1) 144–145,
    159, 162–164, 171–173, 193–194,
    211–212
  attack on Tembue (Zulu 2) 227, 231, 239
  history of 18, 33, 151
  Nyadzonia camp 98–99
  planning for Operation Dingo 86, 91, 133
  Pungwe camp 74
Cannon, John 23–27
cannons
  20-mm cannons 39, 53–54, 75,
    198–199, 229
  30-mm cannons 135, 151–152, 173
  37-mm Chinese twin-barrelled
    cannons 197
captives 83–85, 237–238
Carmichael, George 27–28
Carnation Revolution 59
Carter, Jimmy 95
casualty rates 93, 114, 134–135
Catane 218
CB-470 cluster bombs 251
Cecil Square 154
Central Intelligence Organisation 39, 43,
  48, 61–63, 75, 102
Cessna aircraft 117
Chaminuka 43

chants of ZANLA 42–43
Chapel of Our Lady of the Rampart 38
Chauke, Justin 41
Chibabawa refugee camp 81
chicken run 101
Chifombo camp 62
Chikerema, James 41
Chikondo, Martin 240
chimbwido 56–57
Chimene, Mandi 180
Chimoio Town 66–67
  see also Battle of Chimoio
China 29–30, 36, 86
Chinese astrology 95
Chiswiti army base 219, 223, 226,
  228, 243
Chitepo College 85, 173, 204, 207
Chitepo, Herbert 10, 20–21, 29–32, 41,
  61–63
Chiweshe, Chief 44
Chiweshe Tribal Trust Land 44, 55
CIO *see* Central Intelligence Organisation
Circus Circus Group 251
Clark, Les 235
clouds, impact of 99, 158–159
  see also weather, impact of
code words for Operation Dingo 141, 184,
  187, 222
Cold Comfort Farm 64
Cold War 80
Cole, Barbara 196, 235
College of the Little Flower 147
Collocott, Bruce 100–101
Combined Operations (ComOps) 94,
  102–103, 209
commanders of Operation Dingo
  120–129, 136
ComOps *see* Combined Operations
confidentiality 112–116
Congo 7–8
Conn, Billy 27–28
Constitution of 1961 6–7
convalescents on New Farm 171, 180, 197
Coster, Keith 102
coup d'état, planned, in Rhodesia 248–249
Coventry, Dudley 126
Cranborne 16–17, 89
Crocodile Gang 10–11
C Squadron, SAS 94, 109–111, 126–127
Cuba 73, 132
Culpan, Rick 151
Culpan, Vic 160, 175–176
Curzon Farm 11

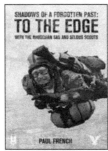
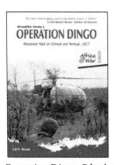

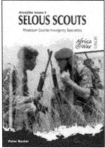

Lightning Source UK Ltd.
Milton Keynes UK
UKHW05f1002231018
331026UK00002B/10/P